MW01089308

"This sobering bo[...]
patriot. Jim Marrs [...]
questions that, whether or not you believe 9/11 was an inside
job, there can be no doubt about the need for us to fight to
win our country back from these thieves and criminals in high
places. This is hair-raising journalism from a fellow Texan
populist."

> — **Jim Hightower**, activist, radio commentator,
> and author of *Let's Stop Beating Around the Bush*

"Jim Marrs is one of our most courageous investigative
journalists, one who is willing to ask the many unanswered
questions about 9/11 that we all want answered, and willing to
keep asking them until he gets to the truth. To heal the wounds
of 9/11, as with any deep emotional wound, it is essential that
we ask these questions and come to know the complete truth
about what really happened. It is only then that the heart of
America can be healed, and only then can we move beyond
fear to create a world of peace at this historic time. *Inside Job*
is an essential contribution to that effort. Read it and share
it with your friends."

> — **John Gray,** author, *Men Are from Mars, Women Are from Venus*

"The primary goal of the National Security Council, the
Federal Reserve Bank of New York, and the Council on Foreign
Relations is not to run the United States. It is to ensure that
the rest of us do not understand how our country is run. As
Jim Marrs describes in *Inside Job*, there is no better example
of this state of affairs than the unanswered questions of 9/11.
If a grand jury is called to review the evidence that Marrs and
his colleagues have presented on 9/11, we could reasonably
anticipate indictments of members of both the Bush and
Clinton administrations for criminal negligence, treason,
and genocide."

> — **Catherine Austin Fitts**, former assistant secretary of housing,
> Bush I; and cofounder, unAnsweredQuestions.org

INSIDE JOB

INSIDE JOB
Unmasking the 9/11 Conspiracies

by

Jim Marrs

Origin Press

San Rafael, California

Origin Press

P.O. Box 151117, San Rafael, CA 94915
OriginPress.com

Visit the official website for *Inside Job*:
InsideJob-911.com

Bulk order discounts are available on request.

Publisher's Cataloging-in-Publication
(Provided by Quality Books, Inc.)

Marrs, Jim.
    Inside job : unmasking the 9/11 conspiracies / Jim
Marrs.
    p. cm.
    Includes bibliographical references
    LCCN 2004106618
    ISBN 1-57983-013-7

    1. September 11 Terrorist Attacks, 2001. 2. War on
Terrorism, 2001- 3. Conspiricies—United States—
History—21st century. 4. United States—Politics and
government—2001- I. Title.

HV6432.7.M345 2004   937.931
                   QBI04-200243

Printed in the United States of America
10 9 8 7 6 5 4

Dedication

*This book is dedicated
to all those who suffered
the horror and fear of
September 11, 2001. They
deserve better than the
superficial and self-serving
pronouncements of federal
officials. They deserve
the truth.*

Acknowledgments

Many dedicated writers and researchers have contributed to our knowledge of 9/11. In the creation of this book, special acknowledgment for assistance over and beyond the call of duty must be given to Gary Beebe, Dan Foster, Les Jamieson, Ken Jenkins, David Kubiak, Thomas J. Mattingly, Mark Mawrence, and Richard Scheck.

Many thanks are also due to George Marsh for his editorial expertise, to Phillip Dizick for his fine cover design and layout, to Paul Goodberg for crucial all-round support, to editor/publisher Byron Belitsos for his foresight and determination, and to that Queen of Tolerance, my wife Carol.

Publisher's note to readers

Knowledge about 9/11 is expanding almost daily. Therefore, Origin Press will be providing periodic updates to the author's findings that are presented in this book. These can be found at the book's official website: **www.insidejob-911.com.**

Contents

Preface by Ellen Mariani

This preface is an open letter to the American people, and it comes straight from my heart. I ask that you read this book and discover for yourself why the attacks of September 11, 2001, were, in fact, an inside job. Jim Marrs makes that case in this book; I intend to prove it in a court of law.

My husband, Neil Mariani, was killed in the attacks. He was a passenger on United Airlines Flight 175, the second of two planes to crash into the World Trade Center. On the awful day, my husband and I were on our way to our daughter's wedding in California from Boston's Logan airport, but we were booked on separate flights. We took separate flights because we were not sure at first that he could afford to fly to his stepdaughter's wedding. So sometime after I had booked my trip, we held a garage sale and raised just enough money to purchase a flight for him two hours later than mine. I will never forget the very last moment I saw him at the airport as I departed to my gate.

Today I am a bereaved widow, but I am a determined one. I am one of about 75 families that did not file for a settlement from the so-called September 11th Victim Compensation Fund, which consisted of taxpayers' money paid out directly from the US Treasury for the first time in history. Rather than accept about $500,000 to be paid to my husband's estate in compensation for my husband's life, I decided to retain my right to speak out.

I don't want this money; I just want *answers.*

By taking money from that fund, which I call the "shut-up and go-away fund," I would have given up my right to sue United Airlines and the federal government. Once I finally overcame my grief for Neil, which took many hard months, I came to believe that the only way I can get information about what happened to him is through the courts. I became the first family member of a victim of 9/11 to file a lawsuit against the government.

My suit is based on the RICO (Racketeering Influenced and Corrupt Organizations) Act, and it is aimed at proving that the September 11 terrorist attacks were no surprise to the government. I believe that many of the highest officials in the federal government were aware the attacks would take place—in fact I am 100 percent sure that they knew.

It was difficult to get a lawyer to take my case. Absolutely no one dared take my case against the government. But then I found a courageous man named Phil Berg, a former deputy attorney general of Pennsylvania.

Our lawsuit is directed against President Bush and a number of other administration members. As Phil Berg has written in the Complaint, the suit "is based upon prior knowledge of 9/11; knowingly failing to act, prevent or warn of 9/11; and the ongoing obstruction of justice by covering up the truth of 9/11; all in violation of the laws of the United States." In addition to President George Bush, we named Vice President Dick Cheney, Attorney General John Ashcroft, Defense Secretary Donald Rumsfeld, and National Security Adviser Condoleezza Rice as defendants, among others. The suit also names the Department of Defense, the Central Intelligence Agency, the National Security Agency, and the Council on Foreign Relations, among other agencies.

Phil Berg and I have agreed to allow Origin Press, the publisher of *Inside Job,* to print highlights of our Complaint in the appendices to this book. Please read this material, and also *Ellen Mariani's Open Letter to Mr. Bush,* which can be found at the website address shown below. And please support us.

I also ask you to read very closely the *23 Questions* of the Family Steering Committee that are also reprinted in the appendices. These 23 queries are among the key questions I seek to have answered in a court of law—and that Jim Marrs so effectively puts forth in this courageous book.

Our lawsuit cannot bring back my husband or the other victims of 9/11. But I believe it can and it will bring forward the truth and justice that is so badly needed at this time, in this country. When you read this book by Jim Marrs, you will surely see why.

Ellen Mariani
(widow of Louis Neil Mariani)
Derry, New Hampshire
May 10, 2004
www.911forthetruth.com

Publisher's Preface

I usually publish books on topics in religion, spirituality, the paranormal, and psychology—crossing over only occasionally to other subjects. When Jim Marrs' 9/11 book came my way, I found it stunning, but I tried to ignore it as being peripheral to my concerns as a publisher. Yet this grim subject would not leave me alone. I had seen pioneer researcher Mike Ruppert speak on 9/11; I had been to many of the 9/11 websites; and I was tracking the other offenses of the Bush administration on a daily basis. The necessity to see Jim's book published was tugging hard at me, but I didn't think I had the courage. Then one night I happened to see *The Last Samurai*, for me a life-changing film about "spiritual warriorship." In the final minutes of the movie, it struck me like a lightening bolt that, given the chance, I simply couldn't turn my back on the opportunity to publish Jim Marrs' exposé. I knew intuitively that I couldn't forgo it and still call myself an American, or even a world citizen.

In this cathartic moment, I also felt directed to publish a second book, which is an Origin Press companion to *Inside Job*. This book is entitled *One Planet: A Progressive Vision of Enforceable Global Law*. I saw in an instant that these two books go together, one stating the problem in stark terms, and the other offering a visionary but achievable solution to the war system—*the abolition of war altogether.*

I had experienced an epiphany watching the performances of Tom Cruise and Ken Watanabe. And in that state of consciousness, I left the movie theatre, which sits in the Yerba Buena Gardens complex, a public facility in downtown San Francisco. I turned left, inadvertently running straight into the Martin Luther King Jr. Memorial that is also located in the complex. It consists of a walkway filled with large backlit photos from the civil rights movement, each featuring Dr. King, plus glass panels inscribed with inspiring words from his best speeches.

Walking through this memorial and gazing at the legacy of this great warrior for love, justice, and forgiveness, I now knew in what spirit I should bring this book into being. And the work on this book has unfolded naturally since then.

Inside Job was originally a HarperCollins book, a somewhat longer book under a different title. As Jim explains in his introduction, Harper did not have the courage to follow through on its commitment to publish this book, even though they had accepted it editorially and had even had a lawyer vet the manuscript.

The second half of that original manuscript, an encyclopedic journalistic investigation of the misdeeds of the Bush administration from the passing of the Patriot Act to the wars in Afghanistan and Iraq in historical context, had become a bit out of date by the time it reached me. Jim plans to update this second part and bring this material out soon as the second book in this series, under the tentative title, *Inside Job: The War on Freedom.*

Meanwhile, Jim and I have worked on updating the first part of the original HarperCollins manuscript, inserting a mountain of new facts and findings, almost up to the minute of printing. That effort has taken the form of this short book, which is really the first book in the *Inside Job* series. To support serious researchers, we also added extensive appendices by other key researchers—notably excerpts from the text of the RICO Act lawsuit recently filed for Ellen Mariani by attorney Phil Berg.

As it has taken gritty determination for Jim Marrs to follow through with this book in a second round, as well as considerable guts to point out the truth about our government, I commend the same spiritual courage to you as you read it. As you do, please keep in mind the memory of Martin Luther King Jr.—and all others who trust in their God enough to stand fearlessly in the truth as they see it—for surely this truth shall make you free.

Byron Belitsos
Publisher, Origin Press
May 25, 2004

P.S. A special note to researchers: Be sure to visit **911Truth.org**, the portal site of the leading researchers, writers, publishers, activists, webmasters, and leaders in the 9/11 truth movement.

Introduction

Knowledge is indeed power.

The information within this book will empower Americans who are ready for some straight talk about the many factual anomalies, conflicting claims, and unanswered questions that still surround the horrific attacks of September 11, 2001.

It was these provocative attacks which provided the underlying justification for all that followed—the hurried passage of The Patriot Act, increases in the defense and intelligence budgets, the invasion and occupation of Afghanistan and Iraq, the creation of the Department of Homeland Security, and the stifling of dissent in a nation that claims to be free.

This knowledge should have been available in print within months of the 9/11 tragedies—but it seems that freedom of the press, at least within the United States, belongs only to those who own the presses.

To those who follow the shadowy side of America's national life, the events of 9/11 immediately raised red flags of warning. Just one day after 9/11, I posted my initial thoughts in a piece on the Internet. Here are some excerpts:

Who's truly behind the attack on America?

Many people have compared the horrendous terrorist attack on New York's World Trade Center and the Pentagon in Washington to the attack on Pearl Harbor in 1941. It is an apt comparison, though not for the reasons most people think.

For true students of history, it is now beyond dispute that certain high-ranking officials in Washington, DC, knew in advance of the Japanese intention to attack the US fleet in Hawaii, yet did nothing to prevent it.

Must the citizens of the United States wait another fifty years to learn that the 9/11 terrorist attack was allowed to take place just like Pearl Harbor? Could such an appalling scenario possibly be true?

Simple countermeasures against such an attack now seem apparent. For example, if the airlines would assign just one armed plainclothes security man to each flight, this tragedy may have been averted since the hijackers were apparently armed only with knives or other type blades. So, how were they able to overpower a planeload of people and, more importantly, gain access to the cockpits? Who taught them to fly jumbo jets?

As in the case of the assassination of President John F. Kennedy, the key to understanding the event lies not in who actually committed the violence but rather who was able to strip away the normal security protection.

Government and airline officials knew immediately that planes had been hijacked, yet no interceptors appeared in the air until after the attacks were completed. Who stripped away the normal security protection of America on 9/11?

At least in this most recent case, the government cannot blame the attack on a lone deranged individual, some Lee Harvey McVeigh. They must deal with a full-blown conspiracy, even though authorities were quick to point the finger at Osama bin Laden. Any investigation of bin Laden must look beyond the man, to his backers and financiers.

The trail of the terrorists will most probably become murky, with plenty of accusations for all concerned. But one thing appears quite clear, the tragic events of 9/11 play right into the hands of persons with an agenda aimed at eroding American liberties and sovereignty.

After decades of bloated and misused defense budgets, there are now calls for doubling our defense allocation. In a time of rising recognition that the CIA is an agency never sought by the public and one which has brought so much condemnation on this nation, there are now cries for doubling its size and budget. If the chief security officer for a large company fails to protect one of its most prized assets, is he more likely to be fired or have his pay doubled?

Watch for more antiterrorist legislation to further shred the US Constitution.

As we all scramble to deal with the effects of terror-ism, are we in danger of losing our few remaining individual liberties?

Also, consider that we are distracted from a faltering economy (the current crisis may require more federal financial controls), a plummeting public opinion of George W. Bush, and surging energy prices.

Would leaders allow a public disaster to happen with an eye toward advancing their agendas? It's happened before—in Nero's burning Rome, Germany's gutted Reichstag, at Pearl Harbor, and again at the Gulf of Tonkin.

While we should grieve for our losses, we must keep our heads. When the emotions of the moment run hot, we must remain cool and thoughtful so that we can find who is truly behind this attack on America.

I believe the basic questions I raised above are as valid today as in September 2001.

And I didn't stop there. Within two months of 9/11 I had gathered much of the material in this book and presented it as a proposal to my publisher, HarperCollins of New York, under the title *The War on Freedom.*

I was told that emotions were too high and the content too "hot" for immediate publication. Foot dragging on a book deal continued until mid-2002. At that time, several employees of the FBI and CIA had come forward to testify that they had tried to warn superiors of an impending terrorist attack. The attitude toward my book proposal softened and I signed a contract to publish the book, along with a sizable advance.

Working feverishly throughout the summer of 2002, I produced a manuscript by October. My editor was elated with the work and predicted it would sell more than a million copies.

The wheels of major publishing grind slowly and it was not until March of 2003 that the book received a legal review. I had already been sent a copy of the cover and publication was just a few weeks away. The legal review, or vetting, is a process in which legal counsel verifies the source material and checks for anything that might cause a legal problem. This hurdle was passed and the last words from the attorney were, "You have satisfied me."

Within two days, however, I was informed that the book had been cancelled by a senior officer who had not even read it. The only justification given was that the officer "did not want to upset the families of 9/11 victims." This was obviously a specious argument as, by today, more than six hundred families have filed lawsuits against either Saudia Arabia or senior members of the Bush administration.

Under normal circumstances, if a book must be cancelled for legal reasons, the author is required to return any payments made in advance. In this case, I was paid the remainder of the entire advance. To me, this was a clear indication that the cancellation of the book was nothing less than outright censorship.

"Why would they want to prevent people from learning truths about 9/11, even if those truths were discomforting to the public and embarrassing to government authorities?" I asked myself, still believing that I lived in a nation which valued free speech.

I proceeded to self-publish *The War on Freedom* and the book's reception was uniformly good. (By sheer coincidence, another book with the same title was published by a scholar named Nafeez Ahmed around the same time as mine. It provides an excellent analysis of the events of 9/11.) As my readers kept expressing astonishment at the book's information, I realized that the knowledge gleaned from a study of published matter, both in print and on the Internet, was indeed painting a dark picture of the persons and forces behind today's current events. I came to see that some force existed which did not want this information available to the general public. It would certainly upset the carefully constructed "official" explanations for the horrors of 9/11.

Today is a new day. The authorized story of 9/11 has been all but discredited in the eyes of an increasingly aware population, thanks to the dedicated work of dozens of journalists and researchers, courageous government whistleblowers, and even revelations from official inquiries.

As I write this in the spring of 2004, we now know that:

— A wide variety of standard defense mechanisms designed to prevent such an attack systematically failed on 9/11. Especially notable are the atypical failures which occurred simultaneously within the Federal Aviation Administration (FAA), the National Military Command Center (NMCC), and the North American Aerospace Defense Command (NORAD), all charged with protecting US airspace.

— Interceptor jets were not scrambled for more than thirty minutes after it was obvious that four airliners had gone off course and were presumably hijacked. In the case of Flight 77, which reportedly slammed into the Pentagon, an hour and forty-five minutes elapsed with no interception.

— Missile batteries designed to protect Washington, DC, failed to stop the strike on the Pentagon, one of the world's most protected structures, and fighter jets on constant alert at Andrews Air Force Base just twelve miles away were never scrambled.

— By a "bizarre coincidence," two government homeland defense agencies (NORAD and the NRO) were practicing war games on the morning of 9/11. The games simulated responses to a scenario in which hijacked planes were crashed into buildings. This fact could explain the government's lack of rapid response to the real hijackings, yet this plausible alibi has never been brought to public attention. One also wonders: How did the hijackers know the time and date of these war games in order to time their attacks to coincide with them?

— President Bush proceeded with a photo op at a Florida elementary school even after he and his aides knew that three planes had been hijacked. He lingered in the classroom for nearly twenty minutes after being informed that a second plane had struck the World Trade Center (WTC).

— Not one steel-framed high-rise building in history has collapsed solely due to fire. The free-fall speed collapse of the Trade Center towers, with attendant melted steel and powdery dust, exhibited all the characteristics of a controlled demolition.

— Just such a controlled demolition apparently occurred about 5 p.m. that same day when, according to the leaseholder of the WTC complex, the 47-story Building 7 was "pulled," i.e., intentionally demolished.

— Vital evidence, including the buildings' structural steel, was destroyed through rapid removal and destruction by US government officials with no investigation. This is only one of the many reasons why *Fire Engineering* magazine called the official investigation "a half-baked farce."

— An eight-mile-long debris trail indicated that Flight 93 was destroyed in the air rather than in the Pennsylvania crash reportedly caused by an onboard struggle between the hijackers and passengers.

— More than a dozen countries firmly warned US authorities that an attack on American soil was imminent, some only days before the events.

— Strong evidence points to complicity in the attacks by senior intelligence operatives from Israel and Pakistan who are closely aligned with American intelligence agencies.

— A classified Congressional report incriminates senior officials in the Saudi Arabian government, showing that they had close ties to the hijackers. The Saudis enjoy long-term business and social ties to the Bush family and close political ties to the US government.

— The US government expedited the swift departure of over 100 Saudis from the country, even as the American public had been denied the right to fly. Two dozen members of bin Laden's own family, presumably potential witnesses, were allowed to leave the country without interrogation.

— Insiders with foreknowledge of the events to come engaged in massive and highly profitable short-selling of shares in American Airlines and United Airlines, as well as other stocks readily affected by the disaster. The public has still not been presented with the final results of official investigations into these transactions—if there are any.

— A growing number of whistleblowers from within the federal government have pointed to evidence that various agencies were well aware of the possibility of attack, and were prevented by seniors officials from mounting full investigations.

— Far from being a mere reaction to 9/11, evidence now proves that the US invasions of Afghanistan and Iraq were the culmination of long-standing plans which only awaited a provocation such as 9/11.

— The official explanations for the invasion of Iraq, such as the need to capture weapons of mass destruction, and to "bring democracy" to the country, have proven false.

— Within a few hours, the FBI released names and photos of the suspected hijackers although later many of those named turned up alive in the Middle East.

— Also within hours of the attacks, FBI agents were scouring the houses, restaurants, and flight schools they frequented. If no one had foreknowledge of the hijackers or their activities, how did they know where to look?

— Far from ordering a full and objective investigation to determine who was responsible for the 9/11 tragedies, the Bush administration dragged its feet and actually took actions to impede a swift and truthful probe into the events of that day. It was nearly two years after the events that mounting pressure from the public, led by families of 9/11 victims, finally forced the creation of an "independent" investigatory commission.

— No one in government has been reprimanded or even scolded for what we are told was the greatest intelligence and homeland-defense failure in US history. In fact, the very agencies which failed the nation watched their budgets increase dramatically, and some of the officials ostensibly at fault were actually promoted.

— No person in government, other than former National Security Council counterterrorism chief Richard A. Clarke, has felt the need to apologize to the American people for the 9/11 security failure.

— President Bush himself declined to apologize for the 9/11 tragedy to either the American public or to victims' families during an April 2004 press conference, despite being presented with the opportunity to do so at least three times.

This is actually a short list of unanswered questions, anomalies, and puzzles concerning the 2001 attacks. These journalistic findings—backed up by a massive outpouring of research data from independent investigations even now under way by hundreds of researchers—have prompted honest thinkers from all across the political spectrum to conclude, reluctantly no doubt, that the tragic attacks of 9/11 were an *inside job.*

You see, one does not have to actively participate in a crime to be part of it. The employee who knowingly unlocks the rear door to a business is just as guilty as the burglars who loot the building later that night.

This is called an *inside job.* It happens all the time in criminal operations.

The 9/11 attacks were without doubt among the most monstrous crimes in history. It is my great hope that this book—along with other volumes of information, the revelations of whistleblowers still to come, and independent citizens' inquiries of all kinds—will motivate the American public to seek out and bring to justice the real perpetrators behind the horrors that chilled the world on September 11, 2001.

Jim Marrs
May 2004

INSIDE JOB

"Let me just be very clear about this. Had we had the information that was necessary to stop an attack, I'd have stopped the attack…if we'd known that the enemy was going to fly airplanes into our buildings, we would have done everything in our power to stop it."

—President George W. Bush to reporters, April 5, 2004

1. The Events of September 11, 2001

Superficially, the attacks of September 11, 2001, horrible and tragic as they were, all appeared to fit the official explanation.

According to these official pronouncements, about nineteen suicidal Middle Eastern Muslim terrorists, their hearts full of hatred for American freedom and democracy, hijacked four airliners, crashing two into the Twin Towers of New York City's World Trade Center and a third into the Pentagon, near Washington, DC. The fourth airliner reportedly crashed in western Pennsylvania after passengers attempted to overcome the hijackers.

However, a closer look at the events of 9/11 brings only a maze of unanswered questions.

As pointed out by thoughtful students of history, one must not be distracted by the *how* of an event but instead should focus on the *who* and the *why*. Accumulate the details, though often contradictory, then concentrate on the overall process by which these events transpired. In other words, consider the overview and try to think like a good police detective: Who benefited from this crime? Who had the means, motive, and opportunity—not only to devise such attacks, but to circumvent normal security measures and hinder any objective investigation? Bear these questions in mind as we launch this inquiry with a brief look at the timeline of these tragic events.

2. A Chronology of Events

Sometime between 7:45 a.m. and 8:10 a.m. on September 11, 2001, American Airlines Flight 11 and United Airlines Flight 175 were hijacked and by 8:15, both were obviously off course. This was known to air traffic controllers.

American Flight 11, a Boeing 767 with 92 persons on board out of a possible 351, had taken off from Boston's Logan International Airport en route to Los Angeles. United Flight 175, another Boeing 767 carrying 65 passengers out of a possible 351, also departed from Logan to Los Angeles.

During that same time frame, American Flight 77, a Boeing 757 with 64 passengers out of a possible 289, took off from Dulles International Airport in Washington destined for Los Angeles, while United Flight 93, a Boeing 757 with 45 passengers out of a possible 289, headed for San Francisco from Newark Airport.

By 8:43 a.m. the Northeast Air Defense Sector (NEADS) of the North American Aerospace Defense Command (NORAD) was alerted to the hijackings of Flights 11 and 175 by the Federal Aviation Administration (FAA) and, according to a NORAD statement, two F-15 jet fighters were scrambled from the Otis Air National Guard Base in Falmouth, Massachusetts.

Moments after 8:45, it was known to authorities that the four airliners had been hijacked, an unprecedented occurrence.

About 8:46, just as the Otis jets were taking off, Flight 11 struck the north face of the 110-story North Tower of the World Trade Center (WTC) at the 96th floor. Also at this time, the two F-15s from Otis were redirected to New York City.

At 8:47, despite having its tracking beacon turned off by the hijackers, air traffic controllers could see that American Flight 77 had reversed course somewhere over West Virginia and was moving back toward the East Coast.

At 9:03 a.m., with the evacuation of the WTC towers proceeding amidst fear and confusion, United Flight 175 careened into the southeast corner of the South Tower at the 80th floor, sending a massive ball of burning fuel into the air over lower New York City. The F-15s were reported as being seventy-one miles away. According to official sources, the jets arrived over New York City at 9:10, seven minutes too late.

At 9:06 a.m., President Bush is at a photo op in Sarasota at Booker Elementary School in a second grade classroom. His chief of staff, Andrew Card, enters the room and whispers into his ear, "A second plane hit the other tower, and America's under attack."

According to the *New York Daily News* of September 12, 2001, at 9:06 a.m., the New York Police Department broadcast this message to key officials, "This was a terrorist attack. Notify the Pentagon." At 9:08, it was added, "Freeze all the airports. Freeze all the airports. Nothing in or out."

Although there were reports of officials inside the Pentagon watching the attack on New York and speculating about the possibility of such attacks on themselves, no one there was warned and the Pentagon was not evacuated.

At 9:30, two F-16 fighters were scrambled from Langley Air Force Base (AFB) in Hampton, Virginia.

At 9:31, President Bush declared the disaster in New York an apparent terrorist attack.

At 9:35, American Flight 77, its transponder turned off, began making a complicated 270-degree spiral turn while descending seven thousand feet. At 9:40, it reportedly crashed into the west side of the concrete and limestone Pentagon, penetrating three of its five rings of offices.

By 9:48, key officials of the White House and the Capitol were evacuated and taken to secure but undisclosed locations. One minute later, in an unprecedented action, the FAA ordered all airline flights across the nation grounded.

Shortly after 10 a.m., the South Tower of the World Trade Center collapsed, covering lower Manhattan with tons of ash, dust, smoke, and debris. At that same time, United Flight 93, also with transponder turned off or disabled, crashed in western Pennsylvania about eighty miles southeast of Pittsburgh near Shanksville after passengers reportedly used cell phones to report that they intended to fight the hijackers. This event was followed about twenty-three minutes later by the collapse of the WTC

North Tower, the upper floors of which had been burning for about an hour and a half.

By noon, there were closings at the United Nations, Securities and Exchange Commission, the stock markets, some skyscrapers in several cities and even some large tourist attractions such as Walt Disney World, Mount Rushmore, the Seattle Space Needle, and St. Louis's Gateway Arch.

At 1:04 p.m., speaking from Barksdale Air Force Base in Louisiana, President Bush proclaimed, "Make no mistake, the United States will hunt down and punish those responsible for these cowardly acts."

At 5:25 p.m. the 47-story Building 7 of the WTC suddenly collapsed—a rather strange occurrence often ignored in the official accounts until brought to the attention of the public by independent researchers.

After about an hour and a half, disaster relief crews began moving into the area searching for survivors.

[*Editor's note to researchers*: very detailed timeline information can be found at **www.cooperativeresearch.org.**]

3. Unresolved Questions Abound

As noted, the attacks have prompted a lengthy list of disturbing questions. In the appendices to this book we have reprinted the list of *23 Questions* posed to the government early in 2004 by the Family Steering Committee, a prominent activist group of relatives of 9/11 victims. At press time for this book in May 2004, almost none of these questions—not to mention any other set of questions, such as those I present in the coming pages—have been satisfactorily answered. Due to the premature cleansing of Ground Zero, which we will examine in detail, most questions about the collapses of the WTC towers will probably never be definitively answered. We will also see how many other pieces of evidence have been systematically withheld or even destroyed.

Years of footdragging and unnecessary secrecy by the Bush administration, widely documented in the mainstream press, has also hampered independent and official inquiries into the truth.

Throughout this difficult process, perhaps the key question remains: How could an obviously sophisticated terrorist plan involving perhaps more than one hundred persons, and in the works for many years, escape the notice of our intelligence services, especially the FBI and CIA?

The fact is, it didn't. Mild admissions of incompetence have been made in official hearings, but a great deal of additional evidence of wrongdoing by these agencies has still not entered mainstream discourse. We'll discuss all this later.

And what about accountability? Why is it that, instead of cashiering those responsible for this intelligence failure, we nearly doubled their budgets? Will we now get twice as much failure as before?

To many thoughtful people, it is also unsettling that *not one* individual within the federal government or military has been fired or even reprimanded for the many obvious government missteps of that day.

And perhaps most important, why did there appear to be such a systematic failure of response on the part of our defense authorities?

Both American Flight 11 and United Flight 175 were known to be off course by 8:15 a.m., yet NORAD was not notified for almost twenty minutes. Why the long delay? It then required another fifteen minutes before jet interceptors were ordered off the ground at Otis AFB, entailing a total delay of more than thirty minutes. None arrived in time for a visual check of the hijacked planes' cockpits.

Yet in October 1999, when golf pro Payne Stewart's Learjet went off course due to a failure of the plane's oxygen system, the air force announced that two F-15s from Elgin Air Force Base, Florida, intercepted the plane within twenty-four minutes after it lost contact with air traffic controllers, and followed it until it crashed after running out of fuel. In 2001, a private plane that merely passed too close to the Bush ranch in Texas was immediately ordered to land.

"It happens all the time," writes investigative journalist William Thomas in a definitive essay on the issue of the 9/11 interceptors. "Between September 2000 and June 2001, the Pentagon launched fighters on sixty-seven occasions to escort wayward aircraft." [*Editor's note:* This important research article is reprinted in its entirety in Appendix A of this book.]

The air traffic controllers who actually handled the hijacked flights on 9/11 may have been able to give a clear picture of what really happened in the hand off to NORAD and other authorities. In fact, according to the inspector general of the Transportation Department, at least six of the controllers had made tape recordings that day describing their experiences. Incredibly, these tapes were destroyed by an FAA quality-assurance manager without making any copies or even a transcript. According to an article in the May 6, 2004, *New York Times,* the manager told investigators he had destroyed the tape because he thought its production was contrary to FAA policy, which calls for written statements, and because he felt that the controllers "were not in the correct frame of mind to have properly consented to the taping" due to stress.

But even more concerning than the aforementioned fatal delays, and the intended or unintended destruction of evidence, is this disturbing fact: The US military had almost an hour and a half lead time to protect Washington after learning that four airliners had been hijacked. Yet no jet interceptors were launched from Andrews AFB where two squadrons of jet fighters are specifically assigned to protect the Pentagon and the White House. F-16s dispatched from the more distant Langley AFB flew at an estimated one-third of their top speed of 1500 mph. Curiously, no antiaircraft or missile installations adjacent to the Pentagon or in the Washington area were activated.

"The attacks . . . could not have succeeded unless some US officials had given 'stand-down' orders for standard operating procedures to be canceled on that particular day," concluded author David Ray Griffin, a distinguished ethicist and theologian at California's Claremont School of Theology, in his landmark analysis of the leading independent and official sources of 9/11 research entitled *The New Pearl Harbor*. We'll further examine this claim of an air force stand-down later in this book.

And more questions:

What are the odds that four transcontinental flights on two major airlines—American Flights 77 and 11 and United Flights 175 and 93—would have 78, 74, 81, and 84 percent empty seats respectively on September 11, 2001?

And how did the terrorists obtain top-secret White House and *Air Force One* codes and signals, the excuse for hustling President Bush from Florida to Louisiana to Nebraska on September 11?

At 9:00 a.m. on September 11, just about the time Flight 175 slammed into the South Tower of the WTC, Secret Service agents in Washington received this chilling message: "*Air Force One* is next." Within minutes Vice President Dick Cheney was hustled from his seat in front of a television down to the president's nuclear-bombproof emergency operations center and the White House evacuated.

The warning was transmitted in that day's top-secret White House code, indicating that whoever was behind the ongoing attacks had access to the highest level of security codes. It meant that whoever had the codes could track and accurately pinpoint the president's plane.

After several days of investigation, the picture grew even darker. Someone had penetrated the National Security Agency's (NSA) hush-hush Echelon surveillance system. In fact, they appeared to have more electronic capability than even the NSA, including the use of "steganography," technology that allows its user to bypass Echelon and other electronic monitoring by hiding messages randomly in otherwise innocent digital files such as music, online advertisements, email headers or even Internet pornography. Such buried messages leave no trace of their presence. The idea that someone had access to such high-level codes provoked speculation that there were "moles," deep-cover secret agents, within the US government. It also meant whoever was behind the attacks had access to our latest and most sophisticated electronic technology.

4. What Did President Bush Know?

Despite the government's systematic failure to respond to the 9/11 attacks themselves, reaction *after the fact* came so swiftly that it lent support to the disconcerting idea that planning for such a reaction had been made months before. Perhaps the most remarkable and puzzling instance of this is the actual behavior of President Bush himself.

About ten minutes after the North Tower of the WTC was struck, Bush arrived at an elementary school in Sarasota, Florida, for a photo op with grade school kids. CNN had already interrupted broadcasting to tell of the strike two minutes after it happened, yet reportedly Bush remained unaware until he was briefed shortly after arriving at the school. Or was he?

On more than one occasion Bush said he saw the first plane strike the WTC North Tower. "I was sitting outside the classroom waiting to go in and I saw an airplane hit the tower—the TV was obviously on, and I used to fly myself, and I said, 'There's one terrible pilot.'" The oddity here is that no video of the strike on the North Tower was available until that evening, when a French camera team revealed they had accidentally filmed the hit while shooting a documentary in Manhattan.

Could Bush have seen the hit via an unannounced private broadcast? This possibility was hinted at when Vice President Cheney, during an interview with *Meet the Press* on September 16, 2001, said, "The Secret Service has an arrangement with the FAA. They had open lines after the World Trade Center was . . ." He ended his statement and moved on to other matters. If Bush indeed witnessed the first strike, why have all later official versions of the school events stated otherwise?

Bush then told the school principal that "a commercial plane has hit the World Trade Center and we're going ahead and . . . do the reading thing anyway." Bush then entered the classroom at about the same time as the second plane struck the WTC South Tower. Moments later, Chief of Staff Andrew Card whispered to Bush, alerting him that a second plane had struck and that this was clearly a terrorist attack. To the later amazement of many,

Bush calmly continued his interaction with the second-graders—even as the rest of country watched terrorist mayhem consume lower Manhattan, and while two additional hijacked planes remained in the air over American territory.

In an effort to address criticism of Bush's lack of immediate action, Card later altered the time frame by telling newsmen that after he informed the president of the second strike, "Not that many seconds later the president excused himself from the classroom." It is now known, however, and supported by video tapes of the photo op, that Bush remained in the classroom until 9:16 a.m., more than *seven hundred* seconds after Card's notification.

To add to this puzzling behavior on the part of the nation's commander in chief is the fact that his security force surely must have realized the danger to the president inherent in a large-scale terrorist attack. Yet, Bush was allowed to finish his chat with the elementary students and calmly leave the school after making general comments to the media. He also left by the same motorcade and along the originally planned route *even after* officials were alerted that White House security codes had been compromised. And finally, *Air Force One* left Florida with no military jet escort—disconcertingly odd behavior considering the potential danger to the president.

Bush was then flown on a series of odd and erratic flight paths to various parts of the country, only surfacing much later that day.

5. Did War Games Aid the Terrorists?

Evidence now available indicates that planning for the 9/11 reaction was indeed set into motion long before September 11.

On May 8, 2001, four months prior to the attacks and a week before convicted Oklahoma City bomber Timothy McVeigh was executed, the Bush administration was already addressing the problem of terrorism. On this day, Bush created a new office dedicated to national preparedness within the Federal Emergency Management Agency (FEMA) and named Vice President Dick

Cheney to head a special task force to study terrorism and guide FEMA's antiterrorism efforts. This new Office of National Preparedness (ONP) placed Cheney in a position to know all aspects of the international terrorist structure and particularly America's nonpublic terrorist attack planning scenarios.

Amazingly enough, pre-9/11 contingency planning may have aided the success of the attacks. Such planning, to include war games, may also provide an answer to the many questions concerning Bush's lack of immediate concern. But such answers raise even more questions.

To begin with, the powerful but little publicized National Reconnaissance Office (NRO) had scheduled a test exercise for the morning of September 11, 2001. The scenario was that of a corporate jet, crippled by mechanical failure, crashing into one of the four towers of the NRO headquarters building in Chantilly, VA, which is about four miles from Washington's Dulles International Airport. No actual planes were to be used in the exercise, but plans called for evacuating most of the three thousand NRO employees.

The exercise, later described as a "bizarre coincidence," was the brain child of CIA officer John Fulton, chief of the NRO's strategic gaming division. In 2002, an announcement for a Department of Homeland Security conference noted the exercise with the comment, "On the morning of September 11, 2001, Mr. Fulton and his team . . . were running a preplanned simulation to explore the emergency response issues that would be created if a plane were to strike a building. Little did they know that the scenario would come true in a dramatic way that day."

The exercise was cancelled when the first plane struck the World Trade Center less than an hour before the test was to begin. All NRO employees, except for certain essential personnel, were sent home for the day, according to NRO officials.

Author Barbara Honegger pointed out the obvious lack of timely response to the 9/11 attacks—especially at the Pentagon—and suggested, "This is beyond comprehension over the nation's capital unless some previous piece of information or mental set led them to assume the Pentagon plane could not be a terrorist vehicle, or at least confuse them as to whether it was or not. If those looking on from inside the Pentagon as 9/11 unfolded believed Flight 77 was, or might be, part of a 'Red Team' counter-terror exercise set for that very morning, it would explain the otherwise incomprehensible delay, almost to the point of paralysis, in effectively scrambling interceptors."

The NRO exercise, astounding in its timing, apparently was either part of—or concurrent with—*an even larger* war game being played out by NORAD's northeast sector, which included the three 9/11 crash sites in New York, Washington, DC, and Pennsylvania. This was recently confirmed by then-NSC counter-terrorism chief Richard A. Clarke. In his 2004 book *Against All Enemies,* narrating his experiences during a video teleconference in the White House Situation Room on the morning of 9/11, Clarke writes: "I turned to the Pentagon screen. 'JCS , JCS [Joint Chiefs of Staff]. I assume NORAD has scrambled fighters and AWACS. How many? Where?'"

Acting chairman of the joint chiefs Richard Myers then responded, "We're in the middle of Vigilant Warrior [other sources state the operation was called Vigilant Guardian], a NORAD exercise, but…Otis has launched two birds toward New York. Langley is trying to get two up now. The AWACS are at Tinker [AFB] and not on alert."

Honegger, who in her well-known 1989 book *October Surprise* revealed the elder Bush's role in a deal with Iranian terrorists to ensure the election of Ronald Reagan in 1980, added that the idea of the 9/11 attacks growing from a homegrown exercise might explain why the leak of a September 10, 2001, NSA intercept message upset Vice President Cheney so much.

That message reportedly was between hijacker leader Mohammad Atta and the purported attack mastermind, Khalid Sheikh Mohammed. It stated, "The Match is about to begin. Tomorrow is zero hour."

"'Match,' of course, is what you would expect if the speaker were referring to his discovery of the date that the US government had selected to conduct its counter-terror simulation/exercise on

the scenario of plane(s) crashing into government buildings—
one that was about to turn very real when the terrorists piggy-
backed their long-planned plot onto it," said Honneger. "[G]iven
the context in which all this finally begins to make sense, Atta was
merely communicating to his boss, or vice versa, the date that the
US government exercise was to take place. Bin al Shibh, Atta, and
Mohammed didn't choose the date. The US government did."

"That's why [Cheney] was in the White House Situation
Room, and why President Bush kept meeting with grammar
school kids in Florida long after he should have instantly broken
it off to perform his emergency duties as commander in chief. The
reason was that Bush 'knew'—or thought he knew—that it was
just a game," she added.

Honegger pointed out that news accounts of the mock
hijackings stated that "exceptions" were made in the scenarios
which concentrated on planes taken over in foreign countries. "It
must be the case that one of these 'exceptions' was used in the war
games of 9/11," she explained. "We know for certain that
NORAD's 'Vigilant Guardian' regional exercise on the morning of
9/11 must have included multiple hijack scenarios because the
'game' participants and organizers were confused as to whether
the hijack alerts coming in from Boston that morning were part of
the game or for real."

Why then have not government officials announced, or at
least leaked this information to explain their lack of response that
morning? Could it be that to acknowledge the exercises would also
acknowledge that someone in high authority must have passed
this information and its timing to the terrorists?

The release of news concerning such exercise proposals also
certainly gives lie to the numerous public statements of President
Bush, National Security Adviser Condoleezza Rice, FBI Director
Louis Freeh, and others who stated, at times under oath, that the
government never considered that terrorists might use airplanes
as weapons.

And there's even more evidence of gaming scenarios. In
2004, it was also reported that in April of 2001 air defense

planners proposed yet another exercise, this one involving an airliner actually being crashed into the Pentagon. According to an email message sent by a NORAD officer in September 2001, and published by the nonprofit watchdog group, Project Government Oversight, "The NORAD exercise developers wanted an event having a terrorist group hijack a commercial airliner (foreign carrier) and fly it into the Pentagon. Joint Staff action officers rejected it as unrealistic."

"What do you want to bet that, when the April 2001 hijacked-plane-into-Pentagon NORAD war game script writer was turned down, that he took his idea to Cheney or one of Cheney's people, who then took it as their own . . ." mused Honegger, ". . . and on September 11, the same scenario that had been turned down in April was embedded in NORAD's own game, 'Vigilant Guardian'?"

It was also learned that as far back as November 3, 2000, the Military District of Washington's Command Emergency Response Training unit conducted a scenario entitled The Pentagon Mass Casualty Exercise, which simulated the crash of an airliner into the courtyard of the Pentagon.

The idea of war games causing the sluggishness of response on 9/11 might also explain why so much of the material on still-missing Khalid Sheikh Mohammed remains classified. He might well be a US intelligence "asset" that was actually working for someone else. This points to the possibility that the 9/11 attacks may indeed have been a conspiracy wrapped inside another conspiracy, a hypothesis considered in the later sections of this book.

Cheney's terrorism task force was scheduled to produce antiterrorism recommendations for Congress by October 1, 2001. Of course, by that time, the nation was well into the new War on Terrorism.

During that same time, Cheney also was in charge of another task force reviewing national energy policy. This panel later became the center of controversy, when California's power woes indicated that corporate energy executives had unduly influenced national policies. Well into 2004, Cheney's task force was still refusing to hand over its internal papers, and a lawsuit over this refusal had made its way up to the Supreme Court.

It is a known fact that Cheney met at least six times with officials of the failed energy company Enron. Some observers, including pioneer 9/11 researcher Mike Ruppert, have argued that smoking-gun documents related to 9/11 may be hidden in the records that Cheney is refusing to make public.

6. Bush Creates the Premise for a War on Terrorism

In prophetic testimony before joint hearings of the Senate Armed Services Appropriations and Intelligence committees in the spring of 2001, Secretary of State Colin Powell explained why Americans should not give up freedoms for the hope of security. "If we adopted this hunkered-down attitude, behind our concrete and our barbed wire, the terrorists would have achieved a kind of victory," he declared.

After the 9/11 attacks, the rhetoric changed completely as new and constitutionally questionable laws and regulations were put into effect. Within days of the 9/11 attacks, President Bush declared a "War on Terrorism." He initially called it a crusade, but that term was quickly dropped when it was pointed out that Muslims, both within and without the Middle East, still remember the history of the word and take offense.

To initiate a war, there first must be a perceived enemy. That one grand enemy was now claimed to be Osama bin Laden and his al Qaeda network. With unbelievable speed, the FBI announced a list of suspected hijackers while at the same time acknowledging that the men used false identity papers. But this list was questioned in many quarters, including government agents.

"There are people within the US intelligence community who doubt that the hijacker list from 9/11 has much truth in it," said one unnamed intelligence source as quoted by Internet writer Jon Rappoport. "They see it as a more-or-less invented list. They know that if you start with men showing false passports (or no passports) to get on four planes on 9/11, you can't assemble a correct list of nineteen suspects within a few days—especially since all those men are presumed dead and missing, untraceable."

"Al Qaeda is being used as a term to convince people that these terrorists are all connected in a vast, very well-organized network that is global in reach, that has a very sophisticated and far-flung communication setup, that issues orders from the top down to cells all over the world," stated the intelligence source. "There are a number of people inside the US intelligence agencies who know this is a false picture. They know that false intelligence is being assembled in order to paint a picture which is distorted, so that the American people will have a single focus on one grand evil enemy."

So began the War on Terrorism, yet few today feel any more secure than before 9/11—in fact many feel far less so.

7. Who Authorized the bin Laden Evacuation?

While hundreds of people around the world were rounded up by national authorities in the wake of the 9/11 attacks and the public denied the right to fly, about 140 Saudis, including two dozen members of Osama bin Laden's own family, were allowed to fly by private jet to a reunion in Washington and then on to Boston. According to *The New Yorker*, the bin Ladens grouped in Boston, from where they eventually were flown out of the country once the FAA reinstated overseas flights. And this curious operation was carried out even as Osama bin Laden was being fingered as the undoubted perpetrator of the attacks.

Initially dismissed as rumor or an urban legend, the reports of the bin Laden family flight were confirmed in an October 2003 *Vanity Fair* interview with Richard A. Clarke, who had resigned earlier that year as chief of the Counterterrorism Security Group of the NSC. Clarke said that he did not recall who requested approval for the flight, but thought it was either the FBI or the State Department. "Someone brought to us for approval the decision to let an airplane filled with Saudis, including members of the bin Laden family, leave the country," he said. "So I said, 'Fine, let it happen.'"

Although both the *Tampa Tribune* and the *New York Times* reported that the Saudis were shepherded to their flights by FBI agents, bureau officials denied such reports. The Saudi flights, which came from ten American cities, including Los Angeles, Washington, DC, and Houston, ended up in Boston where two jumbo jets flew the group to Saudi Arabia in mid-September 2001.

None of the Saudis was seriously interrogated by anyone.

"We were in the midst of the worst terrorist act in history and here we were seeing an evacuation of the bin Ladens..." groused Tom Kinton, director of aviation at Boston's Logan International Airport. "I wanted to go to the highest levels in Washington," he told *Vanity Fair* but realized that the operation had the blessing of top federal officials.

"How was it possible that, just as President Bush declared a no-holds-barred global war on terrorism that would send hundreds of thousands of US troops to Afghanistan and Iraq, and just as Osama bin Laden became Public Enemy No. 1 and the target of a worldwide manhunt, the White House would expedite the departure of so many potential witnesses, including two dozen relatives of the man behind the attack itself?" asked *Vanity Fair* writer Craig Unger.

Numerous bin Laden family members flew out of the US from Logan International on September 18, 2001. The very next day, White House speech writers were formulating President Bush's stirring call for a war on terrorism while at the Pentagon plans were being drawn up for this war to include Iraq. No one yet has pinpointed the authority behind this incredible evacuation, although it is clear this authority must have had control over both the FBI and the FAA.

8. What About the Hijackers Themselves?

A long series of disturbing questions have been raised concerning the hijackers themselves and the people behind them.

The day following 9/11, FBI director Robert Mueller announced some astonishingly swift police work. "We have, in the last twenty-four hours, taken the [passenger] manifests and used them in an evidentiary manner. And have successfully, I believe, identified many of the hijackers on each of the four flights that went down," he told newsmen. Sounding like a 1940s police detective, Mueller added, "We will leave no stone unturned to find those responsible for the tragedies."

Yet, at the same time, Mueller acknowledged that the list of named hijackers might not contain their real names.

An obvious set of questions arises from this scenario: If they used aliases, how did the FBI identify them so quickly? Isn't everyone required to show a photo ID to claim a boarding pass? Where was the normal security? How did the FBI learn the names of five of the hijackers and obtain their photographs the day of the attacks? And where did agents obtain the names and locations of businesses and restaurants used by the hijackers by that same afternoon?

Not one of the accused hijackers' names appeared on the passenger lists made public by American or United airlines. In fact, seven of those named as the culprits in the attacks were soon found alive and well in the Middle East.

Saudi pilot Waleed al-Shehri was identified by the US Justice Department as one of the men who crashed American Flight 11 into the WTC. But a few days later, Waleed al-Shehri contacted authorities in Casablanca, Morocco, to proclaim that he was very much alive and played no part in the attacks. He said he did train as a pilot in the United States but left the country in September 2000, to become a pilot with Saudi Arabian Airlines.

Another man identified as one of the hijackers of Flight 11, Abdulaziz al-Omari, also turned up alive in the Middle East, telling BBC News that he lost his passport while visiting Denver, Colorado. Actually two turned up, as yet another Abdulaziz al-Omari surfaced in Saudi Arabia very much alive and telling newsmen, "I couldn't believe the FBI put me on their list. They gave my name and my date of birth, but I am not a suicide bomber. I am here. I am alive. I have no idea how to fly a plane. I had nothing to do with this."

Yet another man identified as one of the hijackers of United Flight 93, Saeed al-Ghamdi, was reported alive and well and working as a pilot in Saudi Arabia. "You cannot imagine what it is like to be described as a terrorist—and a dead man—when you are innocent and alive," said al-Ghamdi, who was given a holiday by his airline in Saudi Arabia to avoid arrest.

There were even reports that another identified hijacker, Khalid al-Midhar, might also be alive.

"It was proved that five of the names included in the FBI list had nothing to do with what happened," announced Saudi Arabia's foreign minister Prince Saud al-Faisal, after meeting with President Bush on September 20, 2001.

Mueller acknowledged within days of the attacks that the identities of the hijackers were in doubt but this gained little notice in the rush to publicize the culprits. Despite initially saying he was "fairly confident" that the published names of the hijackers were correct, Mueller later admitted, "The identification process has been complicated by the fact that many Arab family names are similar. It is also possible that the hijackers used false identities."

Since Saudi Arabia's foreign minister claimed five of the proclaimed hijackers were not aboard the death planes and in fact are still alive, and a sixth man on that list was reported to be alive and well in Tunisia, why are these names still on the FBI list?

Very soon after the attacks, the stunning news that many of the accused hijackers were in training at American flight schools hit the headlines.

In September 2002, during testimony before a joint congressional committee, Kristin Breitweiser, whose husband, Ronald, died at the WTC, asked a most pertinent question about this admitted fact, a question that continues to go unanswered. She cited a *New York Times* article the day after the strikes stating that FBI agents arrived at flight schools within hours to gather biographies on the terrorists. "How did the FBI know where to go a few hours after the attacks? . . . Were any of the hijackers already under surveillance?"

One promising lead ignored by the FBI but pursued by investigative reporter Daniel Hopsicker concerns the retirement community of Venice, Florida. "Three of the four [accused] 9/11 pilots learned to fly at two flight schools at the tiny Venice Airport. A terrorist trifecta [a race track gambling term meaning the first three places in a race must be predicted in their correct order] out at Venice Airport," noted Hopsicker. "Florida is the biggest 9/11 crime scene that wasn't reduced to rubble. But it hasn't been treated that way. And no one has offered any reason why.

"Both flight schools were owned by Dutch nationals. Both had been recently purchased, at about the same time. A year later terrorists began to arrive, in numbers greater than we have so far been told. All of this must be just a freak coincidence, according to the FBI."

Hopsicker also noted that government officials claimed that the Arab terrorists came to the United States for flight training because it was less expensive, yet, according to aviation experts, they actually paid more than double the cost of training elsewhere.

Further, none of the accused hijackers' names appear on any of the passenger lists and there was a discrepancy of thirty-five names between the published passenger lists and the official death toll on all four of the ill-fated flights. Internet columnist Gary North reported, ". . . the published names in no instance match the total listed for the number of people on board." Why the discrepancy?

To add to this mystery, Dr. Thomas R. Olmsted, a psychiatrist and former navy line officer, filed a Freedom of Information Act request with the Armed Forces Institute of Pathology (AFIP), which had responsibility for identifying all victims in the Pentagon reportedly killed by the crash of Flight 77. Only after the start of the Iraq invasion did Dr. Olmsted finally receive his accounting. "No Arabs wound up on the morgue slab," noted Dr. Olmsted. "However . . . *additional* [emphasis in the original] people not listed by American Airlines sneaked in. I have seen no explanation for these extras."

The airline listed fifty-six persons on Flight 77 yet the AFIP listed sixty-four bodies as passengers on the plane. "And they did not explain how they were able to tell 'victims' bodies from 'hijacker' bodies," added Dr. Olmsted.

Since none of the listed passengers on any of the airlines had Arabic-sounding names, how did the government know who the hijackers were?

Plenty of disturbing questions surround the story of alleged Flight 77 pilot, Hani Hanjour. It is widely known that this young Saudi had a history of great difficulties in his efforts to learn to fly. As late as Aug. 2001, he was unable to demonstrate enough piloting skills to even rent a Cessna 172.

Among other news sources on this subject, *Newsday* revealed the following remarkable facts about Hanjour: "At Freeway Airport in Bowie, Md., 20 miles west of Washington, flight instructor Sheri Baxter instantly recognized the name of alleged hijacker Hani Hanjour when the FBI released a list of 19 suspects in the four hijackings. Hanjour, the only suspect on Flight 77 the FBI listed as a pilot, had come to the airport one month earlier seeking to rent a small plane.

"However, when Baxter and fellow instructor Ben Conner took the slender, soft-spoken Hanjour on three test runs during the second week of August, they found he had trouble controlling and landing the single-engine Cessna 172. Even though Hanjour showed a federal pilot's license and a log book cataloging six hundred hours of flying experience, chief flight instructor Marcel Bernard declined to rent him a plane without more lessons."

Numerous puzzling stories have also emerged about the so-called mastermind of the hijackers, Mohammed Atta.

Atta reportedly left behind in his parked car two suitcases containing incriminating documents, including Atta's passport, driver's license, his last will, a copy of the Koran, flight simulation manuals for Boeing aircraft and a note to other hijackers. But why even take suitcases on a suicide mission? And if the suitcases were camouflage to present the appearance of a normal tourist, why did he leave them behind?

CNN reported on September 16, "In New York, several blocks from the ruins of the World Trade Center, a passport authorities said belonged to one of the hijackers was discovered a few days ago, according to city Police Commissioner Bernard Kerik. That has prompted the FBI and police to widen the search area beyond the immediate crash site." What happened to the passport and this story? Both seemed to have disappeared. Some suspicious researchers smelled planted evidence.

The discovered passport has been widely reported to have belonged to Mohammed Atta but actually was said to have been in the name of Satam al Suqami, supposedly the pilot of Flight 11 which reportedly was consumed within the North Tower after striking it dead on. But how could the "black box" flight recorders on both WTC planes, designed to withstand crashes, have been damaged beyond use but a paper passport be fortuitously found on the ground blocks from the WTC?

Author David Griffin quoted an unnamed high-level intelligence source as saying what was on many people's minds, "Whatever trail was left was left deliberately—for the FBI to chase."

Furthermore, in light of media stories concerning the discovered passport, a Koran left behind, flight school materials, and even "suicide notes," why did FBI director Robert Mueller in an April 19, 2002, speech before the Commonwealth Club in San Francisco declare that the hijackers "left no paper trail"?

On the night before the attacks, according to the *Boston Globe*, four of the suspected hijackers called several escort services asking how much it would cost to acquire prostitutes for the night. Other news sources stated that other suspects spent time in bars and strip clubs in Florida, New Jersey, and Las Vegas. Heavy drinking and a search for hookers by some of the hijackers sound a lot more like mercenaries carousing before a mission than pious religious fundamentalists about to meet their maker.

More discrepancies: Why did the seat numbers of hijackers given by a cell phone call from flight attendant Madeline Amy Sweeney to Boston air traffic control not match the seats occupied by the men the FBI claimed were responsible?

Why did news outlets describe the throat cutting and mutilation of passengers on Flight 93 with box cutters when *Time* magazine on September 24 reported that one of the passengers called home on a cell phone to report, "We have been hijacked. They are being kind."?

In the days following September 11, many major media pundits correctly pointed out that a ragtag bunch of fanatics could not have successfully pulled off the large-scale and well-coordinated attacks by themselves. They must have had the sponsorship of some state, they argued. It was this rationale that provided the foundation argument for the subsequent attacks on Afghanistan and Iraq.

One captured al Qaeda chief may have provided a startling answer to who actually provided state sponsorship for the 9/11 attacks. This "smoking gun" case that links al Qaeda to Saudi Arabia came to light in late March 2002, with the capture of Abu Zubaydah in a middle-class suburb of the Pakistani city of Faisalabad. On April 2, 2002, White House spokesman Ari Fleischer described Zubaydah as the most senior member of al Qaeda captured to that point and stated, "He will be interrogated about his knowledge of ongoing plans to conduct terrorist activities. This represents a serious blow to al Qaeda."

But instead it appears to have been a serious blow to the Saudis. According to a new book by Gerald Posner entitled *Why America Slept*, Zubaydah turned out to be tightly connected with ranking Saudis, including members of the royal family.

Posner, a noted debunker of JFK assassination conspiracies, supported the official version of pre-9/11 intelligence failures in this new book, arguing that despite all the tax dollars spent, federal agencies simply couldn't connect the dots. Posner has admitted being close to friendly CIA sources, which make his ensuing revelations that much more shocking.

According to Posner, when attempts to pry information out of Zubaydah with drugs failed, the al Qaeda chief was flown to an Afghan facility remodeled to look like a Saudi jail cell. Two Arab American Special Forces operatives, disguised as Saudis, then confronted Zubaydah. The idea was to scare him into revealing al Qaeda secrets. Recall that al Qaeda reportedly detests the Saudi royalty.

Yet, when faced by the faked Saudi interrogators, Zubaydah expressed relief rather than fear, according to Posner. He seemed genuinely happy to see them and offered them telephone numbers for ranking Saudi officials. One number was for Saudi Prince Ahmed bin Salman bin Abdul Aziz, a westernized nephew of Saudi King Fahd and a equestrian whose horse, War Emblem, won the 2002 Kentucky Derby. Zubaydah said Prince Aziz would vouch for him and give the interrogators instructions. The disguised Americans were shocked to find the unlisted Saudi numbers valid.

The Saudi Arabian-born al Qaeda leader then proceeded to outline his Saudi connections. He explained that one such contact in Saudi Arabia was intelligence chief Prince Turki al-Faisal bin Abdul Aziz, who met with Osama bin Laden in 1991 and agreed to provide bin Laden with funds in exchange for his pledge not to promote a jihad war in Saudi Arabia. He said his royal Saudi contacts operated through Pakistani Air Marshal Mushaf Ali Mir, a man with close ties to Muslims inside Pakistan's Inter-Services Intelligence (ISI). The ISI has long been suspected of providing al Qaeda with arms and supplies. And according to Posner, this convoluted pipeline was blessed by the Saudis.

Zubaydah went on to claim that 9/11 did nothing to change the relationships between the Saudis, Pakistanis, and al Qaeda. He claimed that while both Prince Ahmed and Mir knew in advance of the attacks, they did not know the specific targets. They also would have been hesitant to reveal their secret agreements.

Posner also noted that not long after Zubaydah's revelations were passed along to the Saudis, the men mentioned by Zubaydah all died within days of each other. Prince Ahmed died of a heart attack at age 43 on July 22, 2002, while two princes, Sultan bin Faisal bin Turki al-Saud and Fahd bin Turki bin Saud al Kabir both were killed in car wrecks within a week of each other. Pakistani Air Marshal Mir died in a plane crash during clear weather. Posner told *Time* the deaths, most convenient to anyone desiring to keep the Saudi–Pakistani–al Qaeda axis hidden, "may in fact be coincidences."

Despite this remarkable information tying al Qaeda to Saudi royals and Pakistani intelligence published in a major US news magazine, very little of such coverage has made its way to the American public.

Bin Laden even had followers within the US military, as evidenced by court records of a former Fort Bragg, North Carolina, sergeant who gathered top-secret materials for more than two years.

Ali A. Mohamed, from 1987 until his arrest in 1989, served for a time at the John F. Kennedy Special Warfare Center and School. Mohamed, who once served as a major in the Egyptian army's special operations forces, was trained at the officer's course for Green Berets at Fort Bragg in 1981. At about that same time, he joined the terrorist group Islamic Jihad, responsible for the 1981 assassination of Egyptian president Anwar Sadat and later became a close adviser to bin Laden. He also tried unsuccessfully to join the CIA but did become a source of information for the FBI, according to Larry Johnson, a former CIA agent and director of counterterrorism at the State Department during the first Bush administration.

The FBI found documents, believed to have come from Mohamed, in the possession of one of the men convicted in the 1993 WTC bombing. Included were top secret papers belonging to the Joint Chiefs of Staff and the commander in chief of the army's Central Command.

One former Special Forces officer said, "There is no doubt that his proximity, in hindsight, was very harmful," adding, "Does this hurt our efforts now? Absolutely."

It must be recalled that Osama bin Laden as well as many of his al Qaeda operatives are Saudis. And this makes for a very troublesome aspect to the War on Terrorism.

To understand the problem, one must bear in mind the fact that the United States, and perhaps most of the industrialized world, is immeasurably dependent on the eight major oil fields of Saudi Arabia. Loss of even a significant portion of this petroleum could mean unthinkable consequences to the economy of both America and the world.

Control over this crucial strategic resource is concentrated in one ruling family, a family line with longstanding and well-documented ties to major players in the oil industry, notably the Bush family.

Media reports to the contrary, Osama bin Laden still receives financial support from his family even if they do not agree with his views and actions.

According to a PBS biography, most of the bin Ladens are faithful Muslims, who are taught that it is a sin to keep something that is not rightfully yours. Whether they agree with their sibling or not, they sincerely believe that bin Laden's share of the family fortune rightfully belongs to him and they see that he receives his due.

So, while the bin Laden assets are held by other family members, who can rightfully argue that bin Laden owns none of it, his share of the profits continue to go to him. Some family members support bin Laden because they feel it is their religious duty. Others are more circumspect, not wishing to offend the Saudi royals, while others still make no effort to hide the fact that they send bin Laden money.

Of all the nations that are the most probable sponsors of bin Laden, first place must go to Saudi Arabia, home of bin Laden, militant Muslims, and the business partners of the Bush family. This may go far in explaining the dearth of reporting on the Saudis in the mainstream media immediately following the 9/11 attacks. It may also explain why the congressional committee investigating 9/11 issued a censored version of its final report, with twenty-eight pages blanked out from the section entitled "Certain Sensitive National Security Matters." We'll later examine claims by numerous sources familiar with the missing pages in the report who said it pointed to a coordinated network of support for the hijackers reaching directly to high levels of the Saudi government.

Also in this connection, Defense Secretary Donald Rumsfeld tried to suppress a mid-2002 special report by the Defense Department naming Saudi Arabia as the "kernel of evil" and stating that Saudi funds support most of the Middle East's terrorist groups because the Saudis have a vested interest in perpetuating tension in the region. According to federal whistle-blower Al Martin, "It has always been a guideline of Republican administrations, starting with Richard Nixon, to suppress the truth about Saudi Arabia."

9. What Really Happened at the Pentagon?

At the Pentagon, again the official story seemed plausible enough—a third hijacked airliner was flown into America's military command center creating a fire that killed more than 185 persons and caused a section of the west wall to collapse. But, as with the rest of the 9/11 account, the closer one looks, the more mysterious becomes the event.

Take the case of April Gallop, who was at work inside the Pentagon's west side when it was struck on 9/11. Gallop was preparing to take her infant son to day care when the building was rocked by an explosion. "I thought it was a bomb," Gallop recalled. "I was buried in rubble and my first thought was for my son. I crawled around until I found his stroller. It was all crumpled up into a ball and I was then very afraid. But then I heard his voice and managed to locate him. We crawled out through a hole in the side of the building. Outside they were treating survivors on the grassy lawn. But all the ambulances had left, so a man who was near the scene stepped up, put us in his private car, and drove us to the hospital. The images are burned into my brain."

Gallop said while in the hospital, men in suits visited her more than once. "They never identified themselves or even said which agency they worked for. But I know they were not newsmen because I learned that the Pentagon told news reporters not to cover survivors' stories or they would not get any more stories out of there. The men who visited all said they couldn't tell me what to say, they only wanted to make suggestions. But then they told me what to do, which was to take the [Victim Compensation Fund] money and shut up. They also kept insisting that a plane hit the building. They repeated this over and over. But I was there and I never saw a plane or even debris from a plane. I figure the plane story is there to brainwash people."

April Gallop is considering joining as a co-plaintiff in the Racketeer Influenced and Corrupt Organizations (RICO) Act lawsuit filed against President Bush and other ranking officials for their failure to foresee and prevent the attack, filed by Ellen Mariani [author of the Preface to this book]. Excerpts from this case can be found in Appendix D of this book.

Unlike the World Trade Center, unaffected witnesses were around the Pentagon, some with digital cameras. One such was Steve Riskus, a 24-year-old computer worker, who said he saw the craft pass over him and strike a lamppost before plunging into the Pentagon. He immediately began snapping photographs from less than 200 yards away and later that day posted his photos on a newly acquired website, **Criticalthrash.com**. His photos, along with others not controlled by the government, caused major problems for the later official version of the Pentagon crash.

They depicted a clean green lawn in front of the damaged wall which contradicted the official claim that the plane hit the ground before entering the building. They also showed one highway lamppost knocked down but not others nearby it within range of the plane's wing span.

One website even posted numerous official photos of the Pentagon crash and challenged viewers to find any trace of the aircraft. Interestingly enough, years after 9/11 neither the mass media nor the FBI had taken any notice of Rickus's pictures or the questions being raised. It is well worth noting here that the FBI confiscated all the security videos in the vicinity of the crash within minutes; somewhat later, the Pentagon released a mere five frames from one of these videos, which show a barely discernable object slamming into the building followed by a huge fireball.

The major mystery in regard to the Pentagon crash centers on what excatly happened to American Flight 77, a Boeing 757 carrying a mere 64 passengers. According to official sources, the entire plane was consumed inside the walls of the Pentagon.

Yet, three years after 9/11 no one had produced any photographs of Boeing 757 fuselage, jet engines, seats, luggage, or other recognizable debris. The one small piece of red, white, and silver metal widely distributed by the major news media has never been firmly identified as coming from a Boeing 757. This now-famous mystery item, categorized as a fake by some foreign press, simply does not appear in any of the pictures taken within the first half hour of the crash.

After any major air disaster, every fragment of the aircraft is assembled to learn the cause and prevent any reoccurrence. One must therefore ask: Why has no one within the government produced any photograph of the wreckage of Flight 77?

Then there are the startling problems with the holes in the Pentagon. The Boeing 757 has a normal wingspan of 124 feet, 10 inches. The official version of the Pentagon crash states that a 757 entered the building at a 45-degree angle. This angle would increase the wing span to 177 feet. Note that the overall height of a 757 is 44 feet, 6 inches and the exterior body width is 12 feet, 6 inches. Yet the hole in the Pentagon cited as the entry point, photographed before the walls collapsed, was only between 15 and 20 feet wide, barely enough to accommodate the width of the craft's body. And the hole height was less then two stories or about 20 feet, *less than half the height of the 757.*

Even after the walls collapsed shortly after 10 a.m., the gaping hole in the building was still not large enough to accommodate the Boeing 757's wing span. Oddly, no evidence of any kind of the plane's wings or tail were found outside the building, other than the small piece of metal mentioned earlier.

Francois Grangier, a French aviation accident investigator, hoping to defend the official version, studied the Pentagon crash carefully but was forced to conclude, "I think the trajectory as far as one can make it out today rules out an impact against the façade…What is certain when one looks at the photo of this façade that remains intact is that it's obvious the plane did not go through there. It's like imagining that a plane of this size could pass through a window and leave the frame still standing."

Just as strange were photographs depicting what officials said was the exit hole caused by the plane as it completed its penetration of the Pentagon. This hole, located on the inside of the building's fourth ring, is barely more than eight feet high; it shows only slight scorching at the top and even unbroken window panes immediately above it. It is most peculiar that the front of a Boeing 757, lacking density in its aluminum-sheathed nose, could have survived the penetration of four hardened concrete walls, while leaving no known remnants behind. The official story claims that a 1500-degree heat caused by the crash was intense enough to immolate the entire plane and occupants. One wonders why the walls to either side of this exit hole are not scorched.

While several witnesses, such as Army Captain Lincoln Liebner, said they distinctly saw an American Airlines jetliner coming toward the Pentagon swiftly and at low altitude, others were not so certain. Steve Patterson told the *Washington Post* that day, "The airplane seemed to be able to hold between eight or twelve persons." Tom Seibert said, "We heard something that made the sound of a missile, then we heard a powerful boom." Mike Walter excitedly told CNN, "A plane, a plane from American Airlines. I thought, 'That's not right, it's really low.' And I saw it. I mean, it was like a cruise missile with wings." Danielle O'Brien told ABC News, "The speed, the maneuverability, the way he turned, we all thought in the radar room, all us experienced air traffic controllers, that that was a military plane."

O'Brien's perceptions were accurate. For whatever plunged toward the Pentagon—reportedly starting 7,000 feet above the ground—was piloted in such a way that it dropped in a downward spiral, forming an almost a complete circle in just more than two minutes. This is an extremely difficult maneuver for the even the most experienced pilot.

The speed, maneuverability, and the high-pitched scream of the jet coupled with the smallness of the hole prompted many researchers to suggest that what struck the Pentagon was nothing less than some sort of winged missile painted to resemble an American Airlines plane.

Could this be why Defense Secretary Donald Rumsfeld inadvertently mentioned a "missile" when describing the Pentagon attack to *Parade* magazine?

Then there are the disturbing statements of another high government official. Testifying under oath before the National

Commission on the September 11 Terrorist Attacks in mid-2003, Transportation Secretary Norman Mineta gave the following account of his experiences on the morning of 9/11:

After stating that he had arrived in the Presidential Emergency Operating Center shortly after the South Tower of the WTC had been struck, Mineta recalled, "During the time that the airplane was coming in to the Pentagon, there was a young man who would come in and say to the Vice President, 'The plane is 50 miles out.' 'The plane is 30 miles out.' And when it got down to 'the plane is 10 miles out,' the young man also said to the Vice President, 'Do the orders still stand?' And the Vice President turned and whipped his neck around and said, 'Of course the orders still stand! Have you heard anything to the contrary?' Well at the time, I didn't know what all that meant . . . [This was the] flight that came into the Pentagon . . ."

Asked if these "orders" were to shoot down the errant airliners, Mineta responded, "Well, I don't know that specifically. I do know that the [interceptor] airplanes were scrambled from Langley or from Norfolk, the Norfolk area, and so I did not know about the order specifically other than to listening to that other conversation. . . . Subsequently, I found that out."

Commission vice chairman Lee Hamilton then asked, "But there were military planes in the air in position to shoot down commercial aircraft?" "That's right," replied Mineta. "The planes had been scrambled, I believe from Otis, at that point."

The strange conversation between Cheney and the "young man" as related by Mineta prompts several puzzling questions. What were these orders? And if the orders were to shoot down captured airliners as later stated by the White House, why weren't they carried out? If fighter jets could not reach the Pentagon in time, what about the antiaircraft missile batteries in place around Washington—indeed, just adjacent to the Pentagon itself?

While researchers have hunted fruitlessly for a stand-down order within the administration to explain the lack of effective response on 9/11, it may be that such orders were much more mundane—a simple matter of slightly changing standard NORAD procedures.

Prior to June 2001, under Department of Defense directives, while the secretary of defense retained approval authority for the release of military jets to support civil air authorities, they also provided that "Nothing in this Directive prevents a commander from exercising his or her immediate emergency response authority…" and that "Requests for an immediate response (i.e., any form of immediate action taken by a DoD Component or military commander to save lives, prevent human suffering, or mitigate great property damage under imminently serious conditions) may be made to any Component or Command. The DoD Components…may initiate informal planning and, if required, immediately respond as authorized in DoD Directive 3025.1 (reference (g))." In other words, in the event of an air emergency, local commanders could initiate a response pending later approval of the secretary of defense.

This all changed on June 1, 2001, with the issuance of Chairman of the Joint Chiefs of Staff Instruction [CJCSI] 3610.01A. This document states, under the heading, "Aircraft Piracy (Hijacking) of Civil and Military Aircraft," that "the NMCC [National Military Command Center] is the focal point within the Department of Defense for providing assistance. In the event of a hijacking, the NMCC will, with the exception of immediate responses as authorized by referenced, forward requests for DoD assistance to the Secretary of Defense for approval."

"Secretary of Defense [Donald] Rumsfeld is personally responsible for issuing intercept orders," noted Internet writer Jerry Russell. "Commanders in the field are stripped of all authority to act . . . it is now clear that [any 'Stand Down' order] was implemented through a routine administrative memo."

Of course, if Flight 77 did not hit the Pentagon, even more questions arise. What happened to the plane and its passengers? Did it cross into Washington air space before a missile was sent into the Pentagon? Was it ditched into the Atlantic as suggested by some? Was a missile or plane guided from an external location as will be discussed later?

All such conjecture could be ended by simply showing the

public the wreckage of the aircraft. But almost three years on, such photos still had not been forthcoming.

Unanswered questions continued to grow in the wake of the 9/11 tragedies. The strange case of the Pentagon crash is among the most puzzling of all.

10. Explosions at the World Trade Center?

Why, according to several experts and numerous independent observers, did the destruction of the World Trade Center towers appear more like a controlled implosion than terrorist-caused destruction?

Such questions concerning the collapse of the towers were advanced by experts in demolition and firefighting immediately, only to die away in the subsequent media blitz of "official" pronouncements. Many people, experts and laymen alike, asked why the South Tower collapsed first when it was not as extensively damaged as the North Tower, which burned for almost an hour and a half before its collapse?

Numerous sources have claimed that bombs rather than the planes caused the collapse of the World Trade Center towers.

Van Romero, vice president for research at the New Mexico Institute of Mining and Technology and a former director of the Energenic Materials Research and Testing Center said televised images of the collapse of the WTC towers suggested that explosives were used to create a controlled demolition.

"My opinion is, based on the videotapes, that after the airplanes hit the World Trade Center there were some explosive devices inside the buildings that caused the towers to collapse," Romero told the *Albuquerque Journal* on September 11, 2001.

Romero, who ironically was in the Washington area during the 9/11 attacks attempting to gain government funding for defense research at his school, said the collapse of the WTC was "too methodical" to be the chance result of airplanes colliding with the structures. He said it appeared more like the controlled implosions used to demolish old buildings.

"It could have been a relatively small amount of explosives placed in strategic points," he said, adding that the detonation of bombs within towers is consistent with common terrorist strategy. "One of the things terrorist events are noted for is a diversionary attack and secondary device. Attackers detonate an initial, diversionary explosion that attracts emergency personnel to the scene, then detonate a second explosion," he explained.

Within 10 days, Romero reversed himself, telling the *Albuquerque Journal* that following conversations with "other experts" he came to understand that "Certainly the fire is what caused the building to fail." He did concede that the final collapse may have been caused when fire reached an electrical transformer or other source of combustion within the building, leaving open the question of explosions. There was no word of whether or not New Mexico Tech received its federal funding requests although it was learned that the school does provide counterterrorism training to firemen, policemen, and first responders.

Many have wondered about the witnesses who claimed to have heard multiple explosions within the buildings. One such witness was the head of WTC security, John O'Neill, who stated shortly before he himself became a victim that he had helped dig out survivors on the 27th floor before the building collapsed. Since the aircraft crashed into the 80th floor, what heavily damaged the 27th floor?

Another of those mentioning bombs was Louie Cacchioli, a fifty-one-year-old fireman assigned to Engine 47 in Harlem. "We were the first ones in the second tower after the plane struck," recalled Cacchioli. "I was taking firefighters up in the elevator to the twenty-fourth floor to get in position to evacuate workers. On the last trip up a bomb went off. We think there were bombs set in the building." The fireman became trapped in an elevator but managed to escape with the use of tools.

Auxiliary Fire Lt. Paul Isaac Jr. also mentioned bombs, telling Internet reporter Randy Lavello that New York firemen were very upset by what they considered a cover-up in the WTC destruction. "Many other firemen know there were bombs in the buildings," he said, "but they are afraid for their jobs to admit it because the higher-ups forbid discussion of this fact." Isaac, who was stationed at Engine 10 near the WTC in the late 1990s, said the higher-ups included the NYFD's antiterrorism consultant, James Woolsey, a former CIA director. "There were definitely bombs in those buildings," Isaac added.

Survivor Teresa Veliz, manager for a software development company, was on the 47th floor of the North Tower when it was struck. "I got off [the elevator], turned the corner and opened the door to the ladies' room. I said good morning to a lady sitting at a mirror when the whole building shook. I thought it was an earthquake. Then I heard those banging noises on the other side of the wall. It sounded like someone had cut the elevator cables. It just fell and fell and fell."

Veliz reached ground level with a coworker when the South Tower collapsed, knocking them down. In near total darkness, she and the coworker followed someone with a flashlight. "The flashlight led us into Borders bookstore, up an escalator and out to Church Street. There were explosions going off everywhere. I was convinced that there were bombs planted all over the place and someone was sitting at a control panel pushing detonator buttons. I was afraid to go down Church Street toward Broadway, but I had to do it. I ended up on Vesey Street. There was another explosion. And another. I didn't know which way to run."

Ross Milanytch watched the horror at the WTC from his office window on the 22nd floor of a building a couple of blocks away. "[I saw] small explosions on each floor. And after it all cleared, all that was left of the buildings, you could just see the steel girders in like a triangular sail shape. The structure was just completely gone," he said.

Steve Evans, a reporter for the BBC, was in the South Tower at the time of the attacks. "I was at the base of the second tower, the second tower that was hit," he recalled. "There was an explosion—I didn't think it was an explosion—but the base of the building shook. I felt it shake . . . then when we were outside, the second explosion happened and then there was a series of explosions. . . . We can only wonder at the kind of damage—the kind of human damage—which was caused by those explosions, those series of explosions."

Fox 5 News in New York City, shortly after 10 a.m. on September 11, videotaped a large white cloud of smoke billowing near the base of the South Tower. The commentator exclaimed, "There is an explosion at the base of the building . . . white smoke from the bottom . . . something has happened at the base of the building . . . then, another explosion. Another building in the World Trade Center complex . . ."

The most compelling testimony came from Tom Elliott, who was already in his office at Aon Corp. on the 103rd floor of the WTC South Tower before the planes struck.

Elliott said he was at his computer answering emails when a bright light startled him shortly before 9 a.m. A rumble shook the building and he could see flames accompanied by dark smoke that appeared to be crawling up the outside of the building. He also felt heat coming through the windows. Strangely, there were no alarms.

"I don't know what's happening, but I think I need to be out of here," Elliott recalled thinking to himself.

Elliott and two others began walking down the building's stairwell when they ran into a few others. The absence of more people and the lack of alarms made them feel they had prematurely panicked.

He recalled that as his small group reached the 70th floor, they heard the announcement that the building was secure and there was no need to evacuate. "Do you want to believe them?" one woman said to Elliott. "Let's go!" He followed the woman down the stairs.

After descending three more floors, Flight 175 crashed into the South Tower. An article in the *Christian Science Monitor* described what happened next:

"Although its spectacularly televised impact was above Elliott, at first he and those around him thought an explosion had come from below. An incredible sound—he calls it an 'exploding sound'—shook the building, and a tornado of hot air and smoke and ceiling tiles and bits of drywall came flying up the stairwell."

"In front of me, the wall split from the bottom up," Elliott said. He said people in the stairwell panicked and tried to flee upward until some men pointed out that the only escape was downstairs. By about 9:40, Elliott managed to stumble out of the South Tower and make his way to his roommate's office in Midtown, where he broke down sobbing upon learning of the tower's collapse.

A CNN video of the scene at the WTC showed smoke boiling up from the street level prior to the collapse of the towers, apparently from the eight-story WTC Building 6, more popularly known as the Customs House building. Nothing of significance had struck street level at that time. Did the billowing smoke come from a premature detonation?

Due to a delayed broadcast, there was some initial confusion about just when the smoke began. However, CNN's Public Affairs Department confirmed that the video footage of an apparent explosion at ground level was made at 9:04, just one minute after Flight 175 struck the South Tower and long before either tower collapsed.

Asked what might have caused the smoke seen in the video, the CNN archivist replied, "We can't figure it out."

According to news reports, the FEMA team of engineers commissioned to investigate the WTC tragedy was barred from entering the Custom House building. FEMA officials reported that because the structure was considered "very dangerous," there was "no data collection" from Building 6. Yet, the FEMA report blithely stated, "Building Five was the only building accessible for observation [by the team of engineers] . . . the observations, findings and recommendations are assumed to be applicable to all three buildings."

A spokesman for the Export-Import Bank of the United States confirmed the 9:04 time of the blast but said all of the eight hundred or so employees of the Customs House building had already been evacuated after the WTC North Tower was struck.

Other occupants of the building, which included the Customs Service, the departments of Commerce, Labor, and

Agriculture and the Bureau of Alcohol, Tobacco and Firearms, declined to explain either the early blast or the massive crater at the center of the Customs House ruins.

No explanation for this explosion or crater has been forthcoming.

But if there were bombs in the towers, how did they get there?

With the buildings turned to powdered ash and the metal quickly hauled away, no one will ever be certain but some interesting theories have been advanced. One is that charges were placed in the towers at the time of their construction to prevent a catastrophe such as 9/11 from causing them to fall over on neighboring buildings, magnifying the destruction. No proof of this has been established. Explosive experts discount this theory, stating that explosives could not have remained effective after an extended period of time. A similar theory postulates that charges were placed in the buildings following the 1993 bombing for the reason stated above.

Yet another theory emerged after Ben Fountain, a financial analyst who worked on the 47th floor of the South Tower, told *People* magazine that in the weeks preceding 9/11 there were numerous unusual and unannounced "drills" in which sections of both towers as well as Building 7 were evacuated for "security reasons." These drills could have provided a perfect cover for persons planting explosives.

Who exactly ordered that broadcast over the loudspeakers in the South Tower as workers were trying to evacuate, "Remain calm, damage is in Tower One. Return to your desks."? Many people lost their lives because of these announcements. Minutes later the towers collapsed unexpectedly.

Yet, apparently New York Mayor Rudolph Giuliani did get word of what was coming. The next morning, he explained to ABC's Peter Jennings he was in a temporary command center at 75 Barkley Street. He said, "We were operating out of there when we were told that the World Trade Center was going to collapse and it did collapse before we could get out of the building."

11. Firefighters Thought the Fires Were Controllable

An audiotape of New York firefighters at the scene, unpubli-
cized until mid-2002, indicated that fire officials managed to reach
the 78th floor of the South Tower—very near the crash scene
which was at the 80th floor—and seemed convinced that the fire
was controllable.

The tape was briefly mentioned by the *New York Times* but
was kept from the public by the US Justice Department, which
claimed it might be needed in the trial of the "twentieth hijacker,"
Zacarias Moussaoui, even though Moussaoui was in custody at the
time of the attacks.

The audiotape was a recording of radio transmissions made
on the morning of September 11, 2001. The tape reportedly was
discovered two or three weeks after 9/11 in offices of the Port
Authority of New York and New Jersey at WTC Building 5.
Apparently, Port Authority personnel were monitoring and
recording the New York Fire Department (NYFD) channel.

Two fire officials mentioned by name in the tape were
Battalion Chief Orio J. Palmer and Fire Marshal Ronald P. Bucca,
both of whom perished when the South Tower collapsed along
with 343 other firefighters, the greatest single loss of firefighters in
one incident in history.

According to the *Times* article, both firemen "showed no
panic, no sense that events were racing beyond their control. . . .
At that point, the building would be standing for just a few more
minutes, as the fire was weakening the structure on the floors
above him. Even so, Chief Palmer could see only two pockets of
fire and called for a pair of engine companies to fight them."

Transcripts released on the Internet provided this statement,
"Battalion Seven . . . Ladder 15, we've got two isolated pockets of
fire. We should be able to knock it down with two lines. Radio
that, 78th floor numerous 10-45 Code Ones."

As noted by reporter Christopher Bollyn, "The fact that
veteran firefighters had a 'coherent plan for putting out' the 'two
pockets of fire,' indicates they judged the blazes to be manageable.
These reports from the scene of the crash provide crucial evidence

debunking the government's claim that a raging steel-melting inferno led to the tower's collapse."

According to Mark Loizeaux, president of Controlled Demolition, Inc., of Phoenix, Arizona, who consulted on removing the WTC debris, "hot spots" of molten steel were found as many as five weeks after the collapse when rubble was removed from the elevator shafts seven levels down.

Loizeaux speculated that steel-melting fires were generated by "paper, carpet and other combustibles packed down the elevator shafts by the towers as they 'pancaked" into the basement." Since construction steel's melting point is about 2800 degrees Fahrenheit, other experts disputed this idea, saying that due to the lack of oxygen, such debris would have been only a smoldering pile.

Speculating further, Loizeaux told the *American Free Press,* "If I were to bring the towers down, I would put explosives in the basement to get the weight of the building to help collapse the structure." Subterranean explosives could explain the "hot spots" discovered under the rubble.

Considering the total destruction, reports from survivors and firemen, and the seismic shocks just prior to the collapse, many people believed that Loizeaux's description was exactly what happened on September 11, 2001.

It is worth noting that Controlled Demolition, Inc., is the same company that hurriedly removed the rubble of the Murrah Federal Building in Oklahoma City following the explosion there in 1996. Both there and at the WTC, crucial structural evidence was removed before any independent examination or investigation.

Strong evidence of ground explosions causing the WTC collapse came from seismographs at Columbia University's Lamont-Doherty Earth Observatory in Palisades, New York, twenty-one miles north of the WTC. Just prior to the collapse of the twin towers, seismic equipment recorded two "spikes" indicating large bursts of energy that shook the ground beneath the WTC towers just before their collapse.

Columbia's seismic equipment recorded a 2.1-magnitude ground shock during the ten-second collapse of the South Tower and a 2.3 quake during the eight-second collapse of the North Tower. However, the strongest shocks, or "spikes," on the data recorder both occurred at the beginning of the tower's collapse, well before falling material struck the ground. The two spikes were more than twenty times the amplitude of the other seismic shock waves associated with the falling buildings. One seismologist said the 1993 truck bomb at the WTC did not even register on seismographs; that massive explosion did not cause detectable shock waves through the ground.

Seismologist Arthur Lerner-Lam, director of Columbia's Center for Hazards and Risk Research, added to this by saying, "During the collapse, most of the energy of the falling debris was absorbed by the towers and the neighboring structures, converting them into rubble and dust or causing other damage—but not causing significant ground shaking." Asked about the two unusual shocks, Lerner-Lam was noncommittal. "This is an element of current research and discussion. It is still being investigated," he told the media.

So the public was left with the official explanation that high-temperature fires caused by burning jet fuel melted structural steel beams, causing the towers to fall. No one will ever know for certain since none of the engineers hired by FEMA inspected or tested the steel before it was hauled away for salvage.

"I am not a metallurgist," explained Dr. W. Gene Corley, head of the FEMA engineer team.

According to FEMA's "Building Performance Assessment," temperatures at the crash site—only two floors above Chief Palmer and Marshal Bucca—were as high as 1700–2000 degrees Fahrenheit, so intense as to melt the structure's steel frame girders.

"If FEMA's temperature estimates are correct, the interiors of the towers were furnaces capable of casting aluminum and glazing pottery," declared researcher and author Eric Hufschmid. Yet the firemen were able to work for an extended period of time in close proximity and believed the fires they encountered were manageable. Furthermore, photographic blowups depicting the jagged gash in the North Tower just before its collapse clearly show survivors peering out through the hole made by the airplane.

"The sooty smoke and the black holes [seen in photographs of the towers prior to their collapse] cannot be dismissed as interesting aspects of the fires, nor as problems with the photography," said Hufschmid. "Rather, they are signs that the air flow was so restricted that the only significant fires were near broken windows. The fires in both towers were probably coating the [structural] columns with soot rather than heating the columns to a high temperature."

Citing a severe fire in Philadelphia's Meridian Plaza in 1991, Hufschmid noted, "The Meridian Plaza fire was extreme, but it did not cause the building to collapse.

"The fire in the South Tower seems insignificant by comparison to both the Meridian Plaza fire and the fire in the North Tower. How could the tiny fire in the South Tower cause the entire structure to shatter into dust after fifty-six minutes while much more extreme fires did not cause the Meridian Plaza building to even crack into two pieces?" The fact still remains that, no other high rise buildings have ever collapsed due to a fire of any size, or of any length—let alone in under one hour.

It was also considered peculiar that both towers dropped within fifteen seconds, essentially free-fall speed. Wouldn't the lower floors have held the weight even if only momentarily?

Massachusetts Institute of Technology Materials Professor Thomas Eager explained to PBS's *NOVA* the WTC fires were so massive that they caused the total collapse of 47 core steel-reinforced columns as well as 236 exterior columns. "If it [fire] had only occurred in one small corner, such as a trashcan caught on fire, you might have had to repair that corner, but the whole building wouldn't have come crashing down," explained Eager. "The problem was, it was such a widely distributed fire, and then you got this domino effect."

He described this domino effect as caused by the failure of angle clips, steel brackets that held the floor trusses between the inner core columns and the exterior columns. "Once you started to get angle clips to fail in one area, it put extra load on the other clips, and then it unzipped around the building on that floor in a matter of seconds," said Eager.

Eager's explanation suffers from the fact that neither tower had fires covering the entire floor and the fact that cross trusses would have prevented, or at least slowed, the "unzippering" effect of the angle clips. His explanation also fails to address the speed of the towers' collapse. Even if one can accept that each floor did not impede the collapsing ones above it, there is no explanation for what shattered the outer walls and inner core columns, threw debris hundreds of feet away from the buildings—as shown in the photo on the cover of this book—and turned most of the concrete to pulverized dust.

Noting that the North Tower collapsed in eight seconds, Hufschmid asked, "How could the debris crush one hundred steel and concrete floors while falling as fast as objects fall through the air?"

Even more peculiar was the sudden and unexplained collapse of WTC Building 7, which apparently had suffered damage only from falling debris that caused a minor fire.

12. What Caused the Collapse of Building 7?

The 47-story Building 7 was an oddity to begin with, as it housed two New York electrical substations which existed there prior to construction of the building. These substations housed ten transformers, 35 feet tall by 40 feet wide. Additionally, Mayor Giuliani's Emergency Command Center was located there along with three 500kW generators for emergency power. Both the command center and other operations in the building stored an estimated 42,000 gallons of diesel fuel for auxiliary generators. Of special interest is the fact that some of that power may have been used by the CIA, Department of Defense, or Secret Service, all of which had offices in Building 7.

Shortly after 4 p.m. on September 11, six hours after the collapse of the South Tower, firemen turned their attention to Building 7 after someone reported small fires. But no firemen were allowed to enter the building as they had in the towers. At 5:25 p.m. the 47-story structure collapsed upon itself.

Although no real explanation of the collapse has been offered, it has been reported that the small fires grew larger, reached the stored fuel and started a conflagration so intense it melted the steel frame of the building causing it to crumple. Hufschmid dismissed this version by noting, "Every photo taken of Building 7 shows only a few tiny fires in only a few windows, and only tiny amounts of smoke were produced," he said. "I would think that a fire of the magnitude necessary to collapse a steel building would have set fire to a lot of the office furniture, carpeting, and other flammable objects. This in turn would have caused a lot of flames to be visible in a lot of windows. I also suspect that such a large fire would have caused many windows to shatter. How could an incredible fire burn in the building without any photos showing evidence of large flames or tremendous plumes of smoke?"

Unlike the twin towers which collapsed from the top down, Building 7 collapsed from the bottom up, the classic form of a typical building demolition. In fact, this might have indeed been the case.

In September 2002, during a PBS documentary entitled "America Rebuilds," WTC leaseholder Larry Silverstein had this to say about Building 7: "I remember getting a call from the, er, fire department commander, telling me that they were not sure they were going to be able to contain the fire, and I said, 'We've had such terrible loss of life, maybe the smartest thing to do is pull it.' And they made that decision to pull and we watched the building collapse."

The idea that a modern 47-story steel building can totally collapse strictly due to fire is something outside of normal experience, yet no serious investigation was undertaken. If Building 7 was "pulled" by demolition, why is it so far-fetched to consider that the towers were felled the same way? Perhaps there are more reasonable explanations for modern buildings to collapse into nothing but dust, but no one will ever know for certain due to lack of investigation and destruction of evidence.

13. FEMA's Report: Cause of WTC Collapses Unknown

The public might know more of what really happened to the WTC if the New York Police Department and New York Fire Department had been allowed to do their jobs. But, as with the JFK assassination, their work was taken from them by federal officials, who immediately closed doors and shut out the public from their consultations. People were even arrested for taking photographs of Ground Zero.

The FBI took charge of the criminal investigation while the little-understood Federal Emergency Management Agency took responsibility for determining what happened to cause the collapse of the twin towers. FEMA seemed determined to haul away the evidence, even before a full and impartial investigation could be made. Such premature destruction of evidence was called into question by Bill Manning, editor of the 125-year-old firemen's publication *Fire Engineering* in its January 2002 issue.

"For more than three months, structural steel from the World Trade Center has been and continues to be cut up and sold for scrap," wrote Manning. "Crucial evidence that could answer many questions about high-rise building design practices and performance under fire conditions is on a slow boat to China, perhaps never to be seen again in America until you buy your next car."

Challenging the theory that the twin towers collapsed as a result of crashed airplanes and fires, Manning added, "*Fire Engineering* has good reason to believe that the 'official investigation' blessed by FEMA and run by the American Society of Civil Engineers (ASCE) is a half-baked farce that may already have been commandeered by political forces whose primary interests, to put it mildly, lie far afield of full disclosure.

"Except for the marginal benefit obtained from a three-day, visual walk-through of evidence sites conducted by the ASCE investigation committee members—described by one close source as a 'tourist trip'—no one's checking the evidence for anything."

The destruction and removal of evidence must stop immediately," Manning declared.

In that same issue, a number of fire officials, including a retired deputy chief from New York's fire department, called on FEMA to "immediately impanel a 'World Trade Center Disaster Review Panel' to coordinate a complete review of all aspects of the World Trade Center incident."

These fire officials noted that the WTC disaster was the largest loss of firefighters ever at one incident; the second largest loss of life on American soil; the first total collapse of a high-rise during a fire in United States history; and the largest structural collapse in recorded history.

"Now, with that understanding, you would think we would have the largest fire investigation in world history," they wrote. "You would be wrong. Instead, we have a series of unconnected and uncoordinated superficial inquiries . . . Ironically, we will probably gain more detailed information about the destruction of the planes than we will about the destruction of the towers. We are literally treating the steel removed from the site like garbage, not like crucial fire scene evidence."

Complaints from the federal investigating team of engineers supported these accusations.

Citing delays by federal agencies and incomplete information, the twenty-six-member team of ASCE engineers that was formed to study the collapse of the WTC towers finally produced a 296-page report by early May 2002.

But even as the report was issued, team leader and structural engineer Dr. W. Gene Corley told Congress there were still many questions left unanswered by his study.

"We didn't have time and resources," Corley complained. He said his team didn't have enough data to create a computer model of the interior damage caused by the aircraft, nor could they model the spread of the fires. The team also griped that federal agencies feuded over funding and to whom the team should be reporting.

The team never had access to 911 emergency calls, which could have helped determine exactly what happened where in the minutes prior to the collapse of the buildings, and—this can not be emphasized enough—they confirmed reports that *much of the structural steel was removed from the site, cut up, and sold as scrap before they had a chance to examine it.*

The team could not even obtain a complete set of building plans until early in 2002. Then they found that floor supports were attached to exterior columns by strong welds and not, as widely believed, relatively small bolts.

The hurried and superficial nature of the FEMA inquiry was evident in the conclusion of its report: "With the information and time available, the sequence of events leading to the collapse of each tower could not be definitively determined."

Corley did say the team learned just enough to know that more answers were desperately needed to design protective measures for similar structures that might be future terrorist targets.

His quest for more answers coupled with congressional outrage over the obstacles thrown in front of the engineering team prompted President Bush to pledge $16 million for a follow-up study by the National Institute of Standards and Technology (NIST).

NIST's National Construction Safety Team, after more than a year of administrative and organizational activity, finally announced in early 2004 that a draft report on the World Trade Center disaster might be "realistic and achievable" by September 2004.

A goodly portion of the NIST team's effort went to study the February 20, 2003, West Warwick, Rhode Island, nightclub fire which claimed one hundred lives and apparently their $16 million budget was taxed. In an initial report to Congress in December 2003, the group complained of the "recurring problem" of insufficient staff for on-site inspections and subsequent research and tests. "The scale and complexity of the current World Trade Center disaster has strained NIST's existing resources," they reported.

They did, however, recommend the creation of a NIST Building and Fire Research Laboratory with a permanent staff funded for $2 million, the establishment of a safety team investigation reserve fund for another $2 million, the establishment of a program to "familiarize local and state investigating authorities about the NCST Act, and a "research program investigating the factors affecting human decision making and evacuation behavior during emergencies in buildings."

The report echoed complaints from the FEMA engineering team by stating the group's major challenges were lack of data ("through most of 2003, significant gaps existed in the data collection related to almost all of the project areas.") and the future need to deploy safety teams immediately to an incident for the collection of physical evidence and witness testimony.

In light of the time lapsed and lack of hard evidence as well as considering the track record of such investigatory panels in the past, many researchers are not holding their breath in expectation of real answers.

As we have seen, the large gaps left by the dismal official record of reporting on the the WTC collapses has been filled by others. Perhaps the best information that we now have about the collapses of the towers comes from independent researchers— notably one named Jim Hoffman, through his detail-rich website **911research.wtc7.net**. In the burgeoning 9/11 truth movement, Hoffman is widely considered to be the leading analyst on this subject.

Observers have long noted that the physical characteristics of the collapses of the two towers were almost identical. That has permitted Hoffman and other researchers to compile the list below that describes principal features of the destruction of both towers. These observations are based on intensive independent study of the surviving evidence, as contrasted with the "official" explanation—although, as we have seen, in truth there is none— of a gravity collapse caused by fire. One can easily see that critical mysteries about the towers' collapse remain unsolved, in large part due to the destruction of evidence and the underfunded investigations earlier noted.

1. *The cores of the towers were obliterated and the perimeter walls were shredded.* According to Hoffman, "there is no gravity collapse scenario" or probable explanation by fire that can account

for the complete leveling of the massive columns that comprised the towers' cores, or the ripping apart of their sturdy perimeter walls. But if not, what scenario *does* explain this?

2. *Nearly all the concrete was pulverized in the air,* so finely that it blanketed parts of lower Manhattan with inches of dust. In a gravity collapse, according to Hoffman, "there would not have been enough energy to pulverize the concrete until it hit the ground, if then." With regard to this observation, the crucial unanswered question becomes: How then was it possible for the non-metallic components of the buildings to turn to dust as fine as flour—and further, to begin to appear so massively at the very outset of the collapse? Independent scientists cited by Hoffman in a highly technical paper have shown that the energy required for the pulverization of this much concrete and for the stupendous expansion of the dust clouds is as much as "100 times greater than could have been produced from each tower's gravitational potential energy" (i.e., mass times height).

3. *Parts of the towers were thrown up to 500 feet laterally* (as discussed earlier, and as the cover image of this book illustrates). Hoffman: "The downward forces of a gravity collapse cannot account for the energetic lateral ejection of pieces." But what forces caused these lateral explosions?

4. *Explosions were visible before many floors had collapsed.* "But in the South Tower collapse," writes Hoffman, "energetic dust ejections are first seen while the top is only slightly tipping, not falling." There is no known source of the dense powder in these clouds of ejected dust. We have also cited numerous eye-witness reports of explosions in the buildings.

5. *The towers' tops mushroomed into thick dust clouds much larger than the original volumes of the buildings.* "Without the addition of large sources of pressure beyond the collapse itself," claims Hoffman, "the falling building and its debris should have occupied about the same volume as the intact building."

6. *The tops fell at nearly the rate of free fall, in less than fifteen seconds.* We've examined this previously. These astounding rates of fall, according to Hoffman's technical explanation, "indicate that

nearly all resistance to the downward acceleration of the tops had been eliminated ahead of them. The forms of resistance, had the collapses been gravity-driven, would include: the destruction of the structural integrity of each story; the pulverization of the concrete in the floor slabs of each story, and other non-metallic objects; and the acceleration of the remains of each story encountered either outward or downward. There would have to be enough energy to overcome all of these forms of resistance and do it rapidly enough to keep up with the near free-fall acceleration of the top."

Even a layman can see that the free-fall scenario based on fires in the buildings has almost no plausible explanation at this time.

14. Tracks of Foreknowledge Revealed

Following the devastating attacks of 9/11, US leaders said we should avoid "finger pointing" to place blame, yet advance warnings were too numerous and specific to do otherwise.

During 2001, the United States spent $30 billion on intelligence gathering plus an additional $12 billion aimed specifically at counterterrorism. This total of $42 billion exceeds most nations' total gross national product, yet Americans were told that none of its two dozen alphabet intelligence agencies had any inkling that we were about to be attacked.

Information available today seriously disputes this claim. It was in fact disputed within days of the attacks by people both in and outside the government.

Questions as to why there had been no warning came quickly. The day after the attacks, Congressional Research Service antiterrorism expert Kenneth Katzman was quoted as saying, "How nothing could have been picked up is beyond me."

But something must have been picked up. How else to explain the fact that the State Department on September 7, 2001, issued a worldwide caution to Americans that they "may be the target of a terrorist threat from extremist groups with links to Osama bin Laden's al Qaeda organization...Such individuals have not distinguished between official and civilian targets. As always, we take this information seriously. US government facilities worldwide remain on heightened alert."

As months passed, more and more evidence accumulated until it became overwhelmingly clear that persons within the federal government were warned of terrorist attacks, including the use of airplanes against buildings.

One year after the attacks, an unusual joint House and Senate investigating committee received testimony that US intelligence agencies had received at least twelve warnings of coming offensive action by terrorists. And, as will be seen, this is a low figure.

By April 2002, leaks in the news media damaging to the official explanation, plus public clamor for an investigation of the 9/11 attacks, prompted congressional leaders to agree to a joint investigation by both the Senate and House Intelligence committees. Limited in scope, the probe was only to review intelligence failures and recommend corrections. It got off to a rocky start when retired CIA inspector general Britt Snider resigned under pressure from committee members who believed his close connection to CIA director George Tenet might interfere with an impartial investigation.

Further frustrating congressional efforts to investigate the attacks was the apparent bumbling and sluggishness of the federal bureaucracy.

According to the *Los Angeles Times*, "Small teams of investigators have been at the Justice Department and the CIA, gathering documents and conducting interviews. They have come back with a litany of complaints about tactics they say are designed to slow their progress and restrict their access to documents and potential informants, sources said."

During these hearings, it was learned that from 1998 onward, both the CIA and FBI had received ever-increasing warnings concerning al Qaeda using hijacked aircraft to attack targets within the United States. Despite the serious nature of the issue of official foreknowledge, the Bush administration continued to stonewall and hamper the congressional investigation, even launching an investigation of the investigators.

After word leaked to the public in June 2002 that communications in Arabic intercepted by the National Security Agency on September 10, 2001, contained phrases such as "Tomorrow is zero hour" and "The match is about to begin," the FBI swung into action.

But instead of going after the authors of the notes indicating foreknowledge, they went after the persons on the joint committee who leaked the information.

Even as White House spokesman Ari Fleischer was calling the notes "alarmingly specific," bureau agents were asking committee members to take lie detector tests regarding the leaks. The *Washington Post* reported that nearly all of the thirty-seven members of the joint committee were questioned. Some members declined to take the lie detector tests, citing constitutional separation of powers and the unreliability of such tests.

Eleanor Hill, staff director of the Joint House and Senate Intelligence Committee, spoke out about advance notice of the attacks passed to ranking leaders. She noted that a briefing for "senior government officials" in July 2001 specifically warned that Osama bin Laden "will launch a significant terrorist attack against US and/or Israeli interests in the coming weeks. The attack will be spectacular and designed to inflict mass casualties against US facilities or interests. Attack preparations have been made. Attack will occur with little or no warning."

She said it was unknown if President Bush received specific information regarding the possibility of airliners being used as flying bombs because the director of the CIA would not declassify the information. The unusual joint hearings were scheduled for June 2002 but then delayed until late September. "Are we getting the cooperation we need? Absolutely not," charged the senior Republican on the Senate Intelligence Committee, Republican Senator Richard Shelby of Alabama.

Florida Democratic Senator Bob Graham echoed Shelby's complaint, saying the Bush administration told them they can "only talk to the top of the pyramid."

"Well, the problem is, the top of the pyramid has a general awareness of what's going on in the organization, but if you want to know why Malaysian plotters were not put on a watch list . . . you've got to talk to somebody at the level where those kinds of decisions were made." Graham referred to Hill's report, which pointed out that two of the hijacking suspects, Khalid al-Midhar and Nawaf al-Hazmi, lived openly in San Diego even after being observed in a Malaysia meeting with known terrorists. Bush and Cheney had long opposed any independent investigation of the 9/11 attacks, claiming it would impede the War on Terrorism by leading to leaks of security measures and tying up personnel needed in the war.

But with the revelations of irregularities in investigations by government agencies that came to light in the spring and summer of 2002, Congress was finally moved to action. "The attacks of September 11 . . . highlighted a failure of national policy to re- spond to the developments of a global terror network implacably hostile to American interests," thundered Senator John McCain, who, along with Senator Joseph Lieberman, cosponsored a bill to create an independent commission to investigate everything from visa procedures to airline security. Legislation authorizing the cre- ation of the ten-person panel, armed with subpoena power and a $3 million budget, was approved by the Senate in a 90/8 vote late in September 2002.

The Hill report, described as preliminary, was based on a review of 400,000 government documents and testimony taken during four months of closed-door hearings. Hill stated that while investigators found no specific warning of the 9/11 attacks, collectively the warnings "reiterated a consistent and critically important theme: Osama bin Laden's intent to launch terrorist attacks inside the United States."

The report showed that in addition to knowing of terrorist plots to use hijacked jets as flying bombs, "senior US officials" were advised two months before the attacks that bin Laden was planning a major operation, possibly inside the United States. Illinois Republican Representative Ray Lahood said it was possible that US intelligence agencies had enough information to have prevented the attacks, but there were "no guarantees."

Actually, warnings of a domestic attack had been coming in for some time—and with increasing frequency right up to 9/11.

In December 2000, the Congressional Advisory Panel to Assess Domestic Response Capabilities for Terrorism Involving Weapons of Mass Destruction issued a report stating, "We are impelled by the stark realization that a terrorist attack on some level within our borders is inevitable."

One clear warning came eight years before the 9/11 attacks in the form of a book written by Yossef Bodansky, director of the US House Task Force on Terrorism and Unconventional Warfare.

In his book, *Target America: Terrorism in the US Today*, Bodansky detailed the airfields in Iran and North Korea where Muslim terrorists trained and noted, "According to a former trainee in Wakiland [Iran], one of the exercises included having an Islamic Jihad detachment seize (or hijack) a transport aircraft. Then, trained air crews from among the terrorists would crash the airliner with its passengers into a selected target."

Wiretaps on suspected al Qaeda terrorists in Italy as far back as 2000 also gave indication of plans for a major attack on the United States involving airplanes and airports. "This will be one of those strikes that will never be forgotten . . ." was the comment recorded from Abdelkader Mahmoud Es Sayed, an Egyptian accused of being a ranking al Qaeda member in Italy and a man convicted of the 1997 massacre of fifty-eight tourists at Luxor, Egypt. Es Sayed also mentioned danger in airports and flying. In another taped conversation on January 24, 2001, a Tunisian terrorist spoke about fake identification papers to Es Sayed and asked, "Will these work for the brothers who are going to the United States?" Es Sayed also stated the war against the enemies of Islam would be fought "with any means we can combat them, using . . . airplanes. They won't be able to stop us even with their heaviest weapons."

According to the *Los Angeles Times*, several US officials said they were unfamiliar with the wiretap messages but "one Justice Department official noted that a small cadre of US intelligence agents might have been privy to them." What is most enlightening

about these Italian wiretaps is not that they evinced foreknowledge—they were too vague to be considered a precise warning—
but that they gave indication of the many and varied alerts
coming into the United States as well as the fact that many foreign
intelligence services were monitoring al Qaeda cells.

Spain got in on the act. In August 2001, the voice of an
unidentified man in London was taped speaking with the head of
a Madrid terrorist cell. The man said he had entered the field of
aviation and was taking flying lessons.

According to a report on MSNBC, just two weeks before the
9/11 attacks, a radio station in the Cayman Islands received an
unsigned letter warning of a major attack against the United States
involving airliners. It was reported that US government officials
went to investigate but no further information was forthcoming.
As will be seen, the Cayman Islands is an offshore banking haven
to many factions, including the CIA and international bankers.

Even the much disparaged Taliban apparently tried to give us
warning. According to a story posted September 7, 2002, by
Independent Digital, an aide to then Taliban foreign minister
Wakil Ahmed Muttawakil tried to warn US authorities weeks
prior to the 9/11 attacks. Muttawakil, unhappy with the glut
of foreign Arab militants in Afghanistan, told his aide he was
concerned over the prospect of US military action against his
country. He was quoted as saying, "The guests are going to destroy
the guesthouse."

The aide, unidentified for his own safety by the British pub-
lication, said Muttawakil was shocked in the summer of 2001 to
learn of a coming attack from fundamentalist Islamic leader Tahir
Yildash. "At first, Muttawakil wouldn't say why he was so upset,"
explained the aide. "Then it all came out. Yildash had revealed that
Osama bin Laden was going to launch an attack on the United
States. It would take place on American soil and it was imminent.
Yildash said Osama hoped to kill thousands of Americans."

The aide said he first traveled across the Pakistan border to
meet with American consul general David Katz late in July 2001.
"They met in a safe house belonging to an old Mujahideen leader

who has confirmed to the *Independent* that the meeting took place," reported the news outlet. Katz declined to discuss the matter.

Next, the aide was sent by Muttawakil to the Kabul offices of the United Nations, where he again issued his warning.

Apparently, since the aide failed to make it clear that he was sent by Foreign Minister Muttawakil, both American and United Nations officials thought his warning more propaganda from the warring factions within Afghanistan and did nothing.

Similar warning signs came from the Far East. In 1995, when Manila authorities answered a fire call they discovered bomb-making materials in the apartment of Ramzi Yousef, later convicted for his role in the 1993 WTC bombing. Yousef escaped but another suspected al Qaeda member, Abdul Hakim Murad, was taken into custody.

Murad told his interrogators that Ramzi had a plan to hijack a commercial airliner in the United States and crash it into CIA Headquarters or the Pentagon. Philippine investigators also found evidence that Ramzi's plan, code-named "Project Bojinka," also involved targeting the White House, Sears Tower in Chicago, the Transamerica Tower in San Francisco, and the World Trade Center.

Apparently Muslim fanatics had already attempted to put Ramzi's plan into effect. On Christmas Eve 1994, four men thought to be connected to bin Laden's terrorist network hijacked Air France Flight 8969 bound from Algiers to Paris. The plane landed in Marseilles, where the hijackers demanded that it be loaded with explosives and extra fuel. Their plan, apparently to crash the craft into the Eiffel Tower, was derailed when commandos stormed the plane and killed all four hijackers.

Warnings continued to pour in from the Philippines, a hotbed of terrorist activity. According to the *Manila Times*, Philippine defense and police intelligence officers warned American authorities of an alliance between Abu Sayyaf (ASG) terrorists there and the al Qaeda network. The paper said American officials ignored the warnings until September 11, 2001.

The report went on to describe a 1994 meeting between ASG cofounder Edwin Angeles and WTC bombing mastermind Ramzi Yousef that included convicted Oklahoma City bombing accomplice Terry Nichols, who was married to a Philippine national. The topics of discussion were terrorist targets. The Murrah Federal Building in Oklahoma City was mentioned as well as another attack on the World Trade Center.

It seemed everyone from the Chinese to our own FBI tried to warn Washington authorities that an attack was imminent, yet nothing was done.

Chinese military officers wrote about just such an attack as 9/11 three years before the fact. In a military manual entitled *Unrestricted Warfare*, People's Liberation Army colonels Qiao Liang and Wang Xiangsui noted, "Whether it be the intrusions of [computer] hackers, *a major explosion at the World Trade Center, or a bombing attack by bin Laden* [emphasis added], all of these greatly exceed the frequency bandwidth understood by the American military . . ."

A CIA translation of this Chinese manual was published on September 11, 2002, the one-year anniversary of the attacks. The manual is a recipe book of unorthodox methods for weaker nations to humble America. It discusses multilevel attacks on America's social, political, and economic systems using strategies involving computer hackers, the infiltration of illegal immigrants, stock market manipulation, and even the use of weapons of mass destruction.

The Chinese leadership, and particularly its military chiefs, has long viewed the United States as their principal enemy, a fact that has been marginalized by both the US Congress and the corporate mass media due to the close business and trade relations between the nations.

Exactly one month following the 9/11 attacks, China was quietly approved as a member of the World Trade Organization after fifteen years of negotiation. It was a move that had previously prompted many and widespread protests due to that Asian nation's abysmal human rights record. This time, with Americans in shock over the 9/11 attacks, little notice was given to this action.

With the heightened security due to the attacks, there was no opportunity for demonstrations against this WTO action. According to CNN, WTO ministers meeting in the Persian Gulf state of Qatar were protected by a US helicopter gunship and naval vessels, and were inside a cordon that included more than two thousand US Marines.

WTO director general Mike Moore declared China's entry into the trade organization "a major historic event," yet there was minimal publicity in the United States.

Even the Russians seemed to be aware that something big was coming.

Dr. Tatyana Koryagina, a senior research fellow for the Institute of Macroeconomic Research under the Russian Ministry of Economic Development and reportedly close to President Putin's inner circle, predicted that an "unusual catastrophe" would strike the United States in late August 2001. Her prediction appeared in a *Pravda* story published on July 12, 2001.

"The US has been chosen as the object of financial attack because the financial center of the planet is located there. The effect will be maximal. The strike waves of economic crisis will spread over the planet instantly and will remind us of the blast of a huge nuclear bomb."

Asked about the discrepancy of dates in a later interview, Dr. Koryagina explained, "I did not make a serious mistake. Indeed, between 15 and 20 August, the dollar started trembling under the pressure of multiple bad news about the US and economy. And within weeks, the Manhattan skyscrapers fell down.

"As a result, a significant part of the world financial network was paralyzed. This strike was aimed at destabilization and destruction of America and (in domino fashion) all the countries making countless billions of dollars." She advised Russian citizens not to invest in American dollars.

She also said the 9/11 attacks were not the work of nineteen terrorists but a group of extremely powerful private persons seeking to reshape the world. This group, she added, has assets of about $300 trillion, which it will use to legitimize its power and create a new world government.

Many persons have taken Dr. Koryagina's comments very seriously when considering both her credentials and her knowledge of Russia's close contacts with nations identified with terrorism, such as Iraq, Iran, Syria, Libya, and North Korea.

As reported by the *Washington Times* on September 28, 2001, "US intelligence agencies have uncovered information that Russian criminal groups have been supplying Osama bin Laden and his al Qaeda terrorist network with components for chemical, biological and nuclear weapons."

Arabic sources too seemed to have been able to discern that bin Laden was preparing to launch a major attack.

In mid-2002, Egyptian president Hosni Mubarak revealed that his intelligence service warned US officials about a week before the 9/11 attacks that bin Laden's organization was in the last stages of preparing a major operation against an American target.

Mubarak said Egyptian intelligence chiefs tried unsuccessfully to thwart the operation using an unnamed agent who had penetrated the al Qaeda network. They passed the information regarding this penetration to US intelligence between March and May 2001, he said, adding, "We informed them about everything."

An American intelligence official told the *New York Times* that they had received no such warning but Mubarak said he was informed that security at the US embassy in Cairo was tightened just before the attacks. Mubarak's interview with the *Times* apparently was the first time that a foreign leader admitted that an intelligence service had penetrated the al Qaeda terrorist network.

The *Times* writers noted dryly, "At a minimum, Mr. Mubarak's account adds detail and drama to a list of warnings about potential terrorist attacks that American intelligence fielded in the days, weeks and months before September 11."

Within hours of the attacks Abdel-Barri Atwan, editor of the London newspaper *al-Quds al-Arabi*, told Reuters News Service, "Osama bin Laden warned three weeks ago that he would attack American interests in an unprecedented attack, a big one... Personally we received information that he planned very, very big attacks against American interests. We received several warnings like this."

Although Atwan said he did not notify the authorities of this warning because he did not take it seriously, it begs the question: If a London newspaper knew of impending attacks, why not the American intelligence services?

An article in the June 23, 2001, issue of *Airjet Airline World News* noted another Arabic source as claiming that "a big surprise" was expected in coming weeks.

A reporter from Arabic satellite television channel MBC who had recently met with bin Laden was quoted as saying, "A severe blow is expected against US and Israeli interests worldwide... There is a mobilization among the Osama bin Laden forces. It seems that there is a race of who will strike first.

"Will it be the United States or Osama bin Laden?"

Another source for a warning may have been an Iranian being held in Germany at the time of the 9/11 attacks. According to the German newspaper *Neue Presse*, prior to 9/11 the man asked to contact American authorities to warn them of an imminent attack. It was reported that when the man told the Secret Service that he was facing deportation from Germany, they hung up on him. On September 14, the man was finally interrogated by US agents.

Closer to home, in a 1993 letter to the *New York Times*, the Middle Easterners who bombed the World Trade Center in that year made it plain that they would try again. Their letter read:

> We, the fifth battalion in the LIBERATION ARMY, declare our responsibility for the explosion on the mentioned building. This action was done in response for the American political, economical, and military support to Israel the state of terrorism and to the rest of the dictator countries in the region.
> Our demands are:
> 1. Stop all military, economical, and political aid to Israel.
> 2. All diplomatic relations with Israel must stop.
> 3. Not to interfere with any of the Middle East countries interior affairs.

If our demands are not met, all of our functional groups in the army will continue to execute our missions against the military and civilian targets in and out the United States.

For your own information, our army has more than hundred and fifty suicidal soldiers ready to go ahead.
The terrorism that Israel practices (which is supported by America) must be faced with a similar one. The dictatorship and terrorism (also supported by America) that some countries are practicing against their own people must also be faced with terrorism.

The American people must know that their civilians who got killed are not better than those who are getting killed by the American weapons and support.

The American people are responsible for the actions of their government and they must question all of the crimes that their government is committing against other people. Or they—Americans—will be the targets of our operations that could diminish them.

The conspirators also drafted a second letter, which was later recovered from an erased file on a computer disc seized from Ayyad's office. This second letter, which the conspirators apparently did not send, proclaimed that the World Trade Center bomb did not do as much damage as had been intended, because their "calculations were not very accurate this time." They warned, however, that they would be more precise in the future and would continue to target the World Trade Center if their demands were not met.

After his arrest, Ramzi Yousef was more specific. He clearly stated that the conspirators had intended for the bomb to topple one of the towers and hoped that it would crash into the other, bringing them both down and killing one quarter of a million people.

It is now clear that the FBI had numerous warnings of what was to come, as we will see in the next section.

15. The FBI Couldn't, or Wouldn't, Connect the Dots

Despite the use of an electronic eavesdropping system originally named Carnivore, the top tier of the FBI couldn't seem to piece together the available information, which would have led any reasonable person to conclude that Middle Eastern terrorists were working diligently on plans to attack the United States.

Just six days after the 9/11 tragedy, FBI director Robert Mueller stated, "There were no warning signs that I'm aware of that would indicate this type of operation in the country."

The Carnivore electronic monitoring system created so much consternation from persons concerned with individual rights and privacy that it is now called simply DCS-1000. In at least one instance, Carnivore actually prevented the bureau from gaining information on a suspected terrorist.

The Electronic Privacy Information Center in May 2002 acquired FBI memos under the Freedom of Information Act, which showed that a 2000 bureau wiretap aimed at an unnamed suspect was ineffective because a low-level FBI technical person destroyed the information.

According to David Sobel, general counsel for the center, "The FBI software not only picked up the emails under the electronic surveillance of the FBI's target . . . but also picked up emails on non-covered targets." One of the obtained memos showed that an FBI supervisor explained, "The FBI technical person was apparently so upset [about intercepting unauthorized emails] that he destroyed all the email take."

The FBI had previously issued assurances that Carnivore could only capture a narrow field of information authorized by a court order. "This shows that the FBI has been misleading Congress and the public about the extent to which Carnivore is capable of collecting only authorized information," Sobel said.

Even a secret court order provoked fallout that may have hampered antiterrorist efforts by the bureau.

When Chief Judge Royce Lamberth, heading the special—and mostly secret—Foreign Intelligence Surveillance Court (FISC), which reviews national security wiretaps, found out that in 2000 the FBI had been misrepresenting information in their requests for eavesdropping, an investigation was ordered forcing many FBI wiretaps to be shut down.

Despite the problems with their Carnivore system and bungled wiretaps, many agents within the bureau were actively working on the problem of terrorism.

Perhaps the most knowledgeable person within the FBI on Middle Eastern terrorism in general and Osama bin Laden in particular was John O'Neill.

In 1995 O'Neill was promoted to head the FBI's counterterrorism section and began working out of FBI headquarters in Washington. One of his initial jobs was the capture of Ramzi Yousef, then a key suspect in several acts of terror including the 1993 bombing of the World Trade Center.

Through the late 1990s, O'Neill, according to Lawrence Wright writing in *The New Yorker*, became "the bureau's most committed tracker of Osama bin Laden and his al Qaeda network of terrorists".

But O'Neill came to believe that his superiors did not carry the same zeal against terrorism as he did. "John had the same problems with bureaucracy as I had," said Richard A. Clarke in a 2002 magazine interview. Clarke had served as White House coordinator for counterterrorism since the Bush administration in the late 1980s. "The impatience really grew in us as we dealt with the dolts who didn't understand."

Despite the 1996 defection of Jamal Ahmed al-Fadl, a long-sought al Qaeda terrorist, and his subsequent detailing of the network to both the CIA and FBI, the State Department refused to list al Qaeda as a terrorist network.

Despite O'Neill's growing ire over perceived indulgence of terrorists by higher authorities and his contentious personality, he accepted the post of special agent in charge of the National Security Division in New York City. Here he created a special "al Qaeda desk" and worked doggedly to pinpoint Osama bin Laden. O'Neill, one of the top-level terrorism experts within the FBI, knew well who and what he was up against.

"Almost all of the groups today, if they chose to, have the ability to strike us here in the United States," O'Neill said in a 1997 Chicago speech.

By the summer of 2001, O'Neill had been passed over for promotion and was growing weary of fighting his superiors on the issue of terrorism. Adding to his disillusionment was O'Neill's experience trying to conduct an investigation of the bombing of the US destroyer Cole, which had been severely damaged by a small boat filled with explosives and two suicide bombers.

O'Neill, commanding about three hundred heavily armed FBI agents, claimed his investigation was being hampered by everyone from Yemen president Ali Abdullah Saleh to US ambassador Barbara Bodine. The FBI force believed they were never given the authority they required to conduct a strenuous investigation.

". . . O'Neill came home feeling that he was fighting the counterterrorism battle without support from his own government," noted Wright in *The New Yorker*. When he tried to return to Yemen in early 2001, O'Neill was refused entry.

"The last two years of his life, he got very paranoid," writer Lawrence Wright was told by Valerie James, a close friend of O'Neill's. "He was convinced there were people out to get him."

In the end, it appears it was his old archenemy, Osama bin Laden, who did get him.

By the summer of 2001, events and O'Neill's career were coming to a head. Someone had leaked information on some of O'Neill's bureau gaffes to the *New York Times* and information on terrorism was pouring into government agencies. "Something big is going to happen," he told a friend.

"It all came together in the third week of June," recalled Clarke. "The CIA's view was that a major terrorist attack was coming in the next several weeks." Clarke said orders to beef up security were passed to the FAA, the Coast Guard, Customs, the INS, and the FBI.

But O'Neill had had enough. By August 23, he had retired from the FBI and accepted a job paying twice his bureau pay—as chief of security for the World Trade Center.

When the first tower was struck, O'Neill ordered the building evacuated but stayed behind to help others in the North Tower. He used a cell phone to speak to a few friends and relatives. He assured them he was okay. He was last seen alive walking toward the tunnel that led to the South Tower.

John O'Neill was not the only FBI agent to see definite warning signs.

Twelve-year FBI veteran Robert G. Wright Jr. in mid-2002 charged the bureau's counterterrorism efforts were ineffective and "not protecting the American people." Going further, Wright charged that FBI superiors had derailed investigations that could have prevented the 9/11 attacks, saying the bureau had evidence that the World Trade Center was a possible target.

On May 9, 2002, Wright, who worked out of Chicago, called a news conference in Washington to publicly accuse the bureau of not properly investigating terrorists in America, despite orders from FBI director Robert Mueller for him to stay home and stay quiet. At the same time he filed a lawsuit against the bureau in Washington's US District Court accusing the bureau of violating his First Amendment rights by prohibiting him from speaking out about FBI wrongdoing.

He charged senior bureau officials "intentionally and repeatedly thwarted and obstructed" efforts to root out terrorists and that they prevented the filing of cases that could have broken up their operations.

Wright's suit was filed just one day after Congress berated the FBI for failing to vigorously act on a July 2001 recommendation from its Phoenix field office that aviation schools should be checked for Middle Easterners seeking flight training.

Counterterrorism experts in Phoenix were concerned after noting that several Middle Eastern men were seeking information on airport operations, security, and flight training. One wrote in a memo to Washington, "FBIHQ should discuss this matter with other elements of the US intelligence community and task the community for any information that supports Phoenix's suspicions."

The memo was written by Phoenix Special Agent Kenneth J. Williams and noted, "Osama bin Laden and Al-Muhjiroun supporters [were] attending civil aviation universities/colleges in Arizona."

FBI officials merely passed the memo, which actually pointed to bin Laden by name, along to about a dozen of its offices for "analysis."

A much more serious issue concerning the FBI arose when five people, including a former and a current agent, were charged in May 2002 with using confidential government information to manipulate stock prices and extort money from businesses.

In indictments brought in Brooklyn, San Diego stock adviser Amr Ibrahim Elgindy was accused of bribing FBI agent Jeffrey A. Royer to give him information on publicly traded companies. Royer, who had worked for the FBI between 1996 and 2000, subsequently left the bureau and went to work for Elgindy's firm, Pacific Equity Investigations. Another FBI agent, Lynn Wingate, was also indicted, accused of passing information to Royer and helping to track investigations of Elgindy through FBI computers. Elgindy reportedly supported Muslim refugees in Kosovo.

According to Assistant US Attorney Kenneth Breen, Elgindy tried to sell $300,000 in stock on September 10, 2001, and told his broker the market was about to drop. Authorities were investigating to see if Elgindy may have had some foreknowledge of the 9/11 attacks.

An FBI spokesman said the bureau was "distressed" by the charges of obstruction of justice, racketeering, extortion, and insider trading.

"I love America, and likewise I love the FBI, particularly its purpose and mission," Agent Wright told newsmen, echoing the thoughts of many bureau personnel. "However, the mission has been seriously jeopardized to the point where American lives have been needlessly lost." "Knowing what I know," Wright added, "I can confidently say that until the investigative responsibilities for terrorism are transferred from the FBI, I will not feel safe."

Former FBI agent Gary Aldrich described the bureau's top management as "incompetent lunkheads and deadheads." Aldrich too said many opportunities to stop the attack were missed.

Aldrich blamed Bill and Hillary Clinton for the breakdown of the FBI as well as other federal agencies. He said the Clintons' blatant disregard for national security procedures made the government weak and vulnerable and that they showed more concern for political opponents than foreign enemies.

According to several FBI sources, when the Clinton administration arrived, emphasis in the bureau shifted from antiterrorism to investigating militias, white supremacists, anti-abortion groups and other "right-wing" extremists.

"When I left [the FBI] in 1998, domestic terrorism was the number one priority," said retired agent Ivan C. Smith, former head of the analysis, budget, and training sections of the FBI's National Security Division. "And as far as I know, it was still a higher priority than foreign terrorism on September 11."

With the advent of the Clintons, FBI probes were aimed everywhere except at foreign terrorists. Veteran agents said some forty boxes of evidence gathered in the 1993 World Trade Center bombing were never analyzed, including almost ten boxes of material from the Philippine side of the investigation.

The Clinton-era disinterest in foreign terrorism was not limited to the FBI. Commerce Department officials told reporter Paul Sperry they were ordered to "sanitize" a Y2K counterterrorism report by removing mention of Islamic threats. Only "right-wing" groups were included in the report.

But on March 23, 2004, Richard A. Clarke, former counterterrorism czar under Clinton and Bush, told CNN's *Inside Politics* a different story about the Clinton administration's terrorism strategy. "I would argue that for what had actually happened prior to 9/11, the Clinton administration was doing a great deal," Clarke said. "In fact, so much that when the Bush people came into office, they thought I was a little crazy, a little obsessed with this little terrorist bin Laden. Why wasn't I focused on Iraqi-sponsored terrorism?" In their appearances before the 9/11 Commission in March 2004, Clarke and former Clinton-era officials defended the Clinton record on al Qaeda, claiming that it was the Bush people and especially Bush's FBI and CIA that dropped the ball immediately after the new administration entered the White House.

By mid-2002, even FBI director Robert Mueller was forced to acknowledge that the FBI had missed many "red flags," including the Phoenix memos as well as two from the Oklahoma City office. There agents and one FBI pilot reported "large numbers" of Middle Eastern men receiving flight training at local airports and warned this activity might be related to "planned terrorist activity."

The revelations of FBI malfeasance prompted an unusual two-hour press conference in late May 2002 in which a defensive Mueller told reporters, "There was not a specific warning about an attack on a particular day. But that doesn't mean there weren't red flags out there, there weren't dots that should have been connected to the extent possible." Mueller even admitted that he had misspoken in fall 2001 when he denied the existence of any pre-9/11 attack warnings.

Mueller outlined his plan to reorganize the FBI, which consisted primarily of shifting agents from the War on Drugs to the War on Terrorism and to create a new Office of Intelligence headed by a CIA analyst. Many observers saw this plan as an attempt to merge the FBI and CIA into a terrorist-fighting force that would only bring more centralized authority to Washington. This same plan—to combine the worst of two worlds—was later echoed in proposals for the new Homeland Security Department.

One government informant, a self-confessed Florida con man named Randy Glass, said he worked undercover for the bureau for more than two years and learned specifically that the World Trade Center twin towers were to be the target of terrorists.

Hoping to lessen a prison term for a conviction of defrauding jewelry wholesalers out of $6 million, Glass in 1998 contacted federal agents and said he could set up illegal arms deals. Aided by veteran Alcohol, Tobacco and Firearms agent Dick Stoltz, Glass began to arrange deals with a variety of persons. He claimed he had acquired heavy weapons such as Stinger and TOW missiles stolen from military facilities.

Business was good but none of the deals seemed to work out until Glass contacted a Pakistani-born New Jersey deli owner. This man helped arrange arms deals with Pakistanis who claimed contacts to Pakistani intelligence, the Taliban, and even Osama bin Laden. Many hours of tapes were made of their meetings.

However, during the lengthy and detailed maneuvering to arrange the financing in early 2001, the Pakistanis grew suspicious and left the country. Only the deli owner and one other man were arrested. The other man pled guilty to trying to sell weaponry and was sentenced to thirty months in jail, while the deli owner went free and his court records were sealed from the public.

ATF agent Stoltz said cases against the men were hampered by the fact that government prosecutors had to remove references to Pakistan in court filings because of diplomatic concerns.

Glass told news reporters that on one occasion in 1999 he met with one of the Pakistanis in the Tribeca Grill in Manhattan. "At the meeting, [he] said Americans are the enemy and they would have no problem blowing up this entire restaurant because it is full of Americans," Glass recounted. "As we left the restaurant, [he] turns and says, 'those towers are coming down.'" The man was indicating the World Trade Center.

Perhaps the most provocative evidence of governmental foreknowledge came from the man who led the prosecution of President Bill Clinton during his impeachment.

Chicago attorney David Schippers, who by mid-2002 was representing Wright and other disgruntled FBI employees, said in a late October 2001 interview that he had been approached by FBI agents a month and a half prior to the 9/11 attacks. The agents revealed that they had knowledge that lower Manhattan was to be the object of a terrorist attack using airplanes as flying bombs and they wanted to prevent this.

They were seeking legal advice because their FBI superiors had ordered them off the case and threatened them with the

National Security Act if they spoke out. Schippers said he tried in vain to warn Attorney General John Ashcroft.

"[A]gain I used people who were personal friends of John Ashcroft to try to get him. One of them called me back and said, 'All right, I have talked to him. He will call you tomorrow morning.' This was like a month before the bombing. The next morning I got a call. It wasn't from Ashcroft. It was from somebody in the Justice Department . . . He said, 'We don't start our investigations at the top. Let me look into this and I will get back to you.' As I sit here today [October 10, 2001], I have never heard from him."

Schippers said interference with official government investigations regarding terrorism is nothing new. He mentioned seeing a warning issued in February 1995 from an unofficial group researching terrorism that a federal facility in America's heartland was to be attacked. Government officials ignored it until the April 19, 1995, bombing of the Murrah Federal Building in Oklahoma City.

The attorney echoed Agent Aldrich's charge that national security precautions were stripped away during the Clinton administration. Speaking of his attempts to warn authorities, Schippers said, "I tried the House, I tried the Senate, I tried the Department of Justice. I didn't go to the FBI because I know there is a roadblock there and I didn't go to the Justice Department until Ashcroft got in there because I know there are roadblocks out there. These are the very same people who put up roadblocks on the attack against the terrorists under Clinton, they are still there. They still constitute, almost like a moat, between the people with the information and the people who should hear the information . . .

"As a human being, as a former prosecutor, as a lawyer and a guy who represents police and agents all over the United States, it is inconceivable to me that those bureaucrats in Washington would turn their back on the obvious for their own purposes," concluded Schippers, "But, I don't know."

One particularly damning indictment of both the bureau and the Bush administration came in 2004 when a woman hired as translator for the FBI with a top-secret security clearance told British reporters that senior US officials knew of al Qaeda's plans to attack targets with aircraft months in advance of 9/11. The important case of FBI whisteblower Sibel Edmonds will be examined later in this book.

It is clear that other bureau employees also tried to send warnings upstairs regarding the flight training of terrorists but got nowhere. In August 2001, the FBI did arrest Zacarias Moussaoui after a Minnesota flight school warned the bureau that Moussaoui appeared to be the type of person who might fly a plane loaded with fuel into a building.

One unnamed FBI agent wrote more than one memo to superiors stating that Moussaoui, a French citizen of Moroccan descent, was the type of individual to take a plane and hijack it, perhaps even fly it into the World Trade Center. It was also report-ed that Moussaoui told a flight instructor that he only wanted to learn to maneuver a Boeing 747 but did not need to learn how to land it.

Although this allegation received widespread media atten-tion and convinced the public of Moussaoui's connection with the hijackers, the *New York Times* of May 22, 2002, quoted Transportation Secretary Norman Mineta as saying it was untrue. Where then did this story come from and why did an erroneous story get such pervasive media coverage? How many other media stories concerning 9/11 are untrue?

There was a general disbelief in the FBI that al Qaeda had much of a presence here," explained White House terrorism coor-dinator Clarke. "It just hadn't sunk through to the organization, beyond O'Neill and [the assistant director of the counterterrorism division]."

In fall 2002, President Clinton's national security adviser, Samuel R. Berger, told a joint congressional committee that the FBI had repeatedly assured the Clinton White House that the al Qaeda organization lacked the ability to launch a strike on US soil.

CBS's *60 Minutes II* reported on May 8, 2002, that a ranking French jurist and terrorist expert sent a report on Moussaoui, a French citizen, to the FBI weeks before 9/11.

US authorities denied there was anything in the report to alert them. One FBI supervisor even questioned the French report, asking how many men named Zacarias Moussaoui must live in France. When informed that there was only one listed in Paris, the supervisory special agent continued to stall any action. Meanwhile, FBI attorneys turned down a request from their agents to search Moussaoui's computer and apartment.

As a result of all this inaction, Moussaoui was simply held on immigration charges until after 9/11 when FBI agents finally were able to make their search. They recovered incriminating financial records linking Moussaoui to al Qaeda, flight simulators, and information on crop dusters.

Moussaoui, whose trial was postponed until early 2003, is known as the "twentieth hijacker" based on the theory that he was to replace an original "twentieth hijacker," Ramzi bin al-Shibh, a former roommate of Mohammed Atta, who reportedly sent $14,000 to Moussaoui. Al-Shibh, who also was unable to gain entry into the United States, was arrested in Pakistan in late September 2002. Moussaoui and al-Shibh were the only two men in custody believed to be directly involved in the 9/11 attacks.

Considering Moussaoui's French citizenship, controversy quickly arose in legal and political circles over how to handle a foreign citizen in an American court with little to link him directly to anyone's death. Further confusion came in September 2002 when the Arab TV station Al-Jazeera aired tapes of the only known contact between Moussaoui and al-Shibh. In another email exchange with al-Shibh, Atta used phrases like, "The first semester starts in three weeks. Nothing has changed. Everything is fine. This summer will surely be hot. Nineteen certificates for private study and four exams." These seem hardly the words necessary to obtain the death penalty that federal prosecutors were seeking.

The feds were further embarrassed in 2002 when government prosecutors left forty-eight classified documents, summaries of FBI interviews, with Moussaoui. They were later found in searches of Moussaoui's Alexandria, Virginia, jail cell. The top-side interference in the Moussaoui case briefly made headlines in the late spring of 2002 with the publication of a scathing thirteen-page letter from FBI special agent and Minneapolis chief division counsel Coleen M. Rowley to Director Robert Mueller. In her May 21 letter, Rowley, a twenty-one-year veteran of the bureau, described a top-heavy FBI management bureaucracy riddled with "many who were failures as street agents" and "careerists" who placed advancing their own careers over integrity and truth.

"I know I shouldn't be flippant about this, but jokes were actually made that the key FBIHQ personnel had to be spies or moles like Robert Hanssen, who were actually working for Osama bin Laden, to have so undercut Minneapolis's effort. . . .

"I have deep concerns that a delicate and subtle shading/skewing of facts by you and others at the highest levels of FBI management has occurred and is occurring in an effort to avoid or minimize personal and/or institutional embarrassment on the part of the FBI and/or perhaps even for improper political reasons," she told Mueller. She added, "I'm hard pressed to think of any case which has been solved by FBIHQ personnel and I can name several that have been screwed up!"

Rowley, after hearing the news media continually quote Director Mueller as saying the bureau would have taken action if only they had had advance warning of the attacks, sent a message informing him of the intelligence sitting in the Minneapolis files. She said when the same denials of knowledge continued, she and other agents again attempted to inform Mueller of the facts.

"Finally, when similar comments were made weeks later we faced the sad realization that the remarks indicated someone, possibly with your approval, had decided to circle the wagons at FBIHQ in an apparent effort to protect the FBI from embarrassment and the relevant FBI officials from scrutiny," Rowley wrote the director.

She also pointed out that the only difference between when informed FBI agents were denied a search warrant on Moussaoui and when one was approved was the fact of the 9/11 attacks, events that certainly could not be swept under the rug.

Rowley was one of many persons who pointed out the fact that FBI headquarters personnel "were privy to many more sources of intelligence information than field division agents." Despite this fact, she said, "key FBIHQ personnel whose job it was to assist and coordinate with field division agents on terrorism investigations continued to, almost inexplicably, throw up road-blocks and undermine Minneapolis's by-now desperate efforts to obtain a FISA [Foreign Intelligence Surveillance Act] search warrant, long after the French Intelligence Service provided its information and probable cause became clear."

Even after the 9/11 attacks had begun, Rowley said higher authorities still would not untie their hands. Taking a call from a bureau superior just after the attacks had begun, Rowley said she told him in light of the attacks it would be the "hugest coinci-dence" if Moussaoui were not involved with the terrorists. Her superior replied that coincidence was the right term; it was just that and the Minneapolis office should not do anything without headquarters' permission because "we might 'screw up' something else going on elsewhere in the country."

Rowley's insightful and damning critique of FBI inefficiency in light of the 9/11 attacks prompted widespread, though brief, mass media coverage. One Internet columnist noted that the Bush administration took advantage of the cover of the "Rowley firestorm" to announce a reversal of some of the government's meager rules against indiscriminate domestic spying, rules prompted by the many abuses of the FBI during the 1960s.

Steve Perry with *Counterpunch*, a biweekly newsletter, commented that the Bush team defused Rowley's revelations by choosing that time to announce plans to reorganize the entire intelligence apparatus. Such a move would be time consuming and require much preparation, yet the administration requested no funding for its proposal this year. According to Perry, this tac-tic indicated that the timing of the announcement may indeed have been meant to distract attention from Rowley's accusations.

It might also be added that any failures at the FBI cannot be laid off on lower level agents and supervisors. In August 2001,

Attorney General Ashcroft, apparently more concerned with the long-lost War on Drugs and pornography, turned down a bureau request for $50 million to beef up its counterterrorism efforts.

All information flowing upward within the FBI ended at Director Mueller and his boss, Ashcroft, both of whom we were told worked closely with President Bush.

16. Missed Opportunities at the CIA

The CIA by all accounts also received a large share of the pre-attack warnings.

Like the FBI, the CIA has its own electronic eavesdropping satellite and computer system. It's called Echelon. This system tracks international calls, faxes and email messages all around the world. It was so secret that the government would neither confirm nor deny its existence until 2001. According to a study by the European Union, Echelon accumulates electronic transmissions like a vacuum cleaner using keyword search software in conjunction with massive computer data banks.

The Echelon system, headquartered in the United States with the National Security Agency at Fort Meade, Maryland, has caused protests in several nations, excluding the United States whose population rarely sees any news concerning this powerful global wiretapping system.

In 2000, French prosecutor Jean-Pierre Dintilhac ordered his country's counterintelligence agency to see if Echelon was being used to steal foreign business secrets, to spy on citizens, and to see if it was "harmful to the vital interests of the nation." The Italian Parliament also opened inquiries into Echelon, saying, "The scope is not military." According to a German newspaper, the *Frankfurter Allgemeine Zeitung*, the Echelon spy system provided both US and Israeli intelligence services warning of the impending terrorist attacks at least three months before the fact. The newspaper reported that Echelon, with its 120 satellites, has been used extensively by Israeli intelligence to monitor Arab terrorist groups.

Largely unreported in the American media was a story that Osama bin Laden himself was overheard telling his stepmother on

September 9, 2001, "In two days you're going to hear big news and you're not going to hear from me for a while." This telephone interception, attributed to a "foreign intelligence service," undoubtedly was the product of Echelon. Yet no one in America was alerted to bin Laden's "big news?"

The CIA also had another high-tech weapon in their arsenal for use against terrorists. The Predator, an unmanned surveillance aircraft, had been used under the Clinton administration to track the movements of Osama bin Laden. There had even been talk of using the craft to unleash Hellfire missiles on the al Qaeda leader. But Donald Rumsfeld, among other things when he took office as secretary of defense, chose not to launch any further Predator drones.

There is enticing evidence that tied Osama bin Laden directly to the CIA back at the time the agency was funding and training fighters against the Soviets in Afghanistan. While it has been widely acknowledged that the CIA helped found and fund the al Qaeda network during the Soviet invasion of Afghanistan, the agency steadfastly denied any direct dealings with bin Laden.

Internet sources claimed that bin Laden, under the name Tim Osman, actually was brought to the United States in the late spring of 1986 for a meeting with government agents at the Hilton Hotel in Sherman Oaks, California. Former FBI senior special agent Ted L. Gunderson confirmed this meeting and said he was one of the attendees.

Gunderson said he was contacted by a "top figure" in the Reagan administration and asked to meet with Afghan insurgents to "see what we might do to help them." The four men at the hotel meeting, according to Gunderson, were himself, a quiet Tim Osman (bin Laden), Michael Riconosciuto, a CIA scientific "asset" with connections in the arms business, and a man identified as Ralph Olberg, who was purchasing weapons on behalf of the Afghan Mujahideen.

Gunderson said conversation during the hour-and-a-half meeting was mostly between Olberg and Riconosciuto while Osman/bin Laden "sat silent in a corner of the room." He added that he was unaware of what, if any, deal was sealed during the meeting but that he is "certain in my own mind" that arrangements were made to provide arms for bin Laden and the Arab fighters.

According to a former staffer of Republican senator David Durenberger, Olberg was a man often seen in the senator's office during the Reagan years talking about the plight of the Afghan people.

Riconosciuto, also tight with Republican bigwigs, had been involved in the development of the PROMIS software initially planned for use against criminals and terrorists.

But by the mid 1990s, the Soviets were out of Afghanistan and the Saudis were our oil friends and, except for certain counterterrorism units, little notice was taken of Osama bin Laden. The CIA, like their brethren in the FBI, apparently became somewhat complacent at the lower levels thanks to the near constant stream of tips, warnings, and information. Workers not actively involved in counterterrorism took a cue from their superiors and never got too serious about terrorism.

Attorney Michael Wildes, who represented one of the Khobar Towers bombers, explained, "You see [there is a] difference between the rank-and-file counterintelligence agents, who are regarded by some as the motor pool of the FBI, who drive diplomats, and the people who are getting the shots called at the highest level of our government—it's unconscionable."

And it wasn't as if prior warnings had all proven false. Almost a year before the deadly 1998 bombings of the US embassies in Kenya and Tanzania, an al Qaeda member had warned CIA officials of the coming attacks. The informant's information was dismissed as unreliable and nothing was done.

Though admittedly vague, there was a warning in a September 1999 National Intelligence Council (NIC) report entitled "Sociology and Psychology of Terrorism: Who Becomes a Terrorist and Why?" The NIC is composed of about a dozen senior intelligence officers and is attached to the CIA.

"Suicide bomber(s) belonging to al Qaeda's Martyrdom Battalion could crash land an aircraft packed with high explosives

(C-4 and semtex) into the Pentagon, the headquarters of the Central Intelligence Agency (CIA) or the White House," stated the report, which was issued exactly two years before 9/11.

"This information was out there," noted Robert L. Worden, chief of the Federal Research Division, which prepared the report from open sources, "certainly to those who study the in-depth subject of terrorism and al Qaeda."

In January 2000, Malaysian security agents conducted surveillance of al Qaeda operatives meeting in Kuala Lumpur at the behest of the CIA. One of the operatives was Khalid al-Midhar. It was determined that al-Midhar had a multiple-entry visa to the United States.

CIA agents also found that al-Midhar was traveling with a Saudi, Nawaf al-Hazmi, who had already entered the United States before. Neither man was placed on the State Department "watch list" until August 23, 2001, far too late to prevent their participation in the 9/11 attacks.

Another example of CIA incompetence, if that's what it was, can be found in the case of Khalid Sheikh Mohammed, who, since the capture of Abu Zubaydah in Pakistan in the spring of 2002, was considered the highest-ranking member of the al Qaeda network still at large, as well as a primary planner of the 9/11 attacks.

Mohammed was so highly placed in bin Laden's organization that the joint congressional committee looking into intelligence failures in the fall of 2002 took special notice of him. But they were so stymied by restrictions on classified material that they could only refer to Mohammed as a "key al Qaeda leader," even though the man was identified as a terrorist chief as far back as 1995.

The joint committee criticized the CIA's handling of Mohammed's case, stating, "there was little analytic focus given to him and coordination amongst intelligence agencies was irregular at best." One US intelligence official disputed this charge but told a *New York Times* reporter, "We had identified him as a major al Qaeda operative before September 11."

Such controversy and contradictions continued when it was reported that Mohammed was captured on March 1, 2003,

following a nighttime shootout in Rawalpindi, Pakistan. US officials expressed jubilation over the arrest but their celebration
faded swiftly as questions arose. Witnesses did not agree with the
official account and foreign media speculated that Mohammed
may have been misidentified, killed at an earlier date, or might
even still be on the loose.

Mohammed Atta, the accused chief hijacker, reportedly was
under surveillance by US intelligence agents for nearly five
months in early 2000, prior to his visit to the United States to take
flying lessons.

The German magazine *Focus* reported that US agents,
referred to as FBI in some accounts and CIA in others, monitored
Atta from January to May 2000 after he was seen buying large
quantities of chemicals thought to be used for making bombs.
According to the article, the US agents never informed German
authorities of Atta's presence or of any suspicions about him.

One of the most outrageous accounts of CIA pre-9/11 activity actually involved Osama bin Laden. One month after the
attacks, the French daily *Le Figaro* reported that bin Laden had
been treated at an American hospital in the Arab emirate of Dubai
in July 2001, and while there was visited by a local CIA agent.
According to this report, bin Laden was flown from the Quetta
airport in Pakistan to Dubai, where he was admitted to the
American hospital located between the Al-Garhoud and Al-
Maktoum bridges. He was taken to the urology department for
treatment of a kidney infection. The article stated that bin Laden
had had mobile kidney dialysis equipment shipped to his hide-
away in Pakistan as far back as early 2000.

Furthermore, it went on to say that during his stay at the
hospital, between July 4 and 14, bin Laden received visits from
family members and prominent Saudis and Emiratis. "During the
hospital stay, the local CIA agent, known to many in Dubai, was
seen taking the main elevator of the hospital to go to bin Laden's
hospital room," stated the *Le Figaro* article, adding, "A few days
later, the CIA man bragged to a few friends about having visited
bin Laden. Authorized sources say that on July 15th, the day after

bin Laden returned to Quetta, the CIA agent was called back to headquarters."

Bin Laden, with both a price on his head and eligible for execution under a last-minute order from outgoing president Bill Clinton, nevertheless was allowed to fly without hindrance from Dubai by private jet on July 14.

The article also reported that in late August, both American and French authorities were notified of the arrest of Djamel Beghal by customs agents in Dubai. Under interrogation, Beghal said he had been ordered to bomb the US embassy in Paris by al Qaeda leader Abu Zubaydah in Afghanistan. "According to Arab diplomatic sources as well as French intelligence, very specific information was transmitted to the CIA with respect to terrorist attacks against American interests around the world, including US soil," stated the French piece. While this story made the rounds in the European media, nothing but a few scattered Internet reports circulated in the United States. In Europe, CIA officials denied the story.

It is either true or false. If it is false, the American public needs to know this, so that such untruths can be stopped during our "War on Terrorism." If it is true, then the American people need to know that their own CIA let the world's most wanted man walk away unmolested two months prior to the deadly 9/11 attacks. Yet no major American media organization apparently could spare one good reporter to travel to Dubai to check with the hospital staff and others to confirm the story.

The story of the CIA and bin Laden in Dubai is reinforced by a story in the December 23, 2001, edition of the *Washington Post* that reported that the CIA had recruited a team of Afghan agents to track bin Laden's movements in their country beginning in early 1998. This effort continued right up until September 11, 2001.

According to the paper, these agents sent the CIA daily reports on bin Laden's whereabouts but the information was often dismissed by agency officials because it sometimes conflicted with other intelligence information.

CIA foreknowledge was also obliquely admitted in April 2002 by its own deputy director, James Pavitt. In a speech to the Duke University Law School Conference, Pavitt was simultaneously trying to excuse his agency's failure to prevent 9/11 while touting its efficiency.

"We had very, very good intelligence of the general structure and strategies of the al Qaeda terrorist organization. We knew and we warned that al Qaeda was planning a major strike. There is no question about that," Pavitt told his audience. His speech later was posted on the CIA's website.

Yet Pavitt tried to echo the administration's claim that there was not enough specific intelligence to prevent the 9/11 attacks. He added that within days of the attacks CIA operatives were "on the ground" operating in Afghanistan. "None of this came easy," he explained. "You cannot learn Pashtun overnight and you can't truly understand the complexities of tribalism, regionalism and personalism in Afghanistan by reading the newspaper or a learned book. My people learned about this by years of study and years of practice often in difficult, hostile and, yes indeed, on the ground in Afghanistan itself.

"If you hear somebody say, and I have, the CIA abandoned Afghanistan after the Soviets left and that we never paid any attention to that place until September 11th, I would implore you to ask those people how we were able to accomplish all we did since the Soviets departed. How we knew who to approach on the ground, which operations, which warlord to support, what information to collect. Quite simply, we were there well before the 11th of September."

One of the strangest cases of apparent foreknowledge involved a man imprisoned in Canada who claimed to be an American intelligence agent who had tried to warn authorities a month or more before the 9/11 attacks.

Delmart "Mike" Vreeland claimed to be a US Navy lieutenant and an agent for the Office of Naval Intelligence in 2000 when he was arrested and jailed in Canada at the behest of US authorities after arriving from a trip to Russia. Canadian authorities charged

Vreeland with credit card fraud and held him on an extradition warrant based on alleged credit card fraud in Michigan.

Following lengthy court hearings, all Canadian charges against Vreeland were dropped, and at this writing he had been granted political refugee status in Canada while the extradition warrant issue was resolved. According to the Canadian court records, running to some 10,000 pages, Vreeland brought back from Moscow intelligence documents in a sealed pouch in December 2000. He said he was simply a courier and was to hand over the documents to a contact in Toronto but the contact failed to arrive.

"The meeting didn't go as planned. I didn't like it, so I basically scanned and copied everything. I opened everything," Vreeland recalled in a June 5, 2002, radio interview. He said that when he returned for a second meeting he was arrested.

The documents, according to Vreeland, were written in Russian, but one contained the Arabic numerals for 9/11/01. Prior to his arrest, he said he had the documents translated and that one specifically referred to attacks in September.

"The initial strike or attack will be started at the WTC on 9/11/01 by our brothers in faith," Vreeland quoted from the documents. "Three Mile Island and Pentagon are as well the goals that we will not miss at the initial terroristic stage of our attack. If everything goes as planned, the attack will work. After Americans who undoubtedly will think that Osama is to be blamed and will start a war with his group, there stands the Russian Empire to gain the first fruit of war and money promised by the Americans."

Vreeland said while incarcerated he wrote about the warning in a letter that was opened three days after the 9/11 attacks and forwarded to authorities in Ottawa. He also said he passed this same information to Canadian authorities via his jailers about a month or more before the 9/11 attacks. "The two officers informed the United States and Ottawa immediately through the RCMP [Royal Canadian Mounted Police]...."

"The Canadians did their job. I think they were pressed down by the US government. They transmitted the information just like they should. I know definitely that the [US] Secret Service had it. I know the FBI had it, I know the DoD [Department of Defense] had it. I know it all went from Ontario to Ottawa, from Ottawa to the Canadian embassy in Washington, DC, and it was just melted everywhere," he added.

The documents, entered into court records at his court hearings, apparently refer to an attack on a nuclear power plant and speak of immediate and deadly radiation within an area of four to seven miles. In a telephone interview from Canada, Vreeland said he believed that Flight 93's objective was Three Mile Island and that the jet was shot down by American fighters to prevent completion of its mission.

In another intriguing aspect to this incredible story, Vreeland's document added the cryptic line "Let one happen, stop the rest." Vreeland said this statement confirmed his belief that US intelligence had penetrated the al Qaeda network and were conducting an operation of their own.

US authorities gave Vreeland's story short shrift, declaring that he was simply a petty criminal who was discharged from the navy for unsatisfactory conduct in 1986. But his records were contradictory and some appeared fabricated. Disclaiming a military operative by special pronouncements and fabricated records is called "sheep dipping," and has been a common intelligence practice in the past.

A Toronto newspaper reported that Vreeland joined the US Navy in 1984 and then joined a special unit operating against drug smugglers. Interestingly, an October 2, 1986, article in the *Los Angeles Times* listed Vreeland as a noncriminal witness to a major cocaine bust by LAPD officers known to have worked with US intelligence agents.

"There is much about Vreeland's past that is objectionable, questionable or both," commented former LAPD officer and researcher Michael Ruppert, who first broke the Vreeland story. "But even in a worst-case scenario, nothing in his past explains how he was able to write a detailed warning of the attacks before they occurred and why the intelligence services of both Canada and the US ignored attempts to warn them while both Vreeland

and his attorneys were nagging down their doors."

Rocco Galati, one of Vreeland's attorneys fighting the extradition orders, told the *Toronto Star*, "Neither myself nor Mr. [Paul] Slansky [another Vreeland attorney] have seen anything as incomprehensibly frustrating, inexplicable, and irresponsibly absurd as the RCMP's position that they are not interested in reviewing Mr. Vreeland's information."

Vreeland's story of a specific warning from Russia gained further support when it was learned that the Russian newspaper *Izvestia* reported the day of the 9/11 attacks that a special messenger of the Russian Intelligence Service met with a deputy director of the CIA and delivered documents and audiotapes containing telephone conversations directly relating to terrorist attacks on Washington and New York.

One of the strangest items indicating foreknowledge of the attacks came in the form of registered Internet domain names.

Two highly suggestive domain names—attackontwintowers.com and worldtradetowerattack.com—were registered more than a year before the 9/11 attacks. Since the registration was allowed to elapse, no one knows who registered the names.

Neil Livingston, who heads Global Options LLC, a Washington-based investigation and counterterrorism firm, said, "It's unbelievable that they [the registration company whose name was withheld] would register these domain names, probably without any comment to the FBI. If they did make a comment to the FBI, it's unbelievable that the FBI didn't react to it."

Incredibly, other domain names registered prior to the 9/11 tragedy included attackamerica.com, horrorinamerica.com, horrorinnewyork.com, nycterroriststrike.com, pearlharborinmanhattan.com, worldtradecenter929.com, worldtradetowerstrike.com, and terroristattack2001.com.

Even from a cursory search of September 11 reports, it would appear as though many people had some inkling of what was to come.

As recounted by Russ Kick, a veteran New York police investigator, numerous Arab Americans in New York heard about the coming attacks. The officer said the number of leads were so overwhelming that it was difficult to tell who had heard about the attacks from a secondhand source and who had heard it from someone who may have been a participant. A Brooklyn detective was quoted as saying that "a serious and major priority" investigation was made into why so many Middle Easterners failed to show up for work at the World Trade Center on September 11.

Even certain schoolkids seemed to have foreknowledge, according to Kick. A Dallas suburb fifth-grader told his teacher on September 10, "Tomorrow, World War III will begin. It will begin in the United States and the United States will lose."

Another schoolkid in Jersey City, home of several of the accused hijackers, told friends to stay away from lower Manhattan on the morning of September 11. One week before the attacks, a Brooklyn high school freshman pointed at the WTC towers and told his class, "Do you see those two buildings? They won't be standing there next week."

There are even telltale signs that some prominent politicians and government officials within the United States had some warning of the September atrocities.

San Francisco mayor Willie Brown was scheduled to fly to New York on the morning of September 11, 2001. But at about 10 p.m. the evening of September 10, he received a phone call at home advising him to be cautious about traveling by air. Brown would only say that the call came from "my security people at the airport," but the warning was clear: don't travel by air. He said the call "didn't come in any alarming fashion, which is why I'm hesitant to make an alarming statement." Brown was preparing to leave for the airport the next morning when instead he joined millions of other Americans in viewing the destruction on TV.

One San Francisco official noted that the FAA routinely issues security notices but added that none had been received in the days before September 11. No one has yet discovered who sent the after-hours warning to Brown.

Newsweek reported on September 24, 2001, that on September 10 "a group of top Pentagon officials suddenly canceled travel plans for the next morning, apparently because of security concerns."

On July 28, 2001, Attorney General John Ashcroft left Washington on a fishing trip to Missouri but it was not on a commercial airliner. CBS news correspondent Jim Stewart reported that Ashcroft had suddenly begun flying only on government-chartered jets in response to what an FBI spokesman called a "threat assessment" by the bureau. Ashcroft was advised to travel only by private jet for the remainder of his term under FBI guidelines.

Former Attorney General Janet Reno and all but the secretaries of interior and energy in the Bush administration had flown by commercial airliners. Asked about this sudden change in policy, Ashcroft said, "I don't do threat assessments myself and I rely on those whose responsibility it is in the law enforcement community, particularly the FBI. And I try to stay within the guidelines that they've suggested I should stay within for those purposes."

But most extraordinary was a comment attributed to a member of Congress. During live coverage of the 9/11 attacks, National Public Radio congressional correspondent David Welna was describing the evacuation of the Capitol.

He reported, "I spoke with Congressman Ike Shelton—a Democrat from Missouri and a member of the Armed Services Committee—who said that just recently the director of the CIA warned that there could be an attack—an imminent attack—on the United States of this nature. So this is not entirely unexpected."

All of the above information stands in sharp contrast to often-repeated Bush administration assertions that no one in government could have imagined an attack such as that on 9/11.

Secretary of Defense Donald Rumsfeld also admitted "there were lots of warnings" in an interview with *Parade* magazine. A transcript of his interview was released by the Department of Defense on October 12, 2001.

Rumsfeld appeared to be laying off blame for the failure to stop the attacks on local officials, strange as that may sound, when he explained, "The intelligence information that we get, it sometimes runs into the hundreds of alerts or pieces of information a week. One looks at the [information] worldwide, it's thousands.

And the task is to sort through it and see what you can find. And as you find things, the law enforcement officials who have the responsibility to deal with that type of thing—the FBI at the federal level, and although it is not, it's an investigative service as opposed to a police force, it's not a federal police force, as you know. But the state and local law enforcement officials have the responsibility for dealing with those kinds of issues."

Of course, local authorities do not normally have access to intelligence from the CIA and FBI. Furthermore, anyone who has served in the military, intelligence services, or law enforcement will confirm that information only flows upward, rarely downward. Thus, lower-level agents can be forgiven their inability to see the bigger picture and connect the dots. Close scrutiny should be leveled at their superiors and, more specifically, the national leaders for whom they manage.

In July 2001, senior government officials received this report on Osama bin Laden: "Based on a review of all-source reporting over the last five months, we believe that [bin Laden] will launch a significant terrorist attack against US and/or Israeli interests in the coming weeks. The attack will be spectacular and designed to inflict mass casualties against US facilities or interests. Attack preparations have been made. Attack will occur with little or no warning."

On July 5, 2001, President Bush received a briefing at his Crawford, Texas, ranch that mentioned the possibility of an airline hijacking as a domestic threat. This information was not made public until nearly nine months after the attacks.

Yet, despite these warnings, when four jetliners went off course on the morning of September 11, there was little or no immediate reaction.

The chairman of the 9/11 Commission, Thomas H. Kean, in early 2004 admitted to the possibility that the attacks could have been prevented but saw no design in the voluminous evidence of foreknowledge.

"My feel is a whole number of circumstances, had they been different, might have prevented 9/11," Kean said during a TV network interview. "They involve everything from how people got into the country to failures in the intelligence system."

Inflated budgets and more manpower will add nothing to the quest for true national security until there is a commitment to such by the highest political leaders.

17. Selling Stocks Short Indicates Foreknowledge

What makes the information concerning foreknowledge even more ominous is the business dealings that entangle former and current American political leaders with wealthy Middle Easterners and the fact that just days after the 9/11 attacks the FBI was asked to investigate the short selling of airline and insurance stocks just prior to September 11. Just as there is growing evidence that many people had foreknowledge of these attacks, there are indications that someone used this prior knowledge for profit. And they were not members of an al Qaeda terrorist cell.

Selling stocks short involves having your broker sell shares you don't even own, betting (or perhaps knowing) you can acquire them later at a lower price and supply them to the buyer within a prescribed short time. If you "bet" right, the difference in price is your profit. You can lose at this game, but you can also win big. Historically, if this precedes a traumatic event, it is an indication of foreknowledge. It is widely known that the CIA uses the *Promis* computer software to routinely monitor stock trades as a possible warning sign of a terrorist attack or suspicious economic behavior.

It was reported by the Interdisciplinary Center, a counterterrorism think tank involving former Israeli intelligence officers, that insiders made nearly $16 million profit by short-selling shares in American and United Airlines, the two airlines that suffered the hijackings, as well as the investment firm of Morgan Stanley, which occupied twenty-two floors of the WTC. According to other sources, profits from this short selling may have netted up to $15 billion worldwide.

A week after the September 11 attacks, the *London Times* reported that the CIA had asked regulators for the Financial

Services Authority in London to investigate the suspicious sales of millions of shares of stock just prior to the terrorist acts. It was hoped the business paper trail might lead to the terrorists. The *Times* said market regulators in Germany, Japan, and the United States all had received information concerning the short selling of insurance, airlines, and arms companies stock, all of which fell sharply in the wake of the attacks.

City of London broker and analyst Richard Crossley noted that someone sold shares in unusually large quantities beginning three weeks before the assault on the WTC and Pentagon. Crossley stated that on the Friday preceding the attacks, more than 10 million shares in the US investment bank Merrill Lynch were sold, compared with 4 million on a normal trading day. He said he took this as evidence that someone had insider foreknowledge of the attacks.

"What is more awful than he should aim a stiletto blow at the heart of Western financial markets?" he added. "But to profit from it. Words fail me."

Stock market regulators in Germany also reported suspicious short selling just prior to September 11.

In the United States, there was an unusually high volume of five-year US Treasury note purchases made just prior to 9/11. The *Wall Street Journal* on October 2, 2001, noted, "Five-year Treasury notes are among the best investments in the event of a world crisis, especially one that hits the US."

"This could very well be insider trading at the worst, most horrific, most evil use you've ever seen in your entire life, or this would be one of the most extraordinary coincidences in the his-tory of mankind, if it was a coincidence," said *Bloomberg Business News* writer Dylan Ratigan.

Just prior to the 9/11 attacks, there were an unusually high number of "put" options purchased for the stocks of AMR Corp. and UAL Corp., the parent firms of American and United Airlines. A put option gives the bearer the right to sell at a specified price before a certain date. Just like short selling, placing a put option is betting that the stock will fall in price.

According to researcher and former LA policeman Michael Ruppert, between September 6 and 7, 2001, the Chicago Board of Options Exchange reported 4,744 put options on UAL but only 396 call options. On September 10, there were 4,516 put options placed on American Airlines compared to only 748 calls. (Calls reflect the belief that the stock will increase in worth.) American's 6,000 percent jump in put options on the day before the attacks was not matched by any other airlines.

"No similar trading in any other airlines occurred on the Chicago Exchange in the days immediately preceding Black Tuesday," Ruppert said in an October 2001 interview. "That means that someone had advance knowledge that only the stocks of these two airlines would be adversely impacted. Had it just been an industry-wide slump, then you would have seen the same kind of activity on every airline, not just these two."

There were other questionable stock trades made just prior to 9/11. According to Ruppert, Morgan Stanley Dean Witter & Co., which occupied twenty-two floors of the WTC, witnessed the purchase of 2,157 put options during the three trading days before the 9/11 attacks as compared to 27 per day prior to September 6. Merrill Lynch & Co., which also had offices in twenty-two floors of the WTC, had 12,215 one-month put options bought during four trading days prior to 9/11 compared to the normal 252 contracts per day.

Alex Popovic, vice president of the Investment Dealers Association of Canada, in early October 2001 confirmed that the US Securities and Exchange Commission had provided a list of thirty-eight companies for scrutiny but said their review need not be limited to those firms listed. "One shouldn't be wearing blinders when looking at that sort of thing," Popovic told the Associated Press.

Earlier this same commitment to an opened-ended investigation was voiced by SEC chairman Harvey Pitt, who stated his agency's "No. 1 priority" was to pursue the possible trading by people associated with the terrorists.

Interestingly enough, one of the thirty-eight companies was Vornado Realty Trust, a New Jersey-based firm that earlier in 2001 lost a bid to lease the World Trade Center complex from its owner, the Port Authority of New York, to real estate developer Larry A. Silverstein. By early 2003, Silverstein was still in court fighting insurers over whether or not the two planes that struck the WTC constituted one or two separate attacks. Leaseholder Silverstein argued that there were two strikes which entitled him to a $7.1 billion total payment, $3.55 billion for each attack.

However, by year's end the story of profiting on terrorism had vanished. Apparently none of the suspicious transactions could be traced to bin Laden, so this news item quietly dropped from sight. But, if the suspicious trading could not be linked to bin Laden, who was at the end of the investigative trail?

Many people wondered if it tracked back to American firms or intelligence agencies. This appears to be the case.

According to the *San Francisco Chronicle*, "[A] source familiar with the United trades identified Deutsche Bank Alex. Brown, the American investment banking arm of German giant Deutsche Bank, as the investment bank used to purchase at least some of these options."

Michael Ruppert said that both the International Policy Institute for Counter Terrorism, an Israeli institute located in Herzliya that studies worldwide terrorism, and European investigators tracked the UAL put options to Deutsche Bank Alex. Brown, a firm formed by the joining of the German central bank with Alex. Brown, the United States' oldest investment banking firm.

Until 1998, the chairman of A.B. Brown was A.B. "Buzzy" Krongard, who on March 26, 2001, was appointed executive director of the CIA. Beginning in 1998, he was counselor to CIA director George Tenet.

Krongard is a man with long-standing and close ties to the financial world. Moving up through the ranks of A.B. Brown, Krongard was elected chief executive officer in 1991 and then chairman of the board in 1994. With the merging of A.B. Brown and Bankers Trust Corp. in 1997, Krongard served as vice chairman of the board until joining the CIA. Bankers Trust was acquired by Deutsche Bank in 1999, becoming the single largest bank in Europe.

Krongard also served as chairman of the Securities Industry Association. A native of Baltimore, he received degrees from Princeton University and the University of Maryland School of Law and served as an infantry officer in the marines.

"Understanding the interrelationships between CIA and the banking and brokerage world is critical to grasping the already frightening implications of [these] revelations," commented Ruppert.

Krongard indeed joined other prominent Americans connected to both the CIA and Wall Street power. These include Clark Clifford (who was a key player in gaining legitimacy for the BCCI, a bank which collapsed in scandal), John Foster Dulles and Allen Dulles (Allen oversaw the failed Bay of Pigs invasion and sat on the Warren Commission, and both Dulles brothers were involved with the Bush-Nazi connection detailed later), William Casey (who moved to the agency after a stint as chairman of the Securities and Exchange Commission), David Doherty (former CIA general counsel, now vice president of the New York Stock Exchange), former president George Herbert Walker Bush (now a paid consultant to the international Carlyle Group, which lists among its clients the bin Ladens), John M. Deutch and Nora Slatkin (Deutch, a former CIA director, and his former executive director Slatkin are both now connected to Citibank and Citigroup) and Hank Greenburg (once nominated as CIA director, he is now chairman of AIG Insurance representing the third largest pool of investment capital in the world).

As detailed in my previous book *Rule by Secrecy*, the CIA historically has been top heavy with members of the Wall Street elite who desire to advance their globalist agenda. It also operates a number of front companies which themselves deal in stocks and bonds.

The CIA's *Promis* computer software to track real-time trades in world stock markets should have alerted them to all this unusual stock trading and perhaps even of the pending 9/11 attacks.

Did former FBI employee and double agent Robert Hanssen deliver an updated version of the purloined computer software *Promis* to his Russian handlers who passed it along to bin Laden, as reported by Fox News? Hanssen's last job before being arrested as a spy was to upgrade the FBI's intelligence computer systems.

The *Promis* software had been developed by a computer program designer named Bill Hamilton, who took his work to the federal government only to have the sophisticated software stolen by President Ronald Reagan's attorney general, Ed Meese. This software, which seemed a promising weapon in tracking criminals and illegal money, was turned into an Orwellian program that integrates databases worldwide, giving its possessor nearly unlimited access to all computer records.

"One of the primary functions of the Central Intelligence Agency, by virtue of its long and very close history of relationships with Wall Street, has been a mandate to track and monitor all financial markets worldwide—and to look for anomalous trades, indicative of either economic warfare, or insider currency trading, or speculation—which might affect the US Treasury, or, as in the case of the September 11 attacks, to look for trades that indicated foreknowledge of attacks like we saw," Ruppert told *OnLine Journal* on October 12, 2001. "I am absolutely convinced that the Central Intelligence Agency had complete and perfect foreknowledge of the attacks, down to the date, time, place and location," he concluded.

Author Don Radlauer, who specializes in stock options and derivatives, noted the suspicious stock trading and stated, "Obviously, anyone who had detailed knowledge of the attacks before they happened was, at the very least, an accessory to their planning; and the overwhelming probability is that the trades could have been made only by the same people who masterminded the attacks themselves."

Who would that be?

The US Government itself was holding the majority of the international and domestic "short" positions, according to commodity trading advisor Walter Burien, a former tenant of the

World Trade Center. According to Burien, government money managers are the primary players within the trillion-dollar international derivative market. "A derivative gives the ability for selling the market 'short' on paper even if you do not own the stock, commodity, currency, bonds, etc.," explained Burien. "The government investment managers over the last thirty years have become very familiar with using this tactic to reap hundreds of billions of dollars each year.

"The government—which controls the economic reports, media coverage and wealth—is in a position to manipulate the above and create an environment to secure substantial revenue while everyone else is lying on the shoulder of the road bleeding to death. For three months prior and going into 9/11, the government investment funds had increased their short positions to the largest diversified short positions ever held by them . . . The airline stock option transaction at issue, and that most people have heard about, is truly minuscule chump change in comparison."

According to Chicago attorney David Schippers the only attempt to truly track and identify the suspicious trading in the United States occurred in Chicago, where money intended for the Hamas terrorist group was stopped by a lawsuit filed by one FBI agent.

In an October 2001 interview Schippers explained, "This agent here in Chicago filed the affidavit where he laid out the whole way that the money moves, the way that it is handled, how it comes out of the Middle East into the Chicago area and into the United States, how it is covered, how the operatives are covered, how the money is transferred back and where it's kept while it's here. And that affidavit ran like thirty pages—laying it out. And he had to go through hell on earth in Washington, he had to fight like a tiger—everybody in his own bureau and in the Department of Justice was against him—and still is."

The suspicious stock market trading indicating foreknowledge of the 9/11 attacks only added to the ever-growing proof that people in high positions knew what was coming in September 2001.

Speaking of all the warnings that poured into government agencies, Jerry Bremer, a former State Department terrorism expert, said, "We all predicted this. We had strategic warning. This is not something the analysts missed."

Despite a barrage of information on the Internet and in the foreign press, the corporate mass media failed to respond until mid-2002, when complaints from CIA and FBI agents and certain members of Congress became too loud to ignore. Even then, they danced around the subject of all the missed clues and cues.

"Because Bush has long insisted he had no inkling of the attacks, the disclosures [in 2002] touched off a media stampede in a capital long deprived of scandal. The fact that the nation's popular war president might have been warned a little over a month before September 11—and that the supposedly straight-talking Bushies hadn't told anyone about it—opened up a serious credibility gap for the first time in the war on terror," wrote *Newsweek* writers Michael Hirsh and Michael Isikoff.

18. What About Israeli Foreknowledge?

Since the September 11 attacks, several media pundits noted that the chief beneficiaries of the terrorism were the Bush administration and Israel. Bush gained welcome relief from bad news in the economy and his own sagging popularity while Israel found a provocation for unleashing its military against the Palestinians.

And there were indications that someone in Israel had foreknowledge of the attacks. Questions also arose concerning the number of Israeli citizens killed on September 11.

A major German newspaper, the *Frankfurter Allgemeine Zeitung*, reported on September 13, 2001, that German intelligence sources stated that both the American and Israeli governments received warnings of the attacks via the Echelon monitoring network. The article said information concerning a plan to hijack commercial airliners to use as weapons against the West was received at least three months prior to the attacks.

There was also a little-noticed story regarding the New York instant messaging firm, Odigo. Odigo officials confirmed soon after the attacks that two of their employees in Israel received text messages warning of the attacks two hours before planes crashed into the WTC.

Odigo's vice president of sales and marketing, Alex Diamandis, said employees in the company's research and development and international sales office in Israel received the warnings from another Odigo user unknown to them. They declined to state exactly what was in the messages or who sent them, saying the FBI was looking into the matter.

Micha Macover, Odigo's CEO, later said that while the company usually zealously protects the privacy of registered users, in this case it provided the FBI with the originating Internet Presence address of the message so the bureau could track down the Internet Service Provider and the originator of the message. There was no further word from the FBI.

Diamandis explained that Odigo offers a "People Finder" program that allows users to seek out and contact others based on common interests. He said it was possible that other Odigo members got the warnings but that the company had not heard from other recipients.

Another small item that raised eyebrows concerned a broken lease at the World Trade Center just days before the 9/11 attacks by a company with close ties to Israel.

The *American Free Press* reported that Zim American Israeli Shipping Co. broke its lease on two floors of the WTC's North Tower when it vacated the rented offices in early September 2001. The company's lease was good until the end of the year and the early pullout cost the company a reported $50,000.

The company is owned by Zim Israel Navigation Co., one of the world's largest container shipping firms. It is jointly owned by the state of Israel and Israel Corp.

Inquiries on the early withdrawal by Zim were routed to the WTC lease owner Silverstein Properties, which in turn passed questions to its public relations firm, Howard J. Rubenstein, which also represents the nation of Israel.

A spokesman for Rubenstein said they had no information on the lease issue.

On September 12, 2001, a *Jerusalem Post* headline read "Thousands of Israelis Missing near WTC, Pentagon." The accompanying story stated, "The Foreign Ministry in Jerusalem has so far received the names of 4,000 Israelis believed to have been in the areas of the World Trade Center and the Pentagon at the time of the attacks. The list is made up of people who have not yet made contact with friends or family."

It should be noted that this 4,000 figure originated not with US news media or Arabic sources but in Israel. The Arab media, however, was quick to seize on it.

A week later, a Beirut television station reported that 4,000 Israeli employees of the WTC were absent the day of the attack, suggesting foreknowledge of the attacks. This information spread across the Internet but was quickly branded a hoax.

On September 19, the *Washington Post* reported about 113 Israelis were missing at the WTC, and the next day, President Bush noted more than 130 Israelis were victims.

Finally, on September 22, the *New York Times* stated that amazingly only one Israeli was killed when the WTC towers collapsed. "There were, in fact, only three Israelis who had been confirmed as dead: two on the planes and another who had been visiting the towers on business and who was identified and buried," reported the *Times*.

But would a staunch friend of the United States like Israel conduct activities detrimental to its ally?

It might be remembered that on the day of the attacks, five Israelis were arrested for "puzzling behavior," namely shouting and dancing just after shooting video of the destruction of the World Trade Center from the roof of the New Jersey building where they worked.

The five, identified as Oded Ellner, Omer Marmari, Yaron Shmuel, and Sivan and Paul Kurzberg, were seen videotaping the WTC attack by neighbors, who interpreted their shouts as jubilation and agreement with the tragedy. Police were notified and later stopped their van bearing the company name Urban Moving Systems. In their van, police found $4,000 in cash and a box cutter. One investigator told the *Bergen Record* on September 12, "There were maps of the city in the car with certain places highlighted. It looked like they're hooked in on this. It looked like they knew what was going to happen." ABC News quoted one of the Israelis as saying, "Our purpose was to document the event."

After the names of two of the five turned up on a CIA-FBI database of foreign intelligence nationals, Marc Perelman of *Forward* reported that the FBI launched a Foreign Counterintelligence Investigation (FCI), which is undertaken quietly at the highest levels of the bureau. One of the men's attorneys, Steven Gordon, confirmed that "counterintelligence officials from the FBI" were involved in the case.

Dominick Suter, owner of the Weehawken, New Jersey, moving company, was questioned by the FBI agents, who took documents and computer hard drives but allowed Suter to go free. A few days later, Suter left the states for Israel.

In late November, the five were quietly released and sent back to Israel, where they charged that American authorities tortured them by keeping them unclothed in solitary confinement, beating them, and depriving them of food.

Irit Stoffer, a spokesperson for the Israeli Foreign Ministry, denied the men were spies and said they were deported for "only visa violations."

Chip Berlet, a senior analyst for Political Research Associates in Boston, explained, "[There] is a backdoor agreement between allies that says that if one of your spies gets caught and didn't do too much harm, he goes home. It goes on all the time. The official reason is always a visa violation."

But was there no real harm done? This case seemed to be just another odd anomaly in the cascading news of the attacks and the subsequent bombing of Afghanistan.

But it turned out to be only the barest tip of an iceberg that was to become public in mid-2002. The story began to surface in early 2002 when a secret report by the Drug Enforcement Agency

(DEA) was leaked to the European media. The report stated that most distribution of the drug Ecstasy was "controlled by organized crime figures in Western Europe, Russia and Israel." According to several reports, a DEA investigation into the Ecstasy supply uncovered a number of Israeli citizens operating in the United States.

"The report shows the clandestine network was engaged in several intelligence operations. It was a long-term project," said Guillaume Dasquie, editor of *Intelligence Online*, which broke the story in March 2002. The French website threatened to publish the entire DEA report if US and Israeli officials continued to deny its existence. The report mentioned investigations of the spy network in Florida, Texas, and California, with many of its participants posing as art students.

Beginning in early 2002, Fox News reporter Carl Cameron began to break the story that the US government was holding more than one hundred Israeli citizens with direct links to foreign military, criminal, and intelligence organizations. A bureau spokesperson would not talk about the case but did not deny it either. He referred reporters to the FBI's National Security Division.

Cameron too said he was hampered in trying to obtain information. "It's very explosive information, obviously, and there's a great deal of evidence that they say they have collected."

Cameron added that the biggest question that investigators shared with him was "How could they [the Israelis] not have known?"

By summer 2002, the estimated number of Israeli nationals being held had climbed to nearly two hundred, yet still the story went largely unreported by America's corporate mass media. One can only imagine what the newspaper headlines and TV crawl tags would look like if a gigantic Iraqi spy ring had been uncovered.

Reportedly, several of the Israelis lived in close proximity to some of the 9/11 terrorists, increasing the speculation that Israel knew more about the attacks than officially admitted. More than one-third of 120 deported Israelis lived in Florida, home to at least

10 of the 19 identified hijackers. At least 5 lived in Hollywood, Florida, home to Mohammed Atta and three other hijackers. Two others lived near Delray Beach, where other hijackers temporarily stayed. Six of the Israelis used cell phones purchased by a former Israeli vice consul in the United States, reported *Le Monde*.

Furthermore, several of the persons involved in this "art student scandal" were observed taking pictures and reconnoitering US military bases and the homes of government officials.

In March 2001, the National Counterintelligence Center (NCIC) issued a warning that "in the past six weeks, employees in federal office buildings have reported suspicious activities concerning individuals representing themselves as foreign students selling artwork."

Paul Rodriguez with *Insight* magazine reported, "Besides federal law enforcement incidents, DEA's I[nternal] S[ecurity] unit found that several military bases also had experienced unauthorized entries by some of the students including two bases from which Stealth aircraft and other supersecret military units operate. Unauthorized photographing of military sites and civilian industrial complexes, such as petroleum storage facilities, also was reported to the DEA, the documents show and interviews confirm."

Many of these young men and women had known connections to Israeli military, intelligence, or even criminal organizations. Some even worked in electronic signal intercept units in the Israeli army.

Most claimed to be art students from Israel's Bezalel Academy or the University of Jerusalem. The Jerusalem university does not exist, and officials with Bezalel Academy said no names of the "art students" turned up in the school's data bank.

According to the prestigious French newspaper *Le Monde*, student art sales were merely a cover for a vast Israeli spy ring whose primary purpose was to track al Qaeda in the United States without informing American authorities. The paper said this was the biggest Israeli spy case in the United States since 1984, when naval intelligence officer Jonathan Pollard, an American Jew, was caught giving military secrets to Israel.

The German newspaper *Die Zeit* reported in late 2002 that the CIA was given a detailed report on the actions of terrorists within the United States by the Mossad but failed to act on the information. According to BBC News, "The paper has uncovered details of a major Israeli spy ring involving some 120 agents for the intelligence service Mossad operation across America and some masquerading as art students. The ring was reportedly hard on the heels of at least four members of the hijack gang, including its leader Mohammed Atta. But the Israeli agents were detected by their American counterparts and thrown out of the country. The US authorities said then that they were students whose visas had expired."

The paper also said that if the CIA had notified German authorities that Ramzi bin al-Shibh, a key logistician for the attacks, had attended the meeting of al Qaeda members in Malaysia more than eighteen months prior to 9/11, the Germans could have prevented him from entering Germany and making contact with the Hamburg cell that planned the 9/11 atrocities.

Central to this tale of spies infiltrating the United States is the fact that the people taken by the FBI in connection with the spy ring included employees of two Israeli-owned high-tech companies that currently perform nearly all official wiretaps in the United States.

Such wiretaps are authorized by the Communications Assistance for Law Enforcement Act (CALEA). Actually wiretaps is a misnomer, because today's communications systems may be accessed by electronic signals rather than physical "taps," but the end result is the same—eavesdropping.

Two firms that handle most of this wiretapping are Amdocs, Ltd. and Comverse Infosys, both identified by Fox News as Israeli telecommunications companies. Amdocs reportedly keeps records of virtually every call made in the United States, although not the content of the calls. Comverse provided custom computers and software that allowed US investigators to intercept, record, store and receive data from the US phone system.

According to **NewsMax.com** reporter Charles R. Smith, "The spy ring enabled criminals to use reverse wiretaps against US intelligence and law enforcement operations. The [spy ring's] illegal monitoring may have resulted in the deaths of several informants and reportedly spoiled planned anti-drug raids on crime syndicates."

Officials at both Amdocs and Comverse denied any knowledge of the Israeli spy ring. Comverse spokesman Paul Baker stated, "In full compliance with the US Department of Defense regulations, this subsidiary's operations are completely segregated from all other Comverse businesses and are insulated from any foreign influence."

The official response to the allegations of widespread spying and even foreknowledge of the 9/11 attacks has prompted overly strenuous denials from US officials and even attacks in the major media. Daniel Pipes in an article for *Jewish World Review*, which was then published as an op-ed piece in the *New York Post*, decried the spy ring story as "conspiracy theories" based on a "crazy-quilt of unsourced allegations, drive-by innuendoes, and incoherent obscurities, but no hard facts." Pipes, director of the Middle East Forum and the author of *Conspiracy: How the Paranoid Style Flourishes and Where It Comes From*, is trotted out from time to time to dispel what he considers conspiracy theories. But Pipes himself holds some extreme political views for a Middle Eastern scholar. The only road to peace in Isreal, he told a recent Zionist conference in Washington, DC, is "an Isreali victory and a Palestinian defeat."

If the major news media are cowed about negative reporting on Israel, US government officials may be worse. *Insight* magazine reporter Paul Rodriguez said one Justice Department official told him, "We think there is something quite sinister here but are unable at this time to put our finger on it." Another official flatly stated, "The higher ups don't want to deal with this and neither does the FBI because it involves Israel." Fox News reported that "investigators within the DEA, INS and FBI have all told Fox that to pursue or even suggest Israel is spying through Comverse is considered career suicide."

Critics have voiced opposition to the wiretapping system. "From the beginning, both the political right and left warned Congress and the FBI that they were making a huge mistake by implementing CALEA, that it would jeopardize the security of private communications, whether it's between a mother and her son or between government officials," said Lisa Dean, vice president for technology policy at the Free Congress Foundation. The foundation's Brad Jansen added, "The CALEA form of massive surveillance is a poor substitute for real law enforcement and intelligence work. Massive wiretapping does not equal security. Instead, we have elected to jeopardize our national security in exchange for poor law enforcement. The current mentality of law enforcement is what failed to protect the US from 9/11. CALEA wiretaps will not protect us from terror attacks in the future. The system does not provide better intelligence information. It actually leads to less security and more crime. We get the worst of both worlds."

Some observers of today's geopolitical scene, especially perennial presidential candidate Lyndon LaRouche, believe that the 9/11 attacks provided a pretext to implement a plan to strengthen Israel, as articulated in a 1996 paper by an Israeli think tank that was influential in the Clinton administration.

The leader of the study group that produced this paper was Richard Perle. In 2002, Perle was chairman of Bush's Defense Policy Board, which reported to Deputy Defense Secretary Paul Wolfowitz. Perle is a ranking member of the Council on Foreign Relations and a key advocate of "neo-conservative" foreign policy.

Perle's 1996 paper, entitled "A Clean Break: A New Strategy for Securing the Realm," was prepared for the Institute for Advanced Strategic and Political Studies (IASPS), a Jerusalem-based think tank with an affiliated office in Washington. The institute issues policy studies and trains Israeli graduates in economic and strategic studies, helping them become research aides in the Israeli Parliament (Knesset) and the US Congress.

The "Clean Break" paper, prepared by IASPS consultants— two of whom were also members of the CFR, stated in 1996 that Israel had an opportunity to make a "clean break" with past policies and formulate "a new strategy to seize the initiative." The paper urged Israeli leaders to "work closely with Turkey and Jordan to contain, destabilize, and roll back some of its most dangerous threats. This implies a clean break from the slogan 'comprehensive peace' to a traditional concept of strategy based on balance of power." This would mean, as the paper goes on to explain, that "Israel can shape its strategic environment, in cooperation with Turkey and Jordan, by weakening, containing, and even rolling back Syria. This effort can focus on removing Saddam Hussein from power in Iraq—an important Israeli strategic objective in its own right—as a means of foiling Syria's regional ambitions."

Perle's paper also calls for changing "the nature of [Israel's] relations with the Palestinians, including the right of hot pursuit for self-defense into all Palestinian areas and nurturing alternatives to Arafat's exclusive grip on Palestinian society."

"The ongoing drive to induce President George W. Bush to launch a war against Iraq is a 1996 Israeli government policy that is being foisted on the President by a nest of Israeli agents inside the US government," declared LaRouche in campaign literature. "This Israeli spy network inside the United States was unable to achieve their objective until President Bush was entrapped by the events of September 11, 2001, and by the falsified account of those events provided by this foreign intelligence apparatus.

"On February 19, 1998, Richard Perle and former congressman Stephen Solarz released an 'Open Letter to the President,' demanding a full-scale US-led drive for 'regime change' in Baghdad. Among the signers of the original Perle-Solarz letter were the following current Bush administration officials: Elliot Abrams (National Security Council), Richard Armitage (State Department), John Bolton (State Department), Doug Feith (Defense Department), Fred Ikle (Defense Policy Board) Zalmay Khalilzad (White House), Peter Rodman (Defense Department), Donald Rumsfeld (Secretary of Defense), Paul Wolfowitz (Defense Department), David Wurmser (State Department), and Dov Zakheim (Defense Department)."

Shortly after the invasion of Iraq began in late March 2003,

Perle resigned as chairman of the Bush administration's Defense Policy Board amid charges of conflict of interest. The *New Yorker* magazine investigative writer Seymour Hersh reported that Perle had met in France with a Saudi arms dealer while soliciting investments for Trireme Partners, a firm he helped create and that planned to profit from homeland security activities. Perle threatened to sue Hersh and called him "the closest thing American journalism has to a terrorist" shortly before resigning.

LaRouche concluded that "President Bush is being pressured —from inside his own national security apparatus—to adopt an Israeli Likud foreign policy! This is a scandalous hoax, far worse than the Gulf of Tonkin affair of the late 1960s."

At least that's LaRouche's view of it. Considering that seven of the eleven men listed above are members of the Council on Foreign Relations, this plan could also be viewed as advancing the stated policy of that organization as well.

But there are other intriguing sources filling in this picture. General Hameed Gul, former director general of the Pakistani intelligence services, who worked closely with the CIA during the years of fighting against the Soviets in Afghanistan, said in an interview with UPI news service that it was his belief that the Israeli Mossad orchestrated the 9/11 attacks with the support of its own assets already within the United States.

While obviously anti-Israel, Gul nevertheless was in an insider's position. His views should be considered when he explained how there was little or no response from security forces on the morning of 9/11. "This was clearly an inside job," Gul said. "Bush was afraid and rushed to the shelter of a nuclear bunker. He clearly feared a nuclear situation."

"Who could that have been?" Gul asked rhetorically, alluding to Israel's nuclear capability.

Gul went on to explain that Israel had grown to detest both President Bush and his father because they are considered "too close to oil interests and the Gulf countries." He noted that Arab sources, through American conduits and "soft money," poured some $150 million into Bush's 2000 campaign, another danger signal to Israeli hardliners.

"Bush conveniently overlooks—or is not told—the fact that Islamic fundamentalists got their big boost in the modern age as CIA assets in the covert campaign to force the Soviets out of Afghanistan.

"All summer long [2001] we heard about America's shrinking surplus and that the Pentagon would not have sufficient funds to modernize for the 21st century. And now, all of a sudden, the Pentagon can get what it wants without any Democratic Party opposition. How very convenient.

"Even [America's] cherished civil liberties can now be abridged with impunity to protect the expansion of the hegemony of transnational capitalism. There is now a new excuse to crush antiglobalization protests. And now the Israelis have given the US the pretext for further expansion into an area that will be critical in the next 25 years—the Caspian basin," Gul stated.

Lest one think that Gul had his own agenda for making such statements, similar ideas were expressed by two former German intelligence chiefs. Eckhardt Werthebach, former president of Germany's domestic intelligence service, *Verfassungsschutz*, and Andreas von Buelow, Germany's former defense minister who also served on a parliamentary commission with oversight over Germany's secret service, both said the 9/11 attacks gave every evidence of being a state-sponsored event. Recall that US Attorney General Ashcroft soon after 9/11 announced that at least three of the hijackers were traced to a terrorist cell that had operated out of Hamburg, Germany, since at least 1999.

Werthebach said a sophisticated operation such as displayed on 9/11 would require a state intelligence service behind it, totally unlike the "loose group" of terrorists reportedly led by Mohammed Atta.

Von Buelow said the 9/11 planner used mercenaries or "guns for hire," such as Palestinian terrorist leader Abu Nidal, whom von Buelow described as an "instrument of the Mossad." Such people as Nidal and other Arab mercenaries are the "working level," according to von Buelow, pointing out the problems with such low-level agents.

He said they were "like assailants who, in their preparations, leave tracks behind them like a herd of stampeding elephants. They made payments with credit cards with their own names; they reported to their flight instructors with their own names. They left behind rented cars with flight manuals in Arabic for jumbo jets. They took with them, on their suicide trip, bills and farewell letters, which fall into the hands of the FBI, because they were stored in the wrong place and wrongly addressed. Clues were left behind like in a child's game of hide-and-seek, which were to be followed!"

He said such an operation is carefully conducted with an eye toward deception that is widely propagated in the mainstream media, creating an accepted version of events.

"Journalists don't even raise the simplest questions," he added. "Those who differ are labeled as crazy."

Von Buelow specified Israel as the most likely sponsor and said that the attacks were designed to turn public opinion against Arabs while boosting military and security spending.

Interestingly enough, the day before the 9/11 attacks, the *Washington Times* ran a story quoting members of the US Army's School of Advanced Military Studies (SAMS). Speaking about the capability of Israel, the paper noted, "Of the Mossad, the Israeli intelligence service, the SAMS officers say: 'Wildcard. Ruthless and cunning. Has capability to target US forces and make it look like a Palestinian/Arab act.'"

While bearing in mind these remarkable statements and allegations, it must be remembered that—in the convoluted world of international covert operations—almost nothing is as it seems. Evidence has also been presented of significant collusion by elements of the *Pakistani government* in the events of 9/11.

This story was first broken by Michel Chossudovsky, author of *War and Globalisation: The Truth Behind 9/11*, professor of economics at the University of Ottawa, and director of the Center for Research on Globalization which hosts **globalresearch.ca**, a critically important background source for 9/11 researchers.

In a little-noticed mainstream television news story cited by Chossudovsky, it was revealed that the FBI had told ABC News in late September 2001 that the 9/11 "ring leader," Mohammed Atta, had been financed by unnamed sources in Pakistan: The FBI had tracked more than $100,000 that had been wired from banks in Pakistan to two banks in Florida, into accounts held by suspected hijack ringleader, Mohammed Atta.

A short time later, according to Chossudovsky, "these findings of the FBI were confirmed by *Agence France Presse* (AFP) and the *Times of India*, quoting an official Indian intelligence report which had been dispatched to Washington. According to these two reports, the money used to finance the 9/11 attacks had allegedly been 'wired to WTC hijacker Mohammed Atta from Pakistan, by Ahmad Umar Sheikh, at the insistence of [ISI Chief] General Mahmoud [Ahmad].' And, according to the AFP (quoting the intelligence source): 'The evidence we have supplied to the US is of a much wider range and depth than just one piece of paper linking a rogue general to some misplaced act of terrorism.'"

As if this were not enough, Chossudovsky discovered that none other than General Mahmoud Ahmad himself, the alleged "money-man behind 9/11," was in the US when the attacks occurred. The ISI chief arrived on the 4th of September, one week before 9/11, on what was described as routine consultations with his US counterparts, including meetings at the Pentagon, the National Security Council, and with CIA Director George Tenet. And on the morning of September 11, Pakistan's chief spy was at a breakfast meeting on Capitol Hill hosted by Senator Bob Graham and Representative Porter Goss, the chairmen of the Senate and House Intelligence committees.

As to which foreign government entity may be behind the events of 9/11—the Saudis, the Israeli Mossad, the Pakistani ISI, or some combination—it can only be said at this point that current evidence points to the likelihood that 9/11 marks the convergence of overlapping and surreptitious agendas of several hidden parties, both international and domestic. Further research will be needed to connect the many dots on the global landscape that have been revealed so far.

19. Remote Controlled Aircraft a Reality

On October 7, 2001, the first operational deployment of Global Hawk spearheaded the American air and missile strikes on Afghanistan.

Global Hawk is the name of the latest version of a high-altitude, long-endurance unmanned air vehicle (UAV); in other words, an unarmed pilotless drone plane that can take off, conduct missions such as photographing battlefields and land by remote electronic control. Armed versions are in the works. The jet aircraft, equivalent in wing size to a Boeing 737 commercial airliner, has a publicly announced range of 14,000 nautical miles (about halfway around the world) and can fly at altitudes of 65,000 feet for about forty hours.

"Working alongside other UAV reconnaissance assets, at least one Global Hawk was used to provide reconnaissance prior to the [Afghanistan] strikes and for successive post-strike battle damage assessment," reported *Jane's Aerospace* on October 8.

This Buck Rogers equipment had been developed in the 1970s and, by several credible accounts, was operational in the 1980s. By the spring of 2001, this unmanned drone, designated the RQ-4A Global Hawk UAV, was capable of flying a mission to Australia.

"On 23 April 2001," according to Australia's Defence Science and Technology Organization (DSTO), "Global Hawk flew nonstop from Edwards Air Force Base, California, to Edinburgh Air Force Base, South Australia, where it was based for nearly two months undergoing a series of demonstration flights. Global Hawk returned to the US on 7 June 2001."

Dr. Brendan Nelson, Australia's parliamentary secretary to the minister of defence, said Global Hawk made aviation history when it became the first unmanned aircraft to fly nonstop across the Pacific Ocean in twenty-three hours and twenty minutes. The previous record had stood for twenty-six years.

During its six weeks of demonstrations in Australia, Global Hawk undertook eleven missions with crews from both the US Air Force and the Royal Australian Air Force. It was the first time the

United States had operated Global Hawk with another nation.

According to the Defense Advanced Research Projects Agency (DARPA), a newly designed Global Hawk aircraft was first flown at Edwards AFB on February 28, 1998. A Defense Department news release said, "The entire mission, including take-off and landing, was performed autonomously by the aircraft based on its mission plan." The craft's ground controllers monitored the status of the flight.

The Global Hawk program is managed by DARPA for the Defense Airborne Reconnaissance Office. The primary contractor is Teledyne Ryan Aeronautical and the principal suppliers are Raytheon Systems, Allison Engine Co., Boeing North American, and L3 Com.

So what does this unmanned flight system have to do with September 11?

Former German secretary of defense Andreas von Buelow, in a January 13, 2002, interview with the newspaper *Tagesspiegel* in speaking about the 9/11 attacks, noted, "There is also the theory of one British flight engineer [and] according to this, the steering of the planes was perhaps taken out of the pilots' hands from outside. The Americans had developed a method in the 1970s whereby they could rescue hijacked planes by intervening into the computer piloting [the electronic flight system]. This theory says this technique was abused in this case." Von Buelow could well have knowledge of this technology as several researchers and websites have stated that Lufthansa, Germany's national airline, was aware of the possibility of electronic capture and had quietly stripped the flight control systems out of American-built jetliners in the early 1990s.

The British flight engineer Von Buelow mentioned is Joe Vialls, a journalist, author, private investigator, and a former member of the Society of Licenced Aeronautical Engineers and Technologists based in London. In an article published on several websites, Vialls claimed, "[T]wo American multinationals collaborated with the Defense Advanced Research Projects Agency (DARPA) on a project designed to facilitate the remote recovery of hijacked American aircraft. Brilliant both in concept and operation, 'Home Run' [Vialls' designation, not its real code name] allowed specialist ground controllers to listen in to cockpit conversations on the target aircraft, then take absolute control of its computerized flight control system by remote means.

"From that point onwards, regardless of the wishes of the hijackers or flight deck crew, the hijacked aircraft could be recovered and landed automatically at an airport of choice, with no more difficulty than flying a radio-controlled model airplane. The engineers had no idea that almost thirty years after its initial design, Home Run's top-secret computer codes would be broken [or passed to unauthorized personnel] and the system used to facilitate direct ground control of four aircraft used in the high-profile attacks in New York and Washington on 11th September, 2001."

Even when news of Global Hawk and its remote-controlled capability was first released, there was speculation that UAV technology might be used to thwart airline hijackings. Once a hijacking took place, the Global Hawk flight technology would be triggered and the electronically captured plane flown to a landing at a safe location regardless of the actions of the flight crew or the hijackers.

The seemingly outlandish suggestion that remote-controlled planes were crashed into American targets is backed by several intriguing facts, beginning with a little-noticed item in the September 28, 2001, edition of the *New York Times* in which President Bush announced his plans to protect air passengers. Along with the usual proposals, such as strengthening cockpit doors and transponders that cannot be turned off, he mentioned "new technology, probably far in the future, allowing air traffic controllers to land distressed planes by remote control." Apparently, Bush was familiar with the Global Hawk technology but chose to present it as technology not yet available. Yet earlier that year, a former chief of British Airways suggested that such technology could be used to commandeer an aircraft from the ground and control it remotely in the event of a hijacking.

After the 2001 attacks, many websites speculated that perhaps Global Hawk's first true operational use might have been
conducted on September 11. After all, as all experienced aviation
and military persons well know, if a technology such as Global
Hawk is publicly revealed, it most probably has been in secret use
for many years.

According to aviation insiders, while it may indeed be years
before air traffic controllers can take control of flying airliners,
such technology already exists in certain modern jumbo jets
equipped with electronic flight control systems, such as the Boeing
757 and 767, both of which were involved in the 9/11 attacks.

This assertion seemed to be confirmed by a technical and
operational analysis white paper published shortly after the 9/11
attacks by two Arizona technology companies, KinetX, Inc., of
Tempe and Cogitek Corp. of Chandler.

These firms were trying to market their version of Global
Hawk as an antihijacker system. "The National Flight Emergency
Response System (NFERS) was developed to prevent the terrorist
incident of 9/11 from ever happening again," stated the companies' white paper. "This system will protect passenger and cargo
aircraft from being used as terrorist weapons. NFERS is essentially the integration of *existing technology* [emphasis added] for the
purpose of transferring cockpit operations to a secure ground
station in case of an emergency. It is important to note that the
essential technology exists now."

The two Arizona companies reported that they could have a
prototype system ready for use in twelve months. If independent
firms could manage a prototype that soon, it is clear that the
government most probably has the same technology operational.

Under such a system, a computer command ground station
could electronically capture a plane equipped with such technology and direct it wherever the controllers wished it to go. Some
experts contended that flying electronic command centers—
Airborne Warning and Control System (AWACS) aircraft—can
perform the same function as a ground station.

Other news items that reinforce the idea that electronically captured planes were used on 9/11 include the tape of Osama bin Laden made public by the CIA in late 2001, in which he revealed that some, if not all, of the hijackers did not realize they were on a suicide mission. This could explain the Boston reports that the hijackers spent their last night drinking heavily and looking for hookers.

Speaking about Flight 77, which reportedly struck the Pentagon, the *Washington Post* noted, "Aviation sources said that the plane was flown with extraordinary skill, making it highly likely that a trained pilot was at the helm, possibly one of the hijackers. Someone even knew how to turn off the transponder, a move that is considerably less than obvious."

This same story noted, "But just as the plane seemed to be on a suicide mission into the White House, the unidentified pilot executed a pivot so tight that it reminded observers of a fighter jet maneuver. The plane circled 270 degrees from the right to approach the Pentagon from the west, whereupon Flight 77 fell below radar level, vanishing from the controller's screens, the sources said."

One Internet source said this was proof that the plane had been electronically captured because software with built-in safety programs would not have allowed such a maneuver. But the software could have been overridden if the craft was taken over electronically as the outside capture would have negated the airliner's safety software.

We have already cited a news story about the suspected pilot of Flight 77, Hani Hanjour, who reportedly had flown so poorly in a flight test just weeks before 9/11 that he was rejected for a small plane rental at a suburban airport. Another news article also pointed out that Hanjour had trained for a few months in Scottsdale, Arizona, but did not finish the course "because instructors felt he was not capable."

Mohammed Atta and Marwan-al-Shehhi, two other hijackers suspected of flying planes, also were reported to be mediocre-to-poor pilots. One flight instructor said neither man was able to pass a Stage 1 rating test.

Suspected hijackers Nawaf al-Hazmi and Khalid al-Midhar both were sent packing from Sorbi's Flying Club in San Diego. "Their English was horrible and their mechanical skills were even worse," commented one flight instructor. "It was like they had hardly even ever driven a car."

Could a capture by Global Hawk and NFERS technology explain why none of the recordings from either air traffic controllers or the cockpit recorders have been made available to the public? Some reports claimed the tapes were blank.

According to some, an electronic capture of the flight control systems would have prevented any normal recordings. Others argue that the recordings were sequestered to prevent the public from hearing how the crews were unable to control their planes.

Investigator Vialls offered this explanation of why the cockpit voice recorder did not send a warning of the hijacking via their transponders. "Technically, a transponder is a combined radio transmitter and receiver which operates automatically, in this case relaying data between the four aircraft and air traffic control on the ground. The signals sent provide a unique 'identity' for each aircraft, essential in crowded airspace to avoid mid-air collisions, and equally essential for Home Run controllers trying to lock onto the correct aircraft.

"Once it has located the correct aircraft, Home Run 'piggy backs' a data transmission onto the transponder channel and takes direct control from the ground. This explains why none of the aircraft sent a special 'I have been hijacked' transponder code. This was the first hard proof that the target aircraft had been hijacked electronically from the ground."

To explain the reported cell phone calls from passengers on the flights, Vialls stated his belief that many of the calls were concocted after the fact. "There are no records of any such calls," he said. "We had the media's invisible 'contact' at an airline who 'said' a hostess called to report a hijacking and we had a priest who 'said' he received a call from a man asking him in turn to call his wife and tell her he loved her."

Vialls said one big reason why electronic capture of jetliners cannot be admitted is the billions of dollars required to replace the flight control systems, an expense the already hard-pressed airlines cannot afford.

"The most innovative antihijacking tool in the American arsenal has now become the biggest known threat to American national security," he lamented.

Vialls' thoughts were echoed by Donn de Grand Pre, a retired US Army colonel and author of *Barbarians Inside the Gates*. Shortly after the 9/11 attacks, Grand Pre, along with several commercial and military pilots, participated in a marathon discussion of the events. He acknowledged that the USA, Russia, China, and Israel all possess AWACS aircraft that "have the capability to utilize electromagnetic pulsing [EMP] to knock out onboard flight controls and communications of targeted aircraft, and then, fly them by remote control.

"The 9/11 activity and horrific destruction of US property and lives was intentionally meant to trigger a psychological and patriotic reaction on the part of the US citizens, which is paving the way for 'combined UN activity' (using the fig leaf of NATO) for striking key targets in both the Middle East/South Asia and the Balkans.

"The goal continues to be the ultimate destruction of all national sovereignty and establishment of a global government," he said.

It is indeed difficult for many people to believe that four jetliners with crews trained in detecting and deflecting a hijacking attempt could all be taken at the same time by a handful of men armed only with knives [some reports said plastic knives] and "box cutters." It is more believable to think that the four craft were captured by electronic technology such as that used on Global Hawk.

One tape, whose authenticity could not be established, was sent through the Internet in the early fall of 2002. It was said to be a conversation between air traffic controllers and Flight 93. In this tape, controllers and other nearby flights heard a male voice speak of a bomb onboard and hostage conditions. Other pilots reported seeing a black plume of smoke coming from the doomed flight.

One Internet user, who identified himself only as "Snake Plissken," offered his "bumble bee" theory:

> The masterminds of the 9/11 attacks kept the airliner passengers artificially low by hacking and manipulating the airlines' computer systems. Once in the air, the pilots were told by radio that an attack on America has taken place and ordered them to turn off their transponders and land at a designated military air base, which they did. The planes are still visible on radar but cannot be identified.
>
> Duplicate jets with remote-control technology have already been sent aloft by the 9/11 masterminds and reach similar altitudes and coordinates and are picked up by air traffic controllers while the original flights descend below radar to the military base.
>
> Once all are on the ground, all passengers are transferred to Flight 93, which is soon airborne under Global Hawk remote control. Duplicate flights 11, 175 and 77 are flown to their targets while original Flight 93 is shot down over Pennsylvania silencing all witnesses.

While this outlandish theory sounds more like a script from the old *Mission Impossible* series than reality, it is an object lesson in turning an event around and looking at it from different angles. This theory also does account for many of the unexplained facts of that day. For example, it would explain the extraordinary piloting by the Arab hijackers who, according to their flight instructors, could barely locate the landing gear; the absence of any recordings on flight data systems; and the fact that transponders were turned off. The inability to control the aircraft might also explain why apparently none of the crews or passengers on the hijacked craft tried to overcome their ill-armed captors, except possibly for Flight 93. And there is an intriguing theory, backed by solid evidence, regarding that doomed flight.

After learning of the WTC and Pentagon attacks and the news that a fourth jetliner was in the air and that fighter jets had been scrambled, many people's first thought upon learning of the Flight 93 crash was that it had been shot down.

The government quickly denied this and, instead, built up the legend of the courageous passengers deciding to attack their captors. This, of course, provided a foundation for the story that the jet crashed during a ferocious battle on board.

However, the last cell phone call received from the doomed flight came from an unidentified male passenger who called the 911 emergency number about eight minutes before the plane crashed. Operator Glen Cramer told the Associated Press on September 11 that the man said he had locked himself in a toilet. "We're being hijacked! We're being hijacked!" the man screamed into his phone.

"We confirmed that with him several times," said Cramer, "and we asked him to repeat what he had said. He was very distraught. He said he believed the plane was going down. He did hear some sort of an explosion and saw white smoke coming from the wing, but he didn't know where. And then we lost contact with him."

The FBI confiscated Cramer's tape and ordered him not to discuss the matter further. No explanation of this cell phone conversation has been offered.

According to an Internet posting by Robb Magley, an earthquake monitoring station in southern Pennsylvania registered a seismic signature somewhat characteristic of a sonic boom at 9:22 a.m. on September 11, 2001. Sonic booms are created by aircraft exceeding the speed of sound. Jumbo airliners do not exceed the speed of sound, but supersonic jet fighters do.

This seismic evidence was thought to suggest that a supersonic jet was in the area just prior to the crash of Flight 93 and added support to a growing suspicion that the airliner was shot down by the US military. After conferring with a NASA scientist, Magley became convinced that the seismic spike was not a sonic boom but perhaps an explosion from a nearby rock quarry. Later, Magley's attention turned to the possibility that Flight 93 may have been the victim of a high-powered microwave (HPM) device rather than an aircraft.

Supporting Magley's original theory of a shoot-down was a statement by top government officials that President Bush had authorized the use of military force early on the morning of September 11.

Speaking on NBC's *Meet the Press* less than a week after the attacks, Vice President Cheney said Bush "made the decision that if the plane [Flight 77, which reportedly struck the Pentagon] would not divert, if they wouldn't pay any attention to instructions to move away from the city, as a last resort, our pilots were authorized to take them out."

Deputy Defense Secretary Paul Wolfowitz acknowledged that the military was closing in on Flight 93. "We responded awfully quickly, I might say, on Tuesday," he said in a PBS interview. "And in fact, we were already tracking in on that plane that crashed in Pennsylvania. I think it was the heroism of the passengers on board that brought it down, but the air force was in a position to do so if we had had to."

General Richard Myers, chairman of the Joint Chiefs of Staff, also confirmed that fighters approached Flight 93, but denied that they fired on the craft.

Several ground witnesses reported sighting a small aircraft circling the area at the time of the Flight 93 crash. Later, the FBI explained that it was a business jet that had been requested by authorities to descend and provide the location of the crash.

This explanation is wanting due to the fact that by then all air traffic had been grounded, the plume of smoke from the wreckage plus numerous calls to 911 would have provided a sufficient location bearing, and the FBI has failed to provide any information concerning this aircraft or its passengers, none of whom has come forward to give their account.

One craft that was in the area was a single-engine Piper piloted by Bill Wright. Wright said he was within sight of Flight 93, in fact so close he could see its United markings. He said he suddenly received orders to get away from the airline and land immediately. "That's one of the first things that went through my mind when they told us to get as far away from it as fast as we could, that either they were expecting it to blow up or they were going to shoot it down," Wright told newsmen.

There is also a question concerning the wreckage. According to the official story, Flight 93 barreled into the ground at close to five hundred miles per hour. Yet, wreckage was strewn for up to eight miles, including paper mail the plane was carrying. One engine, which weighs in excess of one thousand pounds, was found more than two thousand yards from the crash scene, indicating it came loose prior to ground impact.

Wally Miller was the local coroner at the time of the crash and was required by law to establish the cause of death of the victims. "I put down 'murdered' for the 40 passengers and crew, 'suicide' for the four terrorists," Miller told a reporter, adding significantly that he could not prove what actually happened.

Subsequent actions by government authorities did little to dissuade conspiracy theorists. They didn't make public the flight data recordings until April 18, 2002, and then played edited excerpts to the victims' family members, who were ordered not to discuss what they heard. Even then, at least one person said he learned things he hadn't known before. Bureau agents also muzzled Cleveland air traffic controllers involved in the last moments of the flight, ordering them not to speak about what they saw on their radar screens.

Amidst near-hysterical cries of national security, the public was once again asked to blindly accept official pronouncements backed by little, no, or even contradictory evidence. With all hard evidence locked away by the government, speculation has run rampant on the true cause of Flight 93's demise. Countering the official story of the crash occurring during a heroic battle with the hijackers are other equally credible theories.

The most prevalent theory is that a US fighter downed the craft with missile and/or cannon fire, a suspicion firmly supported by all the available evidence. Another theory holds that, since one unauthenticated air traffic controller tape available on the Internet speaks of a bomb on board, one of the hijackers may have detonated such a device in the air.

A more fanciful theory, though backed by solid science, was offered by researchers citing Harvard academic Elaine Scarry. In a series of articles and books, Scarry postulated that some recent airline crashes were caused by high-tech military "electronic warfare" weaponry akin to Global Hawk technology and capable of disrupting an aircraft's control system,. The FBI did confirm that a C-130 military plane was within twenty-five miles of Flight 93, and since 1995 the air force has installed "electronic suites" in twenty-eight of its C-130 aircraft.

This Scarry scenario leads to yet another theory that posits that the plane's passengers were successful in their attempt to regain control of the craft but then found they could not control the plane due to electronic seizure.

Under the theory that all the aircraft were captured and flown remotely using Global Hawk technology, the masterminds behind such a scheme could not possibly allow Flight 93 to land safely and give away the game. Since both the shoot-down orders and the fighters were in place, it would be simply a matter of giving the go-ahead and then sweeping it all under the rug of "national security."

But regardless of what truly happened to Flight 93 or how the hijacked planes were controlled, it is clear that whoever was behind the attacks had information, if not help, from inside the government.

One key question is how at least nineteen foreign terrorists were able to separately evade standard airport security precautions and simultaneously hijack four commercial airliners using only box cutters.

As Internet pundit Gary North stated, "We need a theory of the coordinated hijackings that rests on a plausible cause-and-effect sequence that does not assume the complete failure of both check-in procedures and the onboard seating procedures on four separate flights on two separate airlines. I don't see how anyone can make an accurate judgment about who was behind the attacks until he has a plausible explanation of how hijackers got onto the planes and were not removed."

These terrorists were then able to divert four scheduled flights, all under the nose of air traffic controllers, and there was no immediate response despite the standard response procedures in place. By 8:15 a.m., at the latest, on the morning of September 11, air traffic controllers knew that Flights 11 and 175 were badly off course and probably hijacked. Yet by 8:45 a.m., according to NORAD, fighters were still on the ground. When they did become airborne, standard procedures were ignored.

It was established that the person who called the warning to the White House had access to top-secret government codes, and to many knowledgeable persons the lack of rapid response by the US defense establishment is simply inconceivable.

Military forces had been on a heightened state of alert for several days before the attack. The National Reconnaissance Office had scheduled a training simulation of a jet crashing into a government building the morning of September 11, 2001, either along with or coincidently with a NORAD exercise using a similar scenario.

Yet the US continental defense system consistently failed. Something was very wrong.

If even half of the information outlined in this section is proven in error, the remainder is a damning indictment of official malfeasance. It's much worse than what *Newsweek* termed "a whole summer of missed clues." The totality of the information available today can only lead to two inescapable conclusions: either the highest leadership of the United States is composed of imbeciles and incompetent blunderers or they are criminally negligent accessories to the crimes, if not worse.

Either way, it is clear that such leadership must be changed, and soon, if the traditional standards of freedom and democracy in the United States are to be retained.

20. The Official 9/11 Inquiry: Another Warren Commission?

Earlier we discussed the first official inquiry into 9/11, the Joint Congressional Inquiry, which probed activities of the intelligence community in connection with the attacks. In July 2003, the Bush administration asked Congress to withhold from the press and the public a crucial twenty-eight page section of the inquiry's final report. It was widely reported that these pages pointed to direct ties between the Saudi government—long a loyal client state of the US—and those 9/11 hijackers who were Saudi citizens. And there were also embarrassments for the administration in those portions of the report that were made public.

President Bush staunchly resisted further efforts to investigate the 9/11 attacks until November 2002 when, under intense pressure from the public and especially from 9/11 families, he signed into law a bill creating the National Commission on Terrorist Attacks Upon the United States—which as noted before is usually referred to as the 9/11 Commission. The new commission, intended to pick up where the Joint Inquiry left off, held its first hearings in late March 2003.

In an incident filled with incredible irony, Bush's first choice to head the 9/11 Commission was Henry Kissinger, a prominent secret society member and perhaps the man most responsible for producing the past thirty years of United States foreign policy. It was this deeply flawed foreign policy, mostly thinly disguised neocolonialism and nation looting, that has resulted in worldwide antipathy for America's role in the world in recent years.

Though considered a prominent statesman, there is a darker side to Kissinger, as evidenced by several warrants outstanding in two European countries for war crimes and complicity in murder. In May 2001, for example, during a stay at the Ritz Hotel in Paris, he was visited by the criminal brigade of the French police, and served with a summons. Kissinger made a hasty exit, never to return to France.

Christopher Hitchens, a regular contributor to *Vanity Fair* and author of several noted books, including *The Trial of Henry Kissinger* (Verso: 2001), presents a wealth of documentation showing that Kissinger was the responsible party behind a number of acts that can be considered war crimes, including atrocities during the war in Indochina, planned assassinations in Santiago, Nicosia, and Washington, DC, and genocide in East Timor. For example, in 1970, Kissinger ordered the removal of Chilean army commander in chief Rene Schneider. Schneider was a supporter of Chile's constitution who opposed what later became a right-wing coup against Socialist President Salvadore Allende, and was murdered in 1970 by right-wing plotters within the Chilean military. Former US ambassador to Chile Edward Korry confirmed Kissinger's direct role in these events. Strong evidence ties Kissinger to the actual CIA-sponsored coup itself on September 11, 1973, which resulted in the death of Allende and many hundreds of his left-wing supporters.

Hitchens and many others have raised disturbing questions concerning Kissinger's role in the estimated 700,000 deaths of Cambodian peasants during the Vietnam War era. Edward S. Herman, professor emeritus of the Wharton School at the University of Pennsylvania, wrote extensively on Kissinger's involvement in bringing about the Cambodian "killing fields" and points to his rather dubious achievement as the person responsible for more deaths in Southeast Asia than the infamous Pol Pot. Likewise, it was Kissinger as secretary of state under President Ford who approved Indonesian President Suharto's invasion of East Timor, which resulted in yet another bloodbath.

Upon departing as US secretary of state, Kissinger trucked State Department records to the Rockefeller estate at Pocantico Hills near Tarrytown, New York. These documents were subsequently recovered for their rightful owners, the American public, but not before Kissinger made a substantial amount of money publishing three volumes of memoirs. These writings left out significant issues of his years of service—including deals with China, the loss of Angola in Africa, and the East Timor affair—and even proved to be untrue in some accounts after official documents were later declassified.

After leaving government, Kissinger set himself up as a national security adviser to many nations by forming and serving as chairman of Kissinger Associates. According to author Walter Isaacson, Kissinger started his consulting firm with $350,000 loaned to him by Goldman Sachs and three banks. Early on, he hired Brent Snowcroft and Lawrence Eagleburger, both of whom later left to join the first Bush Administration. It should be noted that Eagleburger has been a member of both the Council on Foreign Relations and the Trilateral Commission.

It is such secret societies as these that form a hidden backdrop to the events most Americans only know about from superficial reporting in the corporate mass media. For a more detailed history of these secretive societies, their role in events from World War I to Vietnam and the 1991 Gulf War, and their "New World Order" agenda for global control, please see my book *Rule by Secrecy* (HarperCollins: 2000).

An excellent example of the influence of such globalist organizations can be found in Kissinger's own meteoric rise to power. In 1955, Kissinger was merely an obscure academic until he attended a meeting at the Marine Corps School at Quantico, VA, hosted by then presidential foreign affairs assistant Nelson Rockefeller. This meeting was the start of a lengthy friendship between the two culminating in a $50,000 outright gift to Kissinger from Rockefeller. Kissinger soon was introduced to David Rockefeller and other prominent members of the Council on Foreign Relations. Through the CFR, Kissinger obtained funding and entree to ranking officials of the Atomic Energy Commission, the three branches of the military, the CIA, and the State Department, which he used to produce a best-selling book entitled *Nuclear Weapons and Foreign Policy*, in which he argued that a nuclear war might be "winnable."

Following a public outcry over Bush's choice to head the 9/11 Commission, Kissinger quickly withdrew, claiming he did not want to make known the client list of Kissinger Associates.

Bush continued to look to the secret societies for appointments, finally settling on former New Jersey Governor Thomas H. Kean and former Indiana Representative Lee Hamilton to chair the commission. Both are members of the Council on Foreign Relations.

Kean's connections to the oil industry go deep. He is currently a director of Amerada Hess, a huge oil company. Hess is a partner with Saudi Arabia's Delta Oil in a joint venture in Azerbaijan. And Delta Oil is part of the joint venture with Unocal for the pipeline through Afghanistan to the Caspian Basin.

Other commission members also were former senior government officials, such as Fred Fielding, former White House counsel to Nixon; Jamie Gorelick, deputy attorney general under Clinton; and John Lehman, Reagan's secretary of the navy.

The commission soon found itself stymied by the Bush administration, which continued to drag its feet in supplying White House intelligence briefing documents to the commission. After a long period of declining its invitations, President Bush in February 2004 finally agreed to meet with the commission. This meeting took place on April 29, but not until White House counsel had negotiated restrictive terms: Vice President Cheney had to be present also, and the two men were not to testify under oath. In addition, no recording was to be made of the session, nor was a stenographer permitted to be in the room. Bush and Cheney also declined to permit notes of the three-hour session to be shared with the 9/11 families.

Through the spring of 2004, commissioners continued to complain that their work was delayed repeatedly because of disputes with the administration over access to documents and other witnesses.

"It's obvious that the White House wants to run out the clock here . . . ," commented former Senator Max Cleland, a Democrat who was widely regarded to be the commission's most vociferous and outspoken critic of the Bush administration. Such activity by Cleland came to a halt almost halfway through the commission's work when he resigned to accept a position on the board of directors of the Export-Import Bank of the United States after being nominated by President Bush on November 21, 2003. Many observers saw Cleland's new job as nothing less than a blatant buy-off by the Bush administration.

Commission chairman Kean said his group might have to restrict its inquiries if Congress did not extend the commission's life, due to end May 27, 2004. "There are many paths to follow, including how intelligence was used, where it came from and what was known by the FBI, CIA, and National Security Council," said Kean, adding that the May deadline could force a report "that we, as commissioners, would feel very frustrated with." The deadline was extended slightly, with the commission agreeing to issue its final report on July 26, 2004.

From the Bush adminstration's point of view, Hamilton was ideal for the job of vice chair. He is a member of the Homeland Security Advisory Council and in years past participated in investigations of both the so-called October Surprise and Iran-Contra scandals. In each case, he was unable to uncover evidence of high-level government malfeasance or criminality.

Commissioner Fielding was named by investigative journalism students at the University of Illinois as being the infamous Deep Throat of Watergate fame, the source that brought down President Nixon and paved the way for Gerald Ford.

The commission's executive director was Philip Zelikow, a member of President Bush's own Foreign Intelligence Advisory Board. He also served as a national security adviser in the Ford and Bush I administrations. Zelikow, who was a member of the Bush-Cheney transition team which helped form the current National Security Council, was considered by many as Bush's "gatekeeper" on the 9/11 Commission.

It was quite apparent that the commission that probed the events of 9/11 was as compromised and controlled as was the Warren Commission of 1964, which declined to ask any hardball questions of the new president or his staff.

Another wrinkle in the progress of the 9/11 Commission came about due to the actual interpretation of its charter by the commissioners. This interpretation was voiced by Vice Chairman Lee Hamilton who explained, "The focus of the commission will be on the future. We're not interested in trying to assess blame; we do not consider that part of the commission's responsibility."

So, it was now openly acknowledged that the commission would not hold key officials accountable for their actions; instead, it would focus on ways to prevent a recurrence in the future. And indeed, on national television and for all to see, the commission has lived up to this charter. This was especially revealed in its forgiving and friendly treatment of government officials testifying under oath.

Attorney General John Ashcroft's appearance before the 9/11 Commission provided one of the best examples of the kid-glove treatment afforded to high administration officials who should be directly in the line of fire for the greatest crime ever committed on American soil.

According to the mainstream Democratic think tank, the Center for American Progress, Ashcroft's testimony was a "deceptive, disingenuous, and dishonest account of his record prior to 9/11 and a Pollyanna-type view of his actions following the attack. Worse, the commissioners largely accepted Ashcroft's testimony at face value and passed on opportunities to aggressively question the attorney general on inconsistencies and inaccuracies in his statements."

The acting FBI director for the three months before 9/11, Thomas Pickard, had just testified to the commission that Ashcroft had waved off an update on the terrorist threat, telling Pickard that he didn't want to hear about the subject anymore.

It fell to former Illinois Governor Jim Thompson—usually the fiercest Republican defender on the commission—to ask the only critical question about this statment. When asked by Thompson about Pickard's claim, Ashcroft replied, "I never said I didn't want to hear about counterterrorism."

But the exchange ended there, with no follow-up question. Obviously, either Ashcroft or Pickard was lying—but the commissioners didn't seem to notice this obvious contradiction. Later in his testimony, Ashcroft insisted that he had added more money to the Justice Department's budget for counterterrorism than for any other function. But according to *Slate* magazine, this claim is patently untrue. "It has been disputed by the commission's staff, several previous witnesses, and public budget documents. Yet none of the commissioners called him on it."

Even Commissioner Richard Ben-Veniste, the Democratic former Watergate prosecutor, went easy on the attorney general. He asked why Ashcroft's top five priorities listed in a policy document of May 10, 2001, did not include fighting terrorism. Ashcroft answered that at the May 9 hearings before the Senate Appropriations Committee he had cited terrorism as his No. 1 priority. Ben-Veniste let Ashcroft go unchallenged, even though the commission staff report released just prior to Ashcroft's testimony revealed that a May 10, 2001, budget guidance he released made no mention of counterterrorism.

Many had predicted before the Ashcroft appearances that the attorney general was so vulnerable on the issue of 9/11 that he might have to be sacrificed as an administration fall guy. But Ashcroft was left unscathed by the commission.

Perhaps the chief embarrassment to the Bush administration during this period of testimony before the commission was the revelations of Richard A. Clarke, the Reagan appointee who was the government's top counterterrorism expert under President Clinton and President George W. Bush. On the CBS television program *60 Minutes*, and in dramatic testimony before the 9/11 Commission that electrified the country, Clarke charged that the Bush administration "failed to act prior to September 11 on the threat from al Qaeda despite repeated warnings." Clarke alleged that the Bush administration received repeated warnings that an al Qaeda attack was imminent, yet it underfunded and subordinated counterterrorism in the months leading up to 9/11—and even after. Among the casualties of this downgrade was "a highly classified program to monitor al Qaeda suspects in the United States," which the White House suspended in the months leading up to 9/11, according to Clarke. Clarke went on to claim that the President was improperly attempting to "harvest a political windfall" from 9/11, charging that the administration began making plans to attack Iraq on 9/11—despite evidence the terror attack had been engineered by al Qaeda.

Clarke's latter assertion was consistent with earlier reports. CBS News had reported on September 4, 2002, that five hours after the 9/11 attacks, "Defense Secretary Donald Rumsfeld was telling his aides to come up with plans for striking Iraq—even though there was no evidence linking Saddam Hussein to the attacks." Similarly, then Secretary of Treasury Paul O'Neill said the administration "was planning to invade Iraq long before the September 11 attacks and used questionable intelligence to justify the war."

National Security Adviser Condoleezza Rice emerged as the administration's point person in its efforts to refute Clarke's accusations. In an opinion piece in the *Washington Post* on March 22, Rice wrote: "Despite what some have suggested, we received no intelligence that terrorists were preparing to attack the homeland using airplanes as missiles, though some analysts speculated that terrorists might hijack planes to try and free US-held terrorists." This claim was restated on numerous TV talk shows, and Rice elaborated on these assertions in her reluctant testimony before the 9/11 Commission; the National Security Adviser of the United States had agreed to testify under oath about the greatest security breach in modern history only after extreme public pressure.

To its credit, pressure from the Commission in connection with the testimony of Rice forced the rather embarrassing release of the President's Daily Briefing (PDB) for August 6, 2001, a document that clearly outlined al Qaeda plans to strike within the United States. The PDB was declassified on Saturday, April 10, 2004. Below is the entire text of the intelligence briefing that was released by the White House. Most remarkable are the chilling revelations in its final two paragraphs.

Bin Ladin Determined To Strike in US

Clandestine, foreign government, and media reports indicate bin Ladin since 1997 has wanted to conduct terrorist attacks in the US. Bin Ladin implied in US television interviews in 1997 and 1998 that his followers would follow the example of World Trade Center bomber Ramzi Yousef and "bring the fighting to America."

After US missile strikes on his base in Afghanistan in 1998, Bin Ladin told followers he wanted to retaliate in Washington, according to a . . . (redacted portion) . . . service.

An Egyptian Islamic Jihad (EIJ) operative told an . . . (redacted portion) . . . service at the same time that Bin Ladin was planning to exploit the operative's access to the US to mount a terrorist strike.

The millennium plotting in Canada in 1999 may have been part of Bin Ladin's first serious attempt to implement a terrorist strike in the US.

Convicted plotter Ahmed Ressam has told the FBI that he conceived the idea to attack Los Angeles International Airport himself, but that Bin Ladin lieutenant Abu Zubaydah encouraged him and helped facilitate the operation. Ressam also said that in 1998 Abu Zubaydah was planning his own US attack.

Ressam says Bin Ladin was aware of the Los Angeles operation. Although Bin Ladin has not succeeded, his attacks against the US Embassies in Kenya and Tanzania in 1998 demonstrate that he prepares operations years in advance and is not deterred by setbacks. Bin Ladin associates surveilled our Embassies in Nairobi and Dar es Salaam as early as 1993, and some members of the Nairobi cell planning the bombings were arrested and deported in 1997.

Al Qaeida members—including some who are US citizens—have resided in or traveled to the US for years, and the group apparently maintains a support structure that could aid attacks. Two al-Qa'ida members found guilty in the conspiracy to bomb our Embassies in East Africa were US citizens, and a senior EIJ member lived in California in the mid-1990s.

A clandestine source said in 1998 that a Bin Ladin cell in New York was recruiting Muslim-American youth for attacks.

We have not been able to corroborate some of the more sensational threat reporting, such as that from a . . . (redacted portion) . . . service in 1998 saying that Bin Ladin wanted to hijack a US aircraft to gain the release of "Blind Shaykh" 'Umar 'Abd al-Rahman and other US-held extremists.

Nevertheless, FBI information since that time indicates patterns of suspicious activity in this country consistent with preparations for hijackings or other types of attacks, including recent surveillance of federal buildings in New York.

The FBI is conducting approximately 70 full field investigations throughout the US that it considers Bin Ladin-related. CIA and the FBI are investigating a call to our Embassy in the UAE in May saying that a group of Bin Ladin supporters was in the US planning attacks with explosives.

A few days after her testimony, a damning response to Rice swiftly came from a major new whistleblower. In public statements intended to directly contradict Condoleezza Rice's testimony before the commission, Sibel Edmonds revealed that she had previously provided information to the panel investigating the September 11 attacks, which she believes proved that senior officials knew of al Qaeda's plans to attack the US with aircraft months before the strikes happened. In three hours during a closed session with the commission, she reiterated that information was circulating within the FBI in the spring and summer of 2001 that strongly suggested that an attack using aircraft was just months away and the terrorists were in place.

Going public to confront Rice's testimony, Edmonds said that by using the word "we," Rice told an "outrageous lie." She went on: "Rice says 'we' not 'I.' That would include all people from the FBI, the CIA and DIA. I am saying that is impossible."

True to form, the Bush administration immediately sought to silence Edmonds, obtaining a gag order from a court. On March 24, 2004, in front of about fifty reporters and a dozen news cameras, Edmonds said: "Attorney General John Ashcroft told me he was invoking 'State Secret Privilege and National Security' when I told the FBI I wanted to go public with what I had translated from the pre-9/11 intercepts."

"I appeared once on CBS's *60 Minutes* but I have been silenced by Mr. Ashcroft. The FBI follows me, and I was threatened with jail in 2002 if I went public," said Edmonds. In March of 2002, Edmonds was abruptly terminated from her job at the FBI, shortly after her immediate supervisors at the bureau learned that she had raised her concerns up the chain of command.

But Edmonds continued to talk to overseas journalists. She told *The Independent*, a London newspaper: "I gave [the commission] details of specific investigation files, the specific dates, specific target information, specific managers in charge of the investigation. I gave them everything so that they could go back and follow up. This is not hearsay. These are things that are documented. These things can be established very easily." She added: "There was general information about the time frame, about methods to be used—but not specifically about how they would be used—and about people being in place and who was ordering these sorts of terror attacks. There were other cities that were mentioned. Major cities—with skyscrapers."

"Most of what I told the commission, ninety percent of it related to the investigations that I was involved in or from working in the department. Two hundred translators side by side, you get to see and hear a lot of other things as well," she told *The Independent*. "President Bush said they had no specific information about 11 September and that is accurate but only because he said '11 September.'"

Such stonewalling and obfuscation by the Bush administration toward 9/11 in general and the 9/11 Commission in particular has proved too much for at least one victim's relative.

Ellen Mariani, whose husband, Louis Neil Mariani, was killed when Flight 175 struck the South Tower of the WTC, on November 26, 2003, filed a federal lawsuit in the United States District Court of the Eastern District of Pennsylvania. Defendants included President Bush, Vice President Cheney, Attorney General Ashcroft, Secretary of Defense Rumsfeld, CIA Director George Tenet, Transportation Secretary Mineta, National Security Adviser Rice, and former President George Herbert Walker Bush. The suit was brought under the Racketeer Influenced and Corrupt Organizations Act (RICO), usually reserved for organized crime figures.

The venue for the suit was changed and an amended complaint was filed in May 2004 in the district court of the District of Columbia. [*Editor's note*: Excerpts from the amended Complaint may be found in Appendix D. See also Ellen Mariani's preface to this book.]

Interestingly, another defendant in the suit was Peter G. Peterson, chairman of the Council on Foreign Relations (CFR). The suit claims that CFR "is believed to have provided Defendant [Bush], et al., while acting under color of federal law, with critical national security advice not believed to be in the best interests of the Plaintiff [Mariani] and the American public."

Mariani's attorney, former Pennsylvania Deputy Attorney General Philip J. Berg, stated he would prove that "these serious RICO Act [charges] claims are bona fide and genuine as provided for under Count II, which will provide specific timelines. Defendants knew, or should have known, the attacks of 9/11 were imminent."

In the conclusion to the suit, Berg wrote, "Defendants must be held to account for their actions prior to and after 9/11 for the good of our nation and our security. Anything less will render the United States Constitution and our leaders' ritual vows 'to preserve and protect our Constitution against all enemies, foreign and domestic' meaningless."

With the filing of this suit and amidst quarrelling between the 9/11 Commission and the Bush administration, it was becoming more widely known that any state sponsorship of the 9/11 terrorists must have come at least in part from Saudia Arabia.

US News & World Report reported on an unnamed government official who had read the twenty-eight pages of classified material in the Congressional Joint Inquiry report, quoting him as saying, "There is so much more stuff about Saudi government involvement, it would blow people's minds."

This statement was clarified by Florida Senator Bob Graham, co-chairman of the report committee. "The reality is that the [Saudi] foreign government was much more directly involved in not only the financing but in the provision of support—transportation, housing, and introduction to a network which gave support to the terrorists." He added, "They were not rogue agents, [but] were being directed by persons of significant responsibility within the government."

According to author Craig Unger, who investigated the elder Bush's role in both the Iran-Contra and Iraqgate scandals, the estranged sister-in-law of Osama bin Laden, Carmen bin Laden, said she thought family members might have provided funds for Osama.

In his recent and widely noted book *House of Bush, House of Saud: The Secret Relationship Between the World's Two Most Powerful Dynasties* (Scribner: March 2004), Unger argues that the seeds for 9/11 were planted nearly thirty years ago in a series of savvy business transactions that subsequently translated into a long-term political union between the Saudi royal family and the extended family of George H. W. Bush.

Unger's book begins with a single question: How is it that two days after September 11, 2001, even as American air traffic was tightly restricted, a Saudi billionaire socialized in the White House with President George W. Bush as 140 Saudi citizens, many immediate kin to Osama Bin Laden, were permitted to return to their country? According to Unger's account, a potential treasure trove of intelligence was allowed to flee the country—including an alleged al Qaeda intermediary who was said to have foreknowledge of the 9/11 attacks. Unger asks, and so do we: Why did the FBI facilitate this evacuation without questioning these people? Why did Saudi Arabia, the birthplace of most of the hijackers, receive exclusive and preferential treatment from the White House even as the World Trade Center continued to burn?

It is well known that Saudi Arabia has long benefited from its cozy relationship with American leaders, always eager to maintain US influence with the world's leading supplier of oil. The Saudis profited most from the 1991 Gulf War. According to London's *Financial Times*, "Saudi Arabia oil revenues have tripled since mid-1990 because of the closure of production in Iraq and Kuwait."

Interestingly enough, it was the elder Bush's own secret society—the Council on Foreign Relations (CFR)—that blew the whistle on his business partners and friends in Saudi Arabia. In a report issued in October 2002, a CFR task force reported that Saudi Arabian officials for years have ignored countrymen and Muslim charities that provided major funding for the al Qaeda network and that US officials had systematically refused to acknowledge this connection.

"Saudi nationals have always constituted a disproportionate percentage of al Qaeda's own membership; and al Qaeda's political message has long focused on issues of particular interest to Saudi nationals, especially those who are disenchanted with their own government," stated the CFR report. Such connections are so numerous and had been so well documented that by late 2002 even the mass media began to question the Saudi role.

Individual Saudis also became the defendants in a $1 trillion lawsuit filed on behalf of more than six hundred families of 9/11 victims in 2002. Since then, many more families have joined the suit, raising the total number of persons involved to about 4,000. Yet to date this story has received scant mention in the mainstream media. The suit was filed by attorney Ron Motley of Charleston, South Carolina, best known for his landmark $350 billion settlement from the tobacco industry in the late 1990s.

"This has become a true mission for me," said Motley. "The individuals that we've sued facilitated the events of September 11." Liz Alderman of Armonk, New York, whose son Peter died in the WTC attack, said she joined the suit because "there is no other way for the truth to come out. I've learned and I believe that an awful lot of the funding that enabled the terrorists to attack America was provided by Saudi Arabia," she said.

Two of the most prominent Saudis named in the suit were Prince Sultan bin Abdul Aziz al-Saud, Saudi Arabia's defense minister, and Prince Turki bin Faisal, a former intelligence chief and ambassador to Britain. The Saudi embassy in Washington had no comment on the suit but, according to the *New York Times*, a State Department source said, "The Saudis have made their concerns known at a senior level [of the US government]."

The *Times* also reported that the Bush administration might well move to dismiss or delay the suit because it might damage the already strained relationship between the two countries. The paper made no mention of the well-documented close business relationships between the Saudis and the Bush family nor the fact that victims' families have implored Bush not to block the suit.

21. What Do We Know Now?

We have come full circle. Our simple and original question now returns to be asked once again: Was 9/11 truly an unprovoked and surprise attack by a handful of Muslim zealots—the official story—or was it yet another case of a provocation contrived to promote an insiders' agenda? Could there have been multiple conspiracies wrapped together, involving both domestic and foreign players, each perpetrating portions of the crime with an eye to their own special agenda?

Undoubtedly, the three primary groups of conspirators behind 9/11 were: (1) those who perpetrated the actual attack upon the United States, i.e., directed the planning for the many details and contingencies involving the hijackings, and flew or controlled the planes; (2) those who must have acted from the inside to suppress or alter normal defense and security precautions, including the responses of President Bush and other key officials at the moment of crisis; and (3) powerful insiders who acted to create and narrate the official story, remove evidence through the premature and hasty cleanup of the 9/11 crime scenes, and thwart or slow official investigations, including the blocking of antiterrorism efforts for years within the FBI and CIA.

We've seen that the goal of powerful interests within the US must have been to create the official version of 9/11 and then use this horrific and fear-drenched story to push its predetermined foreign policy and domestic security agendas through a confused and panicky Congress. And we have also considered the evidence that covert entities within the governments of Israel, Pakistan, and Saudi Arabia surely had foreknowledge of the attacks and most likely had a hand in supporting the perpetrators.

Obviously, all of these players could not and did not engage in *all* of the elements of the crime and the cover-up; perpetrators of one element might not be the perpetrators of another. At the moment, we do not yet know enough to say much more than that in any effort to assign blame—although pending lawsuits and/or courageous new whisteblowers, yet to come, may soon reveal crucial evidence and connect the multiple conspiracy elements with the multiple co-conspirators in unforseen ways.

But the composite result is that the crime and its aftermath—including the acceptance of the chief features of the official story by the population—seems, tragically, to have met with some measure of success. Despite apparently mortal body blows to the official story, found in this and many other studies, the official story, sadly, still remains the consensus reality.

That said, what can we proclaim that we truly know at his point about the 9/11 attacks and their aftermath?

We know that neither simple nor gross incompetence can explain the systematic failure of the normal security protections codified in both the civil aviation and military sectors—and we know that not one single person has yet been reprimanded for such failure. Why did it take more than a year for the public to learn that Vice President Cheney's antiterrorism task force was alerted to the problem and that exercises involving the idea of planes crashing into buildings were scheduled prior to and on September 11, 2001? If a presumption of "just war games taking place" explains the lack of rapid response, why has this plausible alibi not been brought to the public's attention? And how did the hijackers know the time and date of these war games in order to time their attacks to coincide with them?

Furthermore, the evidence of foreknowledge of the attacks, particularly within the FBI and CIA, is overwhelming. This raises the question of who precisely blocked action on this information and why. Why was there no warning to the public or beefed-up security? Who had the power to misdirect and block official investigations?

We also know that actions against the Taliban in general and Osama bin Laden in particular were well underway long before the attacks. How is it that bin Laden remains at large as of this writing, despite what we are told are the best efforts of the world's foremost superpower? Does anyone truly believe that the Mossad, and hence the CIA, has no clue as to bin Laden's whereabouts, especially at a time when every American can be tagged by computer?

It is now clear that the bombing of Afghanistan had more to do with securing oil and gas pipelines and restoring the poppy fields than with apprehending bin Laden. And with the subsequent invasion of Iraq, and its ugly aftermath, it is obvious that the War on Terrorism shifted from finding those responsible for the attacks to enforcing a Pax Americana on the world—exactly as articulated by Cheney, Rumsfeld, Perle, and Wolfowitz, even before President Bill Clinton was elected. Unlike every past American administration, this group has actually proposed a first-strike use of nuclear weapons in this new war.

We know that President Bush has spurned more international treaties than any other world leader of his time, and he even released funds for North Korea's nuclear energy program at a time when he was preparing to seek war with Iraq, claiming Saddam Hussein *might* be capable of building a weapon of mass destruction. In fact, this issue seemed to indicate a schism within the ranks of the New World Order proponents. The Bush forces pushed hard for an attack, while the United Nations worked hard behind the scenes to ensure compliance by Saddam Hussein of UN demands.

We now know that plans to circumvent the Constitution were laid as far back as the Nixon years and that the new Department of Homeland Security carries within it concepts and programs which would have been greeted with howls of protests just a few years ago. And the new technology to identify and classify each individual citizen is now in place. Administration critics cannot be summarily dismissed for using terms like "dictatorship," "1984," and "totalitarianism." Considering the close ties between Prescott Bush, his father-in-law George Herbert Walker, and Hitler's Nazis, it is no stretch of the language to call his grandson's programs "fascist."

Bush and Cheney have consistently fought against having any serious investigation into the tragedies of 9/11. And when popular opinion on this matter turned against them, they turned to one of the most notorious denizens of the secret societies—Henry Kissinger, a leading luminary of the Council on Foreign Relations. Again, a groundswell of public opinion as well as the possibility of dredging up pending war crime charges prompted Kissinger's resignation, even before he began work. Nevertheless, the two men Bush selected to replace Kissinger—Thomas Kean and Lee Hamilton, like Kissinger—are both members of the secretive Council on Foreign Relations.

It is also clear that President Bush is trying to place persons sympathetic to his worldview on the Supreme Court, the place where his father's friends handed him his office. And shifting to a Democrat won't make things better because most of the groundwork for the current "War on Freedom" was laid during the CFR-dominated Clinton administration.

We now know that Bush and most of his cabinet are too locked into the monopolies of energy, pharmaceuticals, telecommunications, and military/aerospace to allow alternative views to be heard. Bush, Cheney, and many others are guilty of the same corporate shenanigans they were forced to criticize in the summer of 2002 following the collapse of Enron, WorldCom, and other major corporations which were also their largest campaign contributors.

We now clearly see that the privatization of US industry, energy, and institutions including health care and education does not fulfill the promise of better service at less cost.

If the game plan of the masterminds behind the 9/11 attacks was to curtail American freedom, centralize more power in the federal government, and set back the social agenda of the United States in favor of an open-ended military and intelligence buildup, then they succeeded admirably. To many long-time researchers, it all has a familiar ring to it.

It is also well worth noting that, in many ways, the aftermath of the 9/11 attacks fits the same template as the aftermath of the assassination of President Kennedy in 1963:

— Within hours, despite a lack of real evidence, one man was blamed for the event along with hints that he was connected to foreign enemies.

— Official pronouncements were widely publicized, only to be quietly admitted as errors later on.

— Although within the jurisdiction of the local authorities, the entire case was usurped by the FBI and CIA, both agencies under the control of a president who benefited from the tragedy.

— A group of specialists (medical in the JFK case and engineers in the WTC) was convened, but limited in what they could view and study, blocked from conducting an objective probe by federal officials.

— Evidence in the case was hastily removed and destroyed, forever lost to an impartial and meaningful investigation.

— More evidence was locked away in government files under the shield of "national security."

— Federal malfeasance was excused by claiming lack of manpower and resources, and no one was disciplined or fired. Federal agency budgets were increased.

— Any alternative to the official version of events was decried as "conspiracy theory" and "unpatriotic."

— The federal government used the event to increase its own centralized power.

— A foreign war (Vietnam in JFK's case and Afghanistan today), which would otherwise have been opposed, was supported by a grieving population.

— Top government leaders (then LBJ and now Bush), formerly under suspicion for election fraud and corrupt business dealings, were suddenly propelled to new heights of popularity.

— Many citizens knew or suspected that the official version of events was incorrect but were afraid to speak out.

— Compliant and sycophantic mass media were content to merely parrot the official version of events and studiously avoided asking the hard questions that might have revealed the truth.

One major difference in the two cases is that following JFK's death, less than ten days went by before President Lyndon Johnson appointed a special commission to investigate the crime. Well more than a year after the events of 9/11, there was still only talk of creating some sort of investigative body, the time lag due primarily to reisitance from President Bush and Vice President Cheney to convening such an inquiry. It was almost two years before an official 9/11 commission was selected and put to work. By then, most of the primary evidence, such as the wreckage of the World Trade Center, was missing or otherwise unavailable.

In the cases of the Pearl Harbor attack, the JFK assassination, and 9/11, a common denominator is the failure of normal security precautions. This is the tip-off.

As Col. L. Fletcher Prouty, former Pentagon-CIA liaison officer, stated in regard to the Kennedy assassination, "The active role is played secretly by permitting it to happen. That was why President Kennedy was killed. He was not murdered by some lone gunman or by some limited conspiracy, but by the breakdown of the protective system that should have made assassination impossible. . . . This is the greatest single clue to the assassination—Who had the power to call off or reduce the usual security precautions that are always in effect whenever a president travels? Castro did not kill Kennedy, nor did the CIA. The power source that arranged that murder was on the inside. It had the means to reduce normal security and permit the choice of a hazardous route. I also had the continuing power to cover up that crime for . . . years."

The same question could be asked regarding the tragedies of September 11, 2001:

Who had the power to call off or reduce normal airline and NORAD security procedures, and who had the power to deflect any meaningful investigation into the events? This kind of power can only be found at the highest levels of government and corporate control. Today's big-time criminals no longer worry about what the government might do to them because, in too many cases, they *are* the government. It therefore becomes essential to identify and connect the inner core elite of the world's secret societies, to demonstrate their ownership and interlocking control over the multinational corporations, and the shadow-government cabals that dominate our national life.

"Most people prefer to believe their leaders are just and fair even in the face of evidence to the contrary, because once a citizen acknowledges that the government under which he or she lives is lying and corrupt, the citizen has to choose what he or she will do about it. To take action in the face of a corrupt government entails risks of harm to oneself and loved ones. To choose to do nothing is to surrender one's self-image of standing for principles. Most people do not have the courage to face that choice. Hence, most propaganda is not designed to fool the critical thinker but only to give moral cowards an excuse not to think at all," noted Internet commentator Michael Rivero.

But the time has come for persons of good heart and conscience to stand up and regain the country handed down to them by men and women who fought for a free and democratic republic by risking their very lives and fortunes.

Look to local leaders, as they are the ones most likely to act for the public welfare. Our democratic republic, with its Constitution and Bill of Rights, is without a doubt the greatest form of government ever initiated during the written history of this planet. Let's make it work as it was intended.

By the time you read this, there is every likelihood that more terrorist threats will have been received and perhaps even another major attack will have taken place—and that some new war for "freedom" will have broken out in some far corner of the world. There will be more "experts" brought forward to generate fear and instruct us on the need to curtail our own freedom to save our democracy.

Do not be stampeded.

We all agree that the true culprits, of this or any future tragedy, must be identified and punished. But we must make certain, through an objective investigation and cool reasoning, that we indeed have in hand the true culprits. We must not be played for suckers as so many times in the past.

The corporate mass media have bombarded the public with facts, statistics, personal opinion, and commentary to the point of distraction and confusion. Partisan politics keeps a great many people squabbling over petty differences in national policies.

Viewed in its broadest perspective, however, the picture of the United States today is both clear and appalling:

The nation in the election year of 2004 is under the control of a dynastic family, blood relatives to virtually all European monarchs, whose patriarch can be shown to have been both in sympathy and in business with Hitler and his Nazis.

The Bush family has been involved with the CIA since before the time of the 1961 Bay of Pigs invasion, with all that implies regarding covert wars, drug smuggling, and assassinations, not to mention the creation of Saddam Hussein as well as Osama bin Laden and his al Qaeda network. One would imagine that the public would finally catch on after realizing that three major world evildoers were financed by the same family.

And each generation has belonged to Skull and Bones, a secret society which, by many and varied accounts, requires its members to swear loyalty to this order over and beyond any later oaths, including one to the US Constitution. This order has been linked to the German Illuminati as well as prominent members of other such societies whose avowed purpose is to end United States sovereignty in favor of globalism. The family has even been linked to accused assassins John Hinckley and Lee Harvey Oswald. What are the odds?

At least two sons were at the heart of the Savings & Loan Scandal which cost every man, woman, and child in the United States thousands of dollars. The eldest son, not elected but selected by a Supreme Court packed by previous Republican presidents including his father, has been linked to Enron, Harken, and other shady oil company dealings and has surrounded himself with men of questionable ethics and truthfulness.

Collectively, this family and their corporate cronies are today seeking what amounts to dictatorial powers to pursue the proclaimed War on Terrorism, despite the growing evidence that the attacks which launched this war were known in advance and allowed to happen to bring about the erosion of individual rights and the centralization of even more power unto themselves. And that description is putting the very best possible light on the affair.

Considering the longstanding connections between this family, the secret societies, the CIA, the bin Laden family, Saddam Hussein, and the al Qaeda network as well as Global Hawk technology, a case can be made that the 9/11 attacks were instigated by persons other than Osama bin Laden.

The nature of public life in the US today has begun to resemble the very despotic societies—Hitler's Third Reich, Stalinist Russia, Communist Eastern Europe, and China—that America contested during the last century.

Such totalitarian regimes stemmed from centralized governments that served themselves rather than the people, that responded more swiftly to policies of the central government than to evidence of criminal activities or public need and used every means at their disposal to spy on and intimidate their citizens. Thoughtful observers see much of that same trend in the United States today.

These are not conjectures or conspiracy theories. These are the facts.

The questions regarding the 9/11 attacks and their aftermath bring only further questions. The greatest of these questions concerns what the American people intend to do about all this.

Will they continue to be led by corporate mass media that deceive by omission more than commission and distract them from the real issues?

Will they continue to reelect politicians who have been in office while all the causes of current problems were put into place?

Will they continue to blindly follow the standards of the two major political parties that have demonstrated that precious little difference exists in their major policies?

Will they continue to support a foreign policy that angers and alienates peoples all across the globe with its thinly disguised goal of empire building?

Will they allow the US military to continue enforcing this foreign policy, and the military-industrial complex to richly profit from it, while losing control over their own nation and lives?

Will the American people continue to permit their nation to be the primary seller of arms to the world and then bemoan the fact that those same arms are now used against them?

Will they finally take a look behind the green curtain of media spin to identify the globalist elites and secret societies who own and control the mass media as well as the government and, hence, the military?

Will they stand up and exercise their own individual right to speak out for the truth, or will they stand idly by—frozen by fear, intimidation, and confusion—while their remaining liberties are irrevocably lost?

Only you, the reader, can answer these questions.

Research support for concerned citizens and activists:

www.911Truth.org

—the portal site for 9/11 information, links, and truth.

Appendices for Further Research

Appendix A

Pentagon Says 9/11 Interceptors Flew: Too Far, Too Slow, Too Late

By William Thomas
Investigative Reporter

www.willthomas.net
December 14, 2003

It happens all the time. When a small private plane recently entered the 23-mile restricted ring around the U.S. Capitol, two F-16 interceptors were immediately launched from Andrews Air Force Base, just 10 miles away. In a similar episode, a pair of F-16 "Fighting Falcons" on 15-minute strip alert was airborne from Andrews just 11 minutes after being notified by the North American Aerospace Defense Command (NORAD) of a Cessna straying towards the White House. [AP Nov11/03; CNN June 20/02]

These were well-practiced routines. With more than 4,500 aircraft continuously sharing U.S. airspace, between September 2000 and June 2001 the Pentagon launched fighters on 67 occasions to escort wayward aircraft. [FAA news release Aug9/02; AP Aug13/02]

But on Sept 11, 2001, NORAD and the FAA ignored routine procedures and strict regulations. In response to a national emergency involving hijacked airliners as dangerous as cruise missiles, interceptors launched late from distant bases flew to defend their nation at a fraction of their top speeds. [NORAD news release Sept18/01]

WHAT NORAD KNEW. A recently resurfaced NORAD news bulletin released seven days after Sept. 11 explains that America's aerial defenders were slow to counter rapidly developing air attacks because they didn't hear from the FAA that American Airlines Flight 11 had been hijacked until 8:40 that fateful morning. [NORAD news release Sept18/01]

But at the National Military Command Center (NMCC) in the basement of the Pentagon, Air Force staff officers monitoring every inch of airspace over the northeastern seaboard would have caught that first hijacking when Flight 11's identification transponder stopped transmitting at 8:20—automatically triggering a radar alarm.

With their capability to monitor developing "situations" by tapping into military and civilian radars, U.S. military commanders would have also seen Flight 175 turn abruptly south 25 minutes later, just as they had watched on radar in October 1999 when pro golfer Payne Stewart's Learjet abruptly departed its flight path while enroute to Dallas. [CNN Oct26/99]

In that legendary intercept, a fighter jet out of Tyndall, Florida was diverted from a training flight to escort the Lear, whose pilot had become incapacitated, trapping Stewart in the stratosphere. An F-16 was reportedly sitting off the left wingtip of Payne's pilotless business jet within 19 minutes of the FAA alert. [ABC News Oct25/99]

If NORAD had been as quick to scramble or divert airborne fighters on Sept. 11, two "anti-terrorist" F-15s on armed alert could have been sent south from Otis Air Force Base on Cape Cod. Flying at full afterburners without edging over the Atlantic to disperse their sonic footprint, two of the fastest fighters on the planet would have broken a few windows. But all the glass in the Twin Towers might have stayed intact had the "fast-movers" intercepted Flight 11 over the Hudson River at least six minutes from Manhattan.

"NO HURRY," SAYS NORAD. Instead, in a stunning admission that received little press scrutiny at the time, NORAD noted that for all interceptions flown against the hijackers on Sept. 11, "Flight times are calculated at 9 miles per minute or .9 Mach." In other words, every interception flown by the world's hottest air-combat aircraft was flown at less than a third of the planes' top speed.

A Defense Department manual insists, "In the event of a hijacking, the NMCC will be notified by the most expeditious means by the FAA." To make this happen, the Federal Aviation Administration permanently posts a liaison officer in the Pentagon air defense room. [CJCSI 3610.01A, June1/01]

Yet, according to NORAD, after air traffic controllers realized that Flight 11 had been hijacked, 38 vital minutes passed before a pair ofF-15s was scrambled from Otis. As they lifted off, American Airlines Flight 11 struck the North Tower of the World Trade Center, 153 air miles away as a Falcon flies. [NORAD Sept18/01]

United Airlines Flight 175 was still 20 minutes out. The F-15 pilots flew "like a scalded ape, topping 500 mph but were unable to catch up to the airliner," Maj. Gen. Paul Weaver later told reporters. [*St. Augustine Times* Sept16/01]

Scalded apes? Airliners fly at 500 mph. An F-15 can fly almost four times faster.

STEP ON IT. One of the Otis intercept pilots dubbed "Duff" later lamented: "We've been over the flight a thousand times in our minds and I don't know what we could have done to get there any quicker."

For starters, he and his wingman could have tried pushing their twin throttles fully forward. Instead of flying two-and-a-half times faster than a bullet, "Nasty" and "Duff" drove their expensive air superiority fighters at a leisurely 447 mph supposedly to intercept a Boeing 767 flying 43 mph faster! Utilizing only 27% power, the F-15s were "eight minutes/71 miles" away, according to NORAD, when Flight 175 struck the South Tower with 56 souls and more than ten tons of fuel onboard. [*Christian Science Monitor* Mar8/02]

HONOR THE THREAT. With both Trade Towers burning, and hijacked United Flight 93 shadowed by a circling F-16 over Pennsylvania, American Airlines Flight 77 was the only threat left in the sky. When that Boeing 757 silenced its transponder signal, made a U-turn over Kentucky and headed directly for the White House and the Pentagon, one billion viewers riveted to the big networks knew this was a kamikaze run. [*Telegraph* Sept13/01]

With no other bogeys on eastern seaboard scopes, air combat doctrine dictates that the two unemployed Otis F-15s already in the area be redirected to "honor the threat" of an incoming flying bomb, 330 miles out. Even loafing along, the fighters would have more than 20 minutes to confront Flight 77 before it neared the Pentagon.

Instead, Pentagon professionals defending their country's nerve centers waited more than an hour after watching Flight 11 go rogue— including 30 critical minutes after Flight 77 turned abruptly toward them and the nearby White House—before scrambling two F-16s out of Langley Air Force Base to protect the capitol.

Nearly half-an-hour after receiving the belated order to scramble, two Falcons coasted in over the burning Pentagon. Slowed down to just 410 mph, it had taken the 1,500 mph-capable fighters 19 minutes to cover the 130 miles from Virginia. It should have taken just over seven minutes to reach the Pentagon at about the time Flight 77 was making a predatory circle overhead. [NORAD Sept18/01; USAF]

GROUNDED. The supersonic jets were flown no faster than WWII prop-driven fighters. But it hardly mattered. Sitting on the Andrews ramp just 10 miles away, were two fully armed and fueled supersonic interceptors tasked with protecting the capitol from airborne terrorist threats on 15 minutes' notice!

Isn't it about time someone asked why those routinely launched Andrews interceptors were "stood down" as Flight 77 bored in toward the headquarters they were supposed to protect? [*San Diego Union-Tribune* Sept12/01]

In the most heavily armed nation on Earth, at least two dozen air force installations were within fast flying time of the World Trade Center and Pentagon. Does anyone else wonder why none of those aircraft were ordered launched—or why none of the armed fighters on training flights or patrolling Air Defense Intercept Zones just off the Atlantic Coast were diverted to intercept four commandeered airliners until after the Pentagon was struck, one hour and 18 minutes after Flight 11 was hijacked? [www.af.mil/sites/alphabetical.shtml#a]

According to NORAD, the F-16s from Langley were still "12 minutes/105 miles" away when the big Boeing they were "chasing" soared past the White House and the Andrews runways. Allegedly flown by an incompetent Egyptian flight student who couldn't solo a Cessna, the 757 peeled off and piled into the Pentagon after an abrupt dive and pull-up that left veteran pilots agape. [*San Diego Union-Tribune* Sept12/01; NBC Nightly News Sept11/01; All Fall Down]

Immediately after the Pentagon was hit, the Andrews alert jets were launched to guard empty skies. [*Mirror* Nov13/03]

ASLEEP AT THE SWITCH. Responding to questions from a Senate confirmation committee two days after this suspicious fiasco, the Joint Chief's acting air defense chief on 9/11 said he was in a meeting while all hell was breaking loose in his sector. Air Force General Richard Myers had not let a TV report about a small plane hitting the World Trade Center interrupt his routine. As jumbo jetliners kept diving into buildings, apparently no one thought to inform the acting commander of U.S. air defenses that his country was under attack. Myers said he came out of his meeting just as the Pentagon was hit.

Asked repeatedly when the brass were first informed of the emergency, and when interceptors were scrambled, Myers repeated a muddled mantra six times, saying "I'll have to get back to you on that." [www.defenselink.mil/news/Oct2001/n10232001_200110236.html]

Instead of being court-martialed like the luckless commanders defending Pearl Harbor, or even reprimanded, General Myers was awarded command of the entire U.S. military as new chairman of the Joint Chiefs of Staff. Bush publicly commended the air force general for his "calm manner, sound judgment, and his clear strategic thinking." [White House press release Oct15/01]

As this bizarre and possibly treasonous story goes to press, the FAA has refused to disclose documents relating to when that agency notified U.S. air defenses about the four hijacked airliners. A second subpoena served on the Pentagon by the National Commission on Terrorist Attacks Upon the United States has been similarly unsuccessful in attaining records concerning whether NORAD responded quickly enough in dispatching interceptors on Sept. 11. [*Washington Post* Nov8/03]

Instead of fingering air traffic controllers for not following procedures, these documents could show that the FAA did follow its own Standard Intercept Procedures and notify NORAD within a few minutes of each hijacking, which would leave the Air Force with even more explaining to do. [AP Oct18/03]

Investigative reporter William Thomas is a former pilot and member of the US military. His book *All Fall Down: The Politics of Terror and Mass Persuasion* details the events of September 11 and the subsequent War on Terrorism.

Appendix B

23 Questions

The Family Steering Committee Statement
Regarding the 9/11 Commission's
Interview with President Bush

Presented to the 9/11 Commission on February 16, 2004

The Family Steering Committee believes that President Bush should provide sworn public testimony to the full ten-member panel of the National Commission on Terrorist Attacks Upon the United States.

Collectively, the Commissioners are responsible for fulfilling the Congressional mandate. Therefore, each Commissioner must have full access to the testimony of all individuals and the critical information that will enable informed decisions and recommendations. Before an audience of the American people, the Commission must ask President Bush in sworn testimony, the following questions:

1. As Commander-in-Chief on the morning of 9/11, why didn't you return immediately to Washington, D.C. or the National Military Command Center once you became aware that America was under attack? At specifically what time did you become aware that America was under attack? Who informed you of this fact?

2. On the morning of 9/11, who was in charge of our country while you were away from the National Military Command Center? Were you informed or consulted about all decisions made in your absence?

3. What defensive action did you personally order to protect our nation during the crisis on September 11th? What time were these orders given, and to whom? What orders were carried out? What was the result of such orders? Were any such orders not carried out?

4. In your opinion, why was our nation so utterly unprepared for an attack on our own soil?

5. U.S. Navy Captain Deborah Loewer, the Director of the White House Situation Room, informed you of the first airliner hitting Tower One of the World Trade Center before you entered the Emma E. Booker Elementary School in Sarasota, Florida. Please explain the reason why you decided to continue with the scheduled classroom visit, fifteen minutes after learning the first hijacked airliner had hit the World Trade Center.

6. Is it normal procedure for the Director of the White House Situation Room to travel with you? If so, please cite any prior examples of when this occurred. If not normal procedure, please explain the circumstances that led to the Director of the White House Situation Room being asked to accompany you to Florida during the week of September 11th.

7. What plan of action caused you to remain seated after Andrew Card informed you that a second airliner had hit the second tower of the World Trade Center and America was clearly under attack? Approximately how long did you remain in the classroom after Card's message?

8. At what time were you made aware that other planes were hijacked in addition to Flight 11 and Flight 175? Who notified you? What was your course of action as Commander-in-Chief of the United States?

9. Beginning with the transition period between the Clinton administration and your own, and ending on 9/11/01, specifically what information (either verbal or written) about terrorists, possible attacks and targets, did you receive from any source?

This would include briefings or communications from:

▶ Outgoing Clinton officials

▶ CIA, FBI, NSA, DoD and other intelligence agencies

▶ Foreign intelligence, governments, dignitaries or envoys

▶ National Security Advisor Condoleezza Rice

▶ Richard Clarke, former counterterrorism czar

10. Specifically, what did you learn from the August 6, 2001, PDB about the terrorist threat that was facing our nation? Did you request any follow-up action to take place?

Did you request any further report be developed and/or prepared?

11. As Commander-in-Chief, from May 1, 2001 until September 11, 2001, did you receive any information from any intelligence agency official or agent that UBL was planning to attack this nation on its own soil using airplanes as weapons, targeting New York City landmarks during the week of September 11, 2001 or on the actual day of September 11, 2001?

12. What defensive measures did you take in response to pre-9/11 warnings from eleven nations about a terrorist attack, many of which cited an attack in the continental United States? Did you prepare any directives in response to these actions? If so, with what results?

13. As Commander-in-Chief from May 1, 2001 until September 11, 2001, did you or any agent of the United States government carry out any negotiations or talks with UBL, an agent of UBL, or al-Qaeda? During that same period, did you or any agent of the United States government carry out any negotiations or talks with any foreign government, its agents, or officials regarding UBL? If so, what resulted?

14. Your schedule for September 11, 2001 was in the public domain since September 7, 2001. The Emma E. Booker School is only five miles from the Bradenton Airport, so you, and therefore the children in the classroom, might have been a target for the terrorists on 9/11. What was the intention of the Secret Service in allowing you to remain in the Emma E. Booker Elementary School, even though they were aware America was under attack?

15. Please explain why you remained at the Sarasota, Florida, Elementary School for a press conference after you had finished listening to the children read, when as a terrorist target, your presence potentially jeopardized the lives of the children?

16. What was the purpose of the several stops of Air Force One on September 11th? Was Air Force One at any time during the day of September 11th a target of the terrorists? Was Air Force One's code ever breached on September 11th?

17. Was there a reason for Air Force One lifting off without a military escort, even after ample time had elapsed to allow military jets to arrive?

18. What prompted your refusal to release the information regarding foreign sponsorship of the terrorists, as llustrated in the inaccessible 28 redacted pages in the Joint Intelligence Committee Inquiry Report? What actions have you personally taken since 9/11 to thwart foreign sponsorship of terrorism?

19. Who approved the flight of the bin Laden family out of the United States when all commercial flights were grounded, when there was time for only minimal questioning by the FBI, and especially, when two of those same individuals had links to WAMY, a charity suspected of funding terrorism? Why were bin Laden family members granted that special privilege—a privilege not available to American families whose loved ones were killed on 9/11?

20. Please explain why no one in any level of our government has yet been held accountable for the countless failures leading up to and on 9/11?

21. Please comment on the fact that UBL's profile on the FBI's Ten Most Wanted Fugitives poster does not include the 9/11 attacks. To your knowledge, when was the last time any agent of our government had contact with UBL? If prior to 9/11, specifically what was the date of that contact and what was the context of said meeting.

22. Do you continue to maintain that Saddam Hussein was linked to al Qaeda? What proof do you have of any connection between al-Qaeda and the Hussein regime?

23. Which individuals, governments, agencies, institutions, or groups may have benefited from the attacks of 9/11? Please state specifically how you think they have benefited.

The Family Steering Committee for
the 9/11 Independent Commission
http://www.911independentcommission.org/

Appendix C

Statement of 9/11 Widow
Mindy Kleinberg to the 9/11 Commission

Presented at the First Public Hearing of the Commission
March 31, 2003

My name is Mindy Kleinberg. My husband Alan Kleinberg, 39 yrs old, was killed in the WTC on September 11, 2001. As I testify here today about the 9/11 attacks, I will begin by saying that my thoughts are very much with the men and women who are involved in armed conflict overseas and their families who wait patiently for them to return.

This war is being fought on two fronts, overseas as well as here on our shores; this means that we are all soldiers in this fight against terrorism. As the threat of terrorism mounts here in the United States, the need to address the failures of September 11 is more important than ever. It is an essential part of "lessons learned."

As such, this commission has an extremely important task before it. I am here today to ask you, the commissioners, to help us understand how this could have happened; help us understand where the breakdown was in our nation's defense capabilities.

Where were we on the morning of September 11th?

On the morning of September 11th my three-year-old son, Sam, and I walked Jacob 10, and Lauren, 7, to the bus stop at about 8:40 a.m. It was the fourth day of a new school year and you could still feel everyone's excitement. It was such a beautiful day that Sam and I literally skipped home oblivious to what was happening in NYC.

At around 8:55 I was confirming playdate plans for Sam with a friend when she said, "I can't believe what I am watching on TV, a plane has just hit the World Trade Center." For some reason it did not register with me until a few minutes later when I calmly asked, "what building did you say?" "Oh, that's Alan's building. I have to call you back."

There was no answer when I tried to reach him at the office. By now my house started filling with people—his mother, my parents, our sisters and friends. The seriousness of the situation was beginning to register. We spent the rest of the day calling hospitals, and the Red Cross, and anyplace else we could think of to see if we could find him.

I'll never forget thinking all day long, "how am I going to tell Jacob and Lauren that their father is missing?"

They came home to a house filled with people but no Daddy. How were they going to be able to wait calmly for his return? What if he was really hurt? This was their hero, their king, their best friend, their father. The thoughts of that day replay over and over in our heads always wishing for a different outcome.

We are trying to learn to live with the pain. We will never forget where we were or how we felt on September 11th.

But where was our government, its agencies, and institutions prior to and on the morning of September 11th?

The Theory of Luck

With regard to the 9/11 attacks, it has been said that the intelligence agencies have to be right 100 percent of the time and the terrorists only have to get lucky once. This explanation for the devastating attacks of September 11th, simple on its face, is wrong in its value. Because the 9/11 terrorists were not just lucky once: they were lucky over and over again. Allow me to illustrate.

The SEC

The terrorists' lucky streak began the week before September 11th with the Securities and Exchange Commission, or SEC. The SEC, in concert with the United States intelligence agencies, has sophisticated software programs that are used in "real-time" to watch both domestic and overseas markets to seek out trends that may indicate a present or future crime. In the week prior to September 11th both the SEC and U.S. intelligence agencies ignored one major stock market indicator, one that could have yielded valuable information with regard to the September 11th attacks.

On the Chicago Board Options Exchange during the week before September 11th, put options were purchased on American and United airlines, the two airlines involved in the attacks. The investors who placed these orders were gambling that in the short term the stock prices of both airlines would plummet. Never before on the Chicago Exchange were such large amounts of United and American airlines options traded. These investors netted a profit of at least $5 million after the September 11th attacks.

Interestingly, the names of the investors remain undisclosed and the $5 million remains unclaimed in the Chicago Exchange account.

Why were these aberrant trades not discovered prior to 9/11? Who were the individuals who placed these trades? Have they been investigated? Who was responsible for monitoring these activities? Have those individuals been held responsible for their inaction?

The INS

Prior to 9/11, our U.S. intelligence agencies should have stopped the 19 terrorists from entering this country for intelligence reasons, alone. However, their failure to do so in 19 instances does not negate the luck involved for the terrorists when it comes to their visa applications and our Immigration and Naturalization Service, or INS.

With regard to the INS, the terrorists got lucky 15 individual times, because 15 of the 19 hijackers' visas should have been unquestionably denied.

Most of the 19 hijackers were young, unmarried, and un-employed males. They were, in short, the "classic overstay candidates." A seasoned former Consular officer stated in *National Review* magazine, "Single, idle young adults with no specific destination in the United States rarely get visas absent compelling circumstances."

Yet these 19 young, single, unemployed, "classic overstay candidates" still received their visas. I am holding in my hand the applications of the terrorists who killed my husband. All of these forms are incomplete and incorrect.

Some of the terrorists listed their means of support as simply "student" failing to then list the name and address of any school or institution. Others, when asked about their means of support for their stay in the U.S. wrote "myself" and provided no further documentation. Some of the terrorists listed their destination in the U.S. as simply "hotel" or "California" or "New York." One even listed his destination as "no."

Had the INS or State Department followed the law, at least 15 of the hijackers would have been denied visas and would not have been in the United States on September 11, 2001.

Help us to understand how something as simple as reviewing forms for completeness could have been missed at least 15 times. How many more lucky terrorists gained unfettered access into this country? With no one being held accountable, how do we know this still isn't happening?

Airline and Airport Security

On the morning of September 11th, the terrorists' luck commenced with airline and airport security. When the 19 hijackers went to purchase their tickets (with cash and/or credit cards) and to receive their boarding passes, nine were singled out and questioned through a screening process. Luckily for those nine terrorists, they passed the screening process and were allowed to continue on with their mission.

But, the terrorists' luck didn't end at the ticket counter; it also accompanied them through airport security, as well. Because how else would the hijackers get specifically contraband items such as box-cutters, pepper spray or, according to one FAA executive summary, a gun on those planes?

Finally, sadly for us, years of GAO recommendations to secure cockpit doors were ignored making it all too easy for the hijackers to gain access to the flight controls and carryout their suicide mission.

FAA and NORAD

Prior to 9/11, FAA and Department of Defense manuals gave clear, comprehensive instructions on how to handle everything from minor emergencies to full blown hijackings.

These "protocols" were in place and were practiced regularly for a good reason—with heavily trafficked air space, airliners without radio and transponder contact are collisions and/or calamities waiting to happen.

Those protocols dictate that in the event of an emergency, the FAA is to notify NORAD. Once that notification takes place, it is then the responsibility of NORAD to scramble fighter jets to intercept the errant plane(s). It is a matter of routine procedure for fighter jets to "intercept" commercial airliners in order to regain contact with the pilot.

If that weren't protection enough, on September 11th, NEADS (or the North East Air Defense System department of NORAD) was several days into a semiannual exercise known as "Vigilant Guardian." This meant that our North East Air Defense system was fully staffed. In short, key officers were manning the operation battle center, "fighter jets were cocked, loaded, and carrying extra gas on board."

Lucky for the terrorists none of this mattered on the morning of September 11th.

Let me illustrate using just Flight 11 as an example.

American Airline's Flight 11 departed from Boston Logan Airport at 7:45 a.m. The last routine communication between ground control and the plane occurred at 8:13 a.m. Between 8:13 and 8:20 a.m. Flight 11 became unresponsive to ground control. Additionally, radar indicated that the plane had deviated from its assigned path of flight. Soon thereafter, transponder contact was lost—although planes can still be seen on radar, even without their transponders.

Two Flight 11 airline attendants had separately called American Airlines reporting a hijacking, the presence of weapons, and the infliction of injuries on passengers and crew. At this point, it would seem abundantly clear that Flight 11 was an emergency.

Yet, according to NORAD's official timeline, NORAD was not contacted until twenty minutes later at 8:40 a.m. Tragically the fighter jets were not deployed until 8:52 a.m.—a full 32 minutes after the loss of contact with Flight 11.

Why was there a delay in the FAA notifying NORAD? Why was there a delay in NORAD scrambling fighter jets? How is this possible when NEADS was fully staffed with planes at the ready and monitoring our Northeast airspace?

Flights 175, 77 and 93 all had this same repeat pattern of delays in notification and delays in scrambling fighter jets—delays that are unimaginable considering a plane had, by this time, already hit the WTC.

Even more baffling for us is the fact that the fighter jets were not scrambled from the closest air force bases. For example, for the flight that hit the Pentagon, the jets were scrambled from Langley Air Force Base in Hampton, Virginia rather than Andrews Air Force Base right outside D.C. As a result, Washington skies remained wholly unprotected on the morning of September 11th. At 9:41 a.m., one hour and 11 minutes after the first plane hijacking was confirmed by NORAD, Flight 77 crashed into the Pentagon. The fighter jets were still miles away. Why?

So the hijackers luck had continued. On September 11th both the FAA and NORAD deviated from standard emergency operating procedures. Who were the people that delayed the notification? Have they been questioned? In addition, the interceptor planes or fighter jets did not fly at their maximum speed.

Had the belatedly scrambled fighter jets flown at their maximum speed of engagement, MACH-12, they would have reached NYC and the Pentagon within moments of their deployment, intercepted the hijacked airliners before they could have hit their targets, and undoubtedly saved lives.

Joint Chiefs Of Staff

The Acting Chairman of the Joint Chiefs of Staff was having a routine meeting on the morning of September 11th. Acting Joint Chief of Staff Meyers stated that he saw a TV report about a plane hitting the WTC but thought it was a small plane or something like that. So, he went ahead with his meeting. "Meanwhile the second World Trade Center was hit by another jet. Nobody informed us of that," Meyers said. By the time he came out of the meeting the Pentagon had been hit.

Whose responsibility was it to relay this emergency to the Joint Chiefs of Staff? Have they been held accountable for their error? Surely this represents a breakdown of protocol.

Secretary of Defense

The Secretary of Defense was at his desk doing paperwork when AA77 crashed into the Pentagon.

As reported, Secretary Rumsfeld felt the building shake, went outside, saw the damage and started helping the injured onto stretchers. After aiding the victims, the secretary then went into the 'War Room.'

How is it possible that the National Military Command Center, located in the Pentagon and in contact with law enforcement and air traffic controllers from 8:46 a.m. did not communicate to the Secretary of Defense also at the Pentagon about the other hijacked planes, especially the one headed to Washington? How is it that the Secretary of Defense could have remained at this desk until the crash? Whose responsibility is it to relay emergency situations to him? Is he then supposed to go to the War Room?

The President

At 6:15 a.m. on the morning of 9/11, my husband Alan left for work; he drove into New York City, and was at his desk and working at his NASDAQ Security Trading position with Cantor Fitzgerald, in Tower One of the WTC by 7:30 a.m.

In contrast, on the morning of September 11, President Bush was scheduled to listen to elementary school children read.

Before the President walked into the classroom, NORAD had sufficient information that the plane that hit the WTC was hijacked. At that time, they also had knowledge that two other commercial airliners, in the air, were also hijacked. It would seem that a national emergency was in progress.

Yet President Bush was allowed to enter a classroom full of young children and listen to the students read.

Why didn't the Secret Service inform him of this national emergency? When is a President supposed to be notified of everything the agencies know? Why was the President permitted by the Secret Service to remain in the Sarasota elementary school? Was this Secret Service protocol?

In the case of a national emergency, seconds of indecision could cost thousands of lives; and it's precisely for this reason that our government has a whole network of adjuncts and advisors to insure that these top officials are among the first to be informed—not the last. Where were these individuals who did not properly inform these top officials? Where was the breakdown in communication?

Was it Luck or No-Fault Government?

Is it luck that aberrant stock trades were not monitored? Is it luck when fifteen visas are awarded based on incomplete forms? Is it luck when Airline Security screenings allow hijackers to board planes with box cutters and pepper spray? Is it luck when Emergency FAA and NORAD protocols are not followed? Is it luck when a national emergency is not reported to top government officials on a timely basis?

To me luck is something that happens once. When you have this repeated pattern of broken protocols, broken laws, broken communication, one cannot still call it luck.

If at some point we don't look to hold the individuals accountable for not doing their jobs properly, then how can we ever expect for terrorists not to get lucky again?

And, that is why I am here with all of you today. Because, we must find the answers as to what happened that day so as to ensure that another September 11th can never happen again.

Commissioners, I implore you to answer our questions. You are the Generals in the terrorism fight on our shores. In answering our questions, you have the ability to make this nation a safer place and in turn, minimize the damage if there is another terrorist attack. And, if there is another attack, the next time our systems will be in place and working and luck will not be an issue.

Mindy Kleinberg is a founding member of September 11th Advocates, a family advocacy group that spearheaded the grassroots effort for the establishment of the independent commission on September 11th.

Her husband Alan Kleinberg was a NASDAQ security trader with Cantor Fitzgerald in the North Tower of the WTC on the 104th Floor. He was 39 and had been a NASDAQ security trader for 15 years.

Mrs. Kleinberg is a Certified Public Accountant. She met her husband when they both worked at Deloitte-Touche, but she left the accounting profession to become a stay-at-home mom. She lives in New Jersey with her three children—Jacob 11, Lauren 8, and Sam 4.

Appendix D

[*Editor's note:* This is an excerpt from an early draft of the Complaint. The complete text of the updated Complaint may be found at **www.911forthetruth.com.**]

IN THE UNITED STATES DISTRICT COURT FOR THE DISTRICT OF COLUMBIA

ELLEN MARIANI, individually and as
Personal Representative of the Estate of
LOUIS NEIL MARIANI, Deceased,
           Plaintiff,

           -against-   COMPLAINT

[1] GEORGE HERBERT WALKER BUSH,   **TRIAL BY JURY**
[2] GEORGE WALKER BUSH,   **DEMANDED**
[3] JOHN "JEB" BUSH,
[4] NEIL MALLON BUSH,
[5] MARVIN BUSH,
[6] RICHARD CHENEY,
[7] DONALD H. RUMSFELD,
[8] COLIN POWELL,
[9] RICHARD ARMITAGE,
[10] CONDOLEEZZA RICE,
[11] JOHN ASHCROFT,
[12] GEORGE J. TENET,
[13] NORMAN Y. MINETA,
[14] TOM RIDGE,
[15] PETER G. PETERSON,
[16] THE COUNCIL ON FOREIGN RELATIONS ...

[*Editor's notes:* Fifty two defendents in all are named; the entire list not included here. Footnotes do not appear in the text; sources used for the actual footnotes are listed at the end of this document for reference.]

Plaintiff, by her attorney Philip Berg, as and for her complaint against the defendants, respectfully alleges:

INTRODUCTION

1.   The plaintiff, Ellen Mariani, is the widow and the duly-appointed personal representative of Louis Neil Mariani, a passenger on United Airlines Flight 175 ("Flight 175") who perished in the terror attacks of September 11, 2001 ("9/11").

2.   While there have been convened two purported "investigations" of 9/11, one by a joint committee of Congress plus a second, "independent" investigation conducted, in the main, by persons with flagrant conflicts of interest, neither investigation has addressed seriously the facts of what really happened on 9/11 to cause the death of plaintiff's decedent, and approximately 2,993 other persons, most of them United States citizens.

3.   Without a true investigation—not a coverup, not a "limited, modified hang-out" restricted to supposed "intelligence failures" plaintiff will be denied justice, and the American people will be denied the truth of the most stunning, catastrophic and consequential event since, at least, the assassination of President Kennedy in 1963. Owing to the Republican Party's control of Congress and the immense power of the defendants at bar, either a true investigation will commence in this court, or it is unlikely to happen in our lifetimes.

4.   Plaintiff does not know all the facts of the catastrophe of 9/11, but her study of facts available in the public domain, most of which come from "conventional" or "mainstream" news media, agencies of the U.S. government, or other sources that, if anything, convince her that the "official story" is a government propaganda exercise, and a deliberate lie.

5.   Plaintiff's study of 9/11 leads her to conclude, and therefore to allege upon information and belief as set forth below, that President George W. Bush, former President George H. W. Bush, Vice President Richard Cheney, Secretary of Defense Donald H. Rumsfeld, National

Security Advisor Condoleezza Rice, then-Acting Chairman of the Joint Chiefs of Staff, General Richard Meyers, then-NORAD chief Gen. Ralph E. Eberhart, then-FEMA Director Joe M. Allbaugh, Senior Political Advisor Karl Rove, and others of the defendants *knew before September 11, 2001 that, on or about that day, one or more commercial airliners would be commandeered, and all on board—including plaintiff's decedent, her husband, would be murdered.*

6.   Plaintiff further alleges on information and belief that defendants not only had foreknowledge that the World Trade Center and other landmark targets would be attacked on 9/11, with mass casualties including the death of plaintiff's husband the intended result, but actively conspired to cause to happen a "new Pearl Harbor" in order to promote a *criminal enterprise classically within the reach of the RICO statute.*

7.   The notorious bank robber, Willie Sutton, told authorities the reason he robbed banks was because "that's where the money is." In today's world, more than in any other sectors, big money is made in the following areas: (1) war preparations, and the international trade in weapons, both legal and illegal; (2) oil, gas, and related energy services; (3) narcotics trafficking; (4) "white collar crime," e.g., securities fraud, insider trading, the illegal manipulation of markets, denuding funds from banks and pension plans, stealing money from government-funded programs, etc. (5) trafficking in humans, in part for forced labor but primarily the abducting and selling women and children for sex; and (6) money laundering, to "cleanse" the (largely) illegal proceeds of the foregoing.

8.   As will be seen, members of the Enterprise alleged herein have been directly involved, or closely associated with persons known to be involved, in all of the aforementioned activities. Their activities have been, and continue to be, largely criminal per se, but even to the extent that some of their business activities are not of themselves illegal (oil and gas investments, investments in defense-related industries) those activities are intertwined with, and supported by, murder, drug-trafficking, financial scams, the blackmailing of politicians, vote-rigging, the waging of wars of aggression and the torture and abuse of prisoners that are crimes under treaties and the law of nations, etc.

9.   Broadly described, defendants' paramount motive in orchestrating the 9/11 attacks was to obtain a "blank check" to conduct wars of aggression, to promote their own financial interests and those

of their RICO "enterprise" which exists and carries out crimes on a scale that "traditional" organized crime could not have dreamed of. In addition, the attacks and the destruction of three buildings at the World Trade Center complex in New York City were intended by the Enterprise alleged herein to destroy records in offices of the Federal Bureau of Investigation in the North Tower, the Security and Exchange Commission in World Trade Center Building 7, and other offices in those buildings, to thwart investigations damaging to the Enterprise, corporations friendly to the Enterprise that were under investigation by the FBI and SEC, Federal Reserve Chairman Alan Greenspan, a number of prominent banks and brokerage houses with strong ties to the Enterprise, the Council on Foreign Relations, and the CIA, and others.

10.   As will be set forth below, in broad terms plaintiff's llegations rest upon three sets of facts. First, the official story of 9/11 promulgated by defendants, and investigated by no one (private researchers aside) is demolished by its internal implausibilities and inconsistencies. As will be explained, the "Osama and the 19 Muslim Zealots" story is flatly incredible, a palpable lie.

11.   Second, a major part of the investigation of any crime of this kind is to ask, *cui bono?* (who benefits?). A review of the facts concerning 9/11 show that the answers to that classic question point to the defendants. Third, the guilt of the defendants is powerfully suggested by their myriad lies, their thwarting of any proper investigation, and their stonewalling and failure to truly cooperate even with the "limited hangout" Kean Commission "investigation" now in progress. It is further confirmed as the most plausible, or even the only rational, explanation as to why the Bush Administration effected a massive reconfiguration of the federal government—conjoining many agencies into a new "Department of Homeland Security" *and then proceeded to starve it for funding, doing almost nothing to truly secure the homeland from terrorist threats from afar, while doing much to attack freedom at home, while aggressively pursuing empire overseas.*

12.   While no doubt many employees of the FBI are loyal to their lawful responsibilities, and not individually part of the criminal enterprise herein alleged, *it is a matter of public record, not disputed, that the Bush Administration had called the FBI off of its investigation of the bin Laden family in the months that preceded the attacks.*

13.   While one would expect that the City of New York would have an interest in thoroughly and honestly investigating the murder

of more than 2,500 persons (to say nothing of the destruction of a number of important office buildings) in its jurisdiction, agents of the Enterprise—acting through FEMA, a shadowy "black budget" agency created not by Congress but by executive order, and which combines ominous, martial-law preparations with benign, disaster-relief functions—were immediately in place, took and maintained strict control over the crime scene, and, with stunning dispatch, removed the principal evidence—the wreckage of the buildings—to Third World countries.

14.   The Department of Justice has not, and will not, conduct a true investigation into 9/11. Indeed, again with a dispatch that defies belief *unless the Attorney General and others within the Department of Justice knew that a "new Pearl Harbor" was impending*—the primary response of the DoJ was to muscle through Congress the grotesquely-misnamed "Patriot Act." That legislation, comprising hundreds of pages and amending dozens of existing laws, was *passed by Congress without hearings and, indeed, without any but a handful of members having read it, or having even been provided with the text before a vote was called in the dead of night.* Attorney General Ashcroft has even acknowledged publicly that he stopped flying on commercial airlines some time before 9/11—which proves that, whether or not Mr. Ashcroft was wholly "in the loop" as to the precise plan of the 9/11 attacks, he clearly knew something major involving airplanes was impending.

15.   A few members of Congress, notably Senators Daschle and Leahy, briefly resisted the "Patriot Act" with its many unconstitutional provisions. Messrs. Daschle and Leahy, however, were thereupon sent potentially fatal dosages of "weaponized" anthrax, from American stores. Congress has been mostly supine since. Curiously, and little reported by the media, the first of the half-dozen fatalities in the October 2001 anthrax attacks was a tabloid newspaper photo editor from Florida, Robert Stevens. While, no doubt, most Americans probably believe these anthrax attacks were the deeds of radical Islamists—notwithstanding that all evidence points to domestic sources—whom had Mr. Stevens offended? The answer is that *he had offended the Bush family,* by selecting for publication in a supermarket tabloid an embarrassing photograph of the President's daughter, Jenna Bush, appearing tipsy and holding a cigarette, while staggering across a dancefloor with a female friend in a nightclub.

16.   Thus, when former Sen. Max Cleland left the "independent" Commission, and Senator Daschle had the opportunity to designate his replacement, he ignored thousands of e-mails urging him to name Kirsten Breitweiser of New Jersey—like the plaintiff, a widow of 9/11— and instead named former Senator Bob Kerrey. While Mr. Kerrey has an impressive résumé, in recent times he has stood out as perhaps the most prominent Democrat to enthusiastically call for the invasion of Iraq to liberate it from Saddam Hussein. Obviously, as 9/11 and the contrived connection between 9/11 and Saddam Hussein led, in a direct line, to an invasion of that country, as a wholehearted supporter of the war, Mr. Kerrey would be distinctly unlikely to stray from the course prescribed for the Commission: to produce a "modified limited hang-out" acknowledging "failures," but not approaching within miles of investigating *actual complicity in the attacks.* That Sen. Daschle named the avidly pro-war Mr. Kerrey to replace the Commission's most skeptical independent member, Mr. Cleland, suggests that the minority leader has been thoroughly sobered by his near-death encounter with U.S. Government anthrax.

17.   In connection with the anthrax attempt on Daschle's life, the *New York Times* reported:

"The dry powder used in the anthrax attacks is virtually indistinguishable in critical technical respects from that produced by the United States military before it shut down its biowarfare program, according to federal scientists and military contractor documents. The similarity to the levels achieved by the United States military lends support to the idea that someone with ties to the old program may be behind the attacks that have killed five people. Its high concentration is surprising, weapon experts said, <u>and far beyond what military analysts once judged as the likely abilities of terrorists</u>. The anthrax sent to the Senate contained as many as one trillion spores per gram. If a lethal dose is estimated conservatively at 10,000 microscopic spores, then a gram in theory could cause about 100 million deaths. <u>The letter sent to Tom Daschle, the Senate Democratic leader, is said to have held two grams of anthrax</u>." [Emphasis added]

18.   Thus, neither the FBI, nor the Justice Department, nor the New York Police Department, nor Congress, nor the "independent" commission has—*or ever will*—conduct a true and thorough investigation into exactly who killed plaintiff's husband, and set in motion events that have brought about the deaths of hundreds of United States military personnel—with no end in sight to the war in

Iraq—and many thousands of Afghan and Iraqi citizens.

19.   The supposedly "independent" commission, apart from
being headed by a blood relative of the President (Thomas A. Kean, a
distant cousin) and comprised in large part of people with resounding
conflicts of interest, has allowed the President and Vice President to
dictate the terms of their testimony and has tiptoed past the critical
issues. As will be described, the Commission—to which the
Administration acceded most reluctantly, and has sought to
stonewall—has been created to produce a foreordained result: that
while there may have been "intelligence failures" (for which no one to
date has been held accountable) the attacks were planned and carried
out by nineteen radical Islamists, with the blessing of Osama bin
Laden, out of hatred for America and resentment over the American
military presence in Saudi Arabia, its support of Israel, and its
perceived opposition to Islam. Plaintiff has every expectation that this
lawsuit will be met by attempts on the part of the enormously powerful members of the Enterprise seeking to steamroller the plaintiff—if
not by covertly killing her or her attorney (and making the death[s]
appear to be accidents or suicides) then by obstructions to disclosure
being made, in the name of "executive privilege" and "national
security." *If we do not live already in a de facto police state, there is no
"privilege" that protects mass murder, or even gross misfeasance that
permits attacks on the scale of 9/11.* As for "national security," even if
the Administration figures can be seen as having been only grotesquely
negligent, rather than actively complicit, in the attacks of 9/11, the
words should stick in their throats. *Having—at the very least—failed
so abjectly in their primary task, which is the protection of American
lives, the defendants cannot be allowed to hide their misdeeds behind the
curtain of "national
security."*

[*Editor's note:* A lengthy list of claims follows; most of these are
excised here. We pick up the Complaint with these following
sections, which are deemed as being pertinent to this book.]

**THE EVIDENCE SHOWS THAT THE AIR FORCE AND AIR
NATIONAL GUARD WERE ORDERED TO "STAND DOWN"
AS THE 9/11 HIJACKINGS BECAME KNOWN AND THAT
MOST OR ALL OF THE HIJACKED AIRCRAFT COULD
HAVE BEEN INTERCEPTED BY A TIMELY RESPONSE.**

515. Despite all of the warnings and the obvious fact that Washington, D.C., as the nation's capital, and New York City, its most populous city and a primary media and financial center, would be at the top of the list for any intended terrorist attack, officially as of 9/11 there were only two (2) bases in the northeastern U.S. that were part of NORAD's defensive system. One was Otis Air National Guard Base on Cape Cod, about 188 miles distant from New York City. The other was Langley Air Force Base near Norfolk, Virginia, about 129 miles distant from Washington, D.C.

516. During the Cold War, the U.S. had literally thousands of fighters on alert. By 9/11, the number was supposedly reduced to only fourteen in the entire continental U.S. However, web pages for a number of other Air National Guard units boasted of five minute alert status, meaning that from the moment they were ordered into the air, they could be airborne within five minutes. These websites used terms like "combat ready," "five minute alert," "highest state of readiness" and so on. Indeed, the web site for Andrews Air Force Base, about ten miles from Washington, D.C., stated that it hosted two "combat ready" squadrons, "capable and ready response forces for the District of Columbia in the event of a natural disaster or civil emergency." The District of Columbia Air National Guard—also stationed at Andrews—claimed that its mission was "to provide combat units in the highest possible state of readiness." On September 12, 2001—as the Enterprise needed to cover up that it had caused the U.S. military air defense system to "stand down" and permit the 9/11 attacks to be carried out—both websites were sanitized, with phrases suggesting quick response capability being expurgated.

517. As of sunrise on the East Coast on 9/11, NORAD was taking part in "Vigilant Guardian," the war game that had begun a few days before. Because of this, NORAD was fully staffed and alert, with senior officers manning stations throughout the U.S. when the first real-life hijacking was reported. Because of the war game, NORAD "had extra fighter planes on alert." Colonel Robert Marr, in charge of NORAD's northeastern U.S. sector, said "We had the fighters with a little more gas on board. A few more weapons on board."

FLIGHT 11 (NORTH TOWER WTC) COULD HAVE BEEN INTERCEPTED. A FIFTEEN MINUTE "GAP" AND OTHER SUSPICIOUS CIRCUMSTANCES THAT SHOW COMPLICITY.

518.   Edited transcripts of cockpit transmissions from Flight 11 indicate that the last routine communication with Boston air traffic control was at 8:13:47. The loss of communications was quickly noticed; flight controllers can be heard discussing it at 8:15. Furthermore, "just moments" after the radio contract was lost, Flight 11's transponder was turned off as well. The transponder identifies the jet on the air traffic controller's screen, gives its exact location and altitude, and permits an emergency hijack code to be sent. Boston air traffic manager Glenn Michael later said, "We considered [Flight 11] at that time to be a possible hijacking."

519.   Flight 11's pilot, Captain John Ogonowski, did not press the Emergency Locator Transmitter button, nor did the pilots of Flights 77 and 93; it has been surmised that this was because hijackers were already in the cockpits (for example, as guest pilots sitting in the cockpit's extra seat) when the hijackings began. Captain Ogonowski is believed to have turned the "talk-back" button off and on, enabling flight controllers to hear what was being said, and also enabling them to learn that something was wrong. This continued intermittently most of the way to New York, until about 8:38 A.M.

520.   Flight controllers suspected something was wrong, but may have been confused because Flight 11's ELT button had not been activated. At 8:20 A.M., however, Flight 11 stopped transmitting its IFF ("Identify Friend or Foe") beacon signal and the plane was clearly off course by that time. As a result, at "about 8:20" Boston flight control decided that Flight 11 had probably been hijacked. Beginning at 8:24:38, Boston flight controllers heard what they understood to be the hijackers in Flight 11's cockpit, broadcasting a message to the passengers: "We have some planes. Just stay quiet and you will be OK. We are returning to the airport." A flight controller responded, "Who's trying to call me?" The apparent hijacker continued, "Everything will be OK. If you try to make any moves you'll endanger yourself and the airplane. Just stay quiet." A Boston flight controller later said that, immediately after hearing this voice, "he knew right then that he was working a hijack."

521.   At 8:25 exactly, Boston flight control notified other flight control centers of the apparent hijacking of Flight 11. This was twenty-six minutes before the impact at the World Trade Center North Tower. Astonishingly, according to NORAD, it was not told of the hijacking until 8:40 A.M.—fifteen minutes after other flight control

centers were notified that Flight 11 had been hijacked, and twenty
minutes from the shutoff of Flight 11's IFF beacon, which gave rise to
suspicions that it had been hijacked.

522.   Thus, the nation's air defense system was somehow not
working as of 8:20 A.M. on 9/11. FAA regulations in force at the time
state, "Consider that an aircraft emergency exists . . . when: . . . There is
unexpected loss of radar contact with any aircraft." The regulations
state further, "If . . . you are in doubt that a situation constitutes an
emergency or potential emergency, handle it as though it were an
emergency."

523.   According to an MSNBC report, a significant course deviation is "considered a real emergency, like a police car screeching down a
highway at 100 miles an hour" and leads to fighters being quickly
dispatched to see what the problem might be. However, for reasons
as yet unexplained, on 9/11 "There doesn't seem to have been alarm
bells going off . . . There's a gap there that will have to be investigated."

524.   This fifteen-minute gap from 8:25 to 8:40 is critical, as if
NORAD had taken five minutes to process the alarm and scramble
fighters at Otis ANG Base, the pilots had taken an additional five
minutes to get aloft, and they had traveled the approximately 188
miles to Manhattan at slightly better than half of their F-15 fighters'
top rated speed of 1875 mph. Fighters could have been in New York
City before the North Tower was struck at 8:46.

525.   And, even if fighters from Otis could not have arrived in
New York in time to intercept Flight 11, of particular import to the
plaintiff at bar is that indisputably, if aware at 8:25 A.M. that Flight 11
was hijacked, and off course heading in the direction of New York
City, it beggars belief that fighters could not have been scrambled
before Flight 175, carrying plaintiff's husband, allegedly struck the
South Tower of the World Trade Center at 9:03 A.M. Allowing five
minutes (from 8:25 to 8:30) for NORAD to confirm and forward the
information to Otis, and six minutes (from 8:30 to 8:36) for the pilots
to get aloft, they would have had 27 minutes to cover the 188 miles
from Otis to New York City. That would have required the F-15s,
which have a top speed of 1875 mph, to travel at an average speed
slightly in excess of 6.96 miles per minute—or about 417 mph, an
almost leisurely, subsonic speed for that aircraft.

526.   Upon information and belief, the "official" NORAD
account that it was not notified of the hijacking of Flight 11 until 8:40

A.M. on 9/11 is a lie. ABC News reported that the FAA notified NORAD employee Lt. Col. Dawne Deskins at 8:31 A.M., not 8:40. A different version of the ABC News report has it that "Shortly after 8:30 A.M., behind the scenes, word of a possible hijacking reached various stations of NORAD. Certainly, it is difficult to believe that the FAA would have delayed so greatly in informing NORAD of the diversion of Flight 11. And, so far as has been made public, no air traffic control or FAA employees have been fired, suspended, reprimanded or otherwise disciplined for failure to give timely notice to NORAD on 9/11.

527.   Other, critical aspects of the NORAD account of its actions on 9/11 cannot withstand scrutiny. NORAD's story was set forth in a press release on September 18, 2001. It claimed that after being told of the hijacking of Flight 11 at 8:40 A.M. on 9/11, it waited six minutes to give the scramble order to the pilots at Otis. Then, it took the pilots an additional 6 minutes to take off. Thus, according to NORAD, two fighter planes, F-15s, left Otis at 8:52 A.M. headed toward New York. A NORAD commander claimed the planes were stocked with extra fuel. One of the Otis pilots, Lt. Col. Timothy Duffy, stated that he flew "full-blower," which is to say at top speed, all the way. An F-15 can travel over 1875 MPH. Lt. Col. Duffy later said that he flew at supersonic speeds, headed for the airspace over Kennedy Airport in New York City. Maj. Gen. Larry Arnold stated that the Otis pilots headed straight for New York City, at about 1100 to 1200 MPH. Maj. Gen. Paul Weaver, director of the Air National Guard, claimed that the Otis pilots headed toward New York "like a scalded ape" but could not arrive in time to prevent the South Tower from being struck at 9:03 A.M.

528.   The complete untruth and cynicism of these statements is confirmed by simple arithmetic. To cover 188 miles in 11 minutes, the F-15s would have had to travel at an average speed of 17.09 miles per minute, or 1,025.45 MPH. That speed is only 54.7% of "full blower," or the 1,875 MPH that the F-15 is capable of traveling. Thus, even leaving Otis as late as 8:52 A.M., it is inexplicable that the F-15s failed to reach New York before 9:03 A.M.

529.   NORAD cannot reconcile its "scalded ape," "full-blower" claims with its story that it took the F-15s from Otis nineteen minutes to reach New York City. Traveling 188 miles in 19 minutes means that these 1875 MPH fighters responded to this crisis flying at an average speed of about 594 MPH, a distinctly subsonic speed, a fraction of the F-15's capabilities, and barely faster than the passenger airliner itself.

THE FAILURE TO INTERCEPT FLIGHT 175, CARRYING PLAINTIFF'S HUSBAND, BEFORE THE SOUTH TOWER IMPACT AND MORE REASONS WHY THE OFFICIAL STORY IS UNBELIEVABLE.

529a. Flight 175, with plaintiff's husband on board, took off from Boston Logan Airport at 8:16 A.M. Its last routine communication occurred four seconds before 8:42. One minute later, a Boston flight controller said of Flight 175, "He's off about 9 o'clock and about 20 miles looks like he's heading southbound but there's no transponder no nothing and no one's talking to him." By this time, notifying NORAD of the hijacking of Flight 175 was redundant, because NORAD technicians had their headsets linked to Boston flight control to hear about Flight 11, and thus learned about Flight 175 at the same time Boston did. NORAD's timeline in its press release of September 18, 2001 admitted that it received notice about Flight 175 at 8:43 A.M. Any doubt that Flight 175 had been hijacked ought to have evaporated at 8:44:05, at which time Boston (with NORAD listening in) was told by a nearby airliner that it had heard Flight 175's Emergency Locator Transmitter go off.

530.   However, testifying (although not under oath) before the Commission on May 22, 2003, a NORAD spokesman made the bizarre claims (1) that NORAD learned only at 9:05 A.M. from the FAA of the "possible" hijacking of Flight 175, and (2) that Flight 175's transponder was never turned off. As shown, NORAD was listening in at 8:43 A.M. when Boston was told that Flight 175's radio had been cut off, the transponder had been turned off, and the plane was seriously off course.

531.   Flight 175's transponder, after being off briefly, was turned on but changed to a signal not designated for any plane on that day. This enabled controllers to track Flight 175 easily throughout the final 20 minutes before the South Tower was struck at 9:03 A.M.

532.   Indeed, neither Flight 11 nor Flight 175 was at any time lost to Boston flight control's radar. When Flight 11's transponder was turned off at 8:14 A.M., that only prevented Boston from determining the plane's exact altitude, but it could still be tracked using primary radar. At some point before the plane turned south toward New York City at 8:28 A.M., the FAA had tagged Flight 11's radar dot for easy visibility, and at American Airlines headquarters, "all eyes watched as the plane headed south." Boston flight controller Mark Hodgkins later

said that he had watched Flight 11 "all the way down." Accordingly, from at least 8:28 A.M. until the North Tower (8:46 A.M.) and South Tower (9:03 A.M.) impacts, a number of persons watched as the planes diverged from their flight paths, and headed inexorably toward New York.

533. "Several minutes" after the first impact at 8:46 A.M., Boston flight control reported to NORAD that it was Flight 11 that had crashed into the North Tower. "Within minutes" of the first impact at 8:46 A.M., two open telephone conference calls were established among the FAA, NORAD, the Secret Service, and a number of other government agencies. Indeed, even President Bush and Vice President Cheney were occasionally overheard on these open lines.

534. Based on the foregoing, it defies belief that, as NORAD claimed in testimony before the Commission on May 23, 2003, it was not notified of Flight 11 striking the North Tower of the World Trade Center until 9:05 A.M.

535. No less unbelievable is NORAD's claim that it learned that Flight 175 had "possibly" been hijacked only two minutes after the impact at the South Tower of the World Trade Center.

536. NORAD, plainly, cannot keep its lies straight, and has acted throughout like an entity having much to hide, but also extreme confidence that it will never be made to account for its acts and its falsehoods concerning them. Indeed, its entire story of having scrambled planes first from Otis and, later, from Langley appears to be a fabrication, intended to cover that—plaintiff alleges due to a "Stand Down" order, given with the knowledge and approval of defendants including, at least, all of President George W. Bush, ex-president and presidential advisor George H. W. Bush, Vice-President Cheney, and Generals Myers and Eberhart—NORAD did <u>nothing</u> between 8:40 A.M., at which hour it admits receiving word that Flight 11 had been hijacked, for at least *57 minutes,* until some time after the Pentagon was struck, at 9:37 A.M. In other words, in order to deceive the public into thinking that attempts had been made to intercept Flight 175 (with fighters scrambled from Otis) and Flight 77 (with F-16s scrambled from Langley) NORAD created a fiction that fighters were scrambled but, despite flying like "scalded apes," could not prevent the South Tower and the Pentagon from being struck.

537. As shown above, even allowing for the improbable delays in NORAD being notified of the hijacking of Flight 11, it is not

credible that planes were, in truth, scrambled, but were not able to reach their destinations in time.

538. Gen. Richard Myers was acting Chairman of the Joint Chiefs of Staff on 9/11. Two days after 9/11, testifying under oath before the Senate Armed Services Committee, Myers was asked when the order to scramble planes was first given. Given the magnitude of the attacks, that the same had occurred on his watch, and that he was testifying at his own confirmation hearing, one would suppose that the General would come prepared, have the facts, and—if he could not testify truthfully—at least avoid egregious lies, that he might have to account for later. He responded, "That order, to the best of my knowledge, was after the Pentagon was struck [at 9:37 A.M.]"

539. If Gen. Myers' testimony just quoted was correct, then NORAD'S claim to have ordered the scrambling of jets at 8:46 A.M. is off by at least fifty-one minutes. So far as plaintiff is aware, neither President Bush, nor Vice President Cheney, nor General Myers has been asked in public to explain how Gen. Myers came to form the belief that no planes were scrambled until at least 9:37 A.M., and whether it is true that two fighters left Otis for New York City at 8:52 A.M., but arrived only nineteen minutes later.

540. While, again, it seems improbable in the extreme that, had fighters really been scrambled as NORAD now claims, General Myers would not have known of that fact when he appeared at his confirmation hearing on September 13th, NORAD spokesman, Marine Maj. Mike Snyder, also claimed that no fighters were scrambled until after the Pentagon was hit. Only then, according to Maj. Snyder, did the military realize the scope of the attacks, and order fighters into the air.

541. Had the attacks of 9/11 been fully under the control of Islamist fanatics intent on inflicting the greatest damage on the United States, it is curious that Flight 11 and Flight 175 both bypassed the Indian Point nuclear power complex in Buchanan, New York in Westchester County. Plaintiff believes, and alleges on information and belief, that while the Enterprise did not require casualties and property damage on the truly massive scale that would have resulted had two planes been flown into nuclear power facilities, it did calculate that to qualify as a "catastrophic and catalyzing event" that would "shock and awe" Congress and the American public into the Orwellian Patriot Act, and a blank check for warmaking in the oil lands of the world, both towers at the World Trade Center would have to be struck, and a few thousand fatalities at least inflicted.

542.   Consistent with plaintiff's analysis is that, while President Bush, Vice President Cheney, NORAD, the FAA, the Secret Service and other agencies had a conference call "within minutes" of 8:46 A.M. by which time all participating in the call had to know (1) that the North Tower had been struck; and (2) that Flight 175 was bearing down on New York City, from all indications it occurred to none of these devoted guardians of the public safety to notify New York City officials. As a result, from about 8:55 A.M. until shortly before the second impact, a public announcement was broadcast inside the South Tower of the World Trade Center, saying that the building was safe, and people could return to their offices.   Again, the Enterprise did not want quite so much "shock and awe" as would result from twin strikes at Indian Point nuclear power plant, but it had a pretty clear idea regarding how much shock and awe—and how many dead bodies—it needed to achieve its aims.

543.   Flight controllers in New York City complained afterward that the crash of Flight 11 was confirmed to them only a minute or two before Flight 175 crashed at 9:03. They also were not told that there was a concern with Flight 175 until right before it crashed.   Even the fighter pilots who may, or may not, have been en route to New York from Otis appear to have been uninformed.   One pilot, Maj. Daniel Nash, stated that he could not recall actually being told of the Flight 11 crash.   Both Lt. Col Duffy and Maj. Nash (the two supposed F-15 pilots from Otis) deny they were told of the hijacking of Flight 175 until after the South Tower impact.   Maj. Nash suggested that, even if he had reached New York City before Flight 175, he could not have shot that plane down, because a decision to do so assertedly had to be made by the President, who by 9:03 A.M. was preoccupied with a classroom of children in Florida.

544.   Even viewed in the light most favorable to the Enterprise defendants, the foregoing shows the following. There is a huge, unexplained gap between when NORAD should have learned of the diversion of Flight 11—by 8:25 A.M.—and the time it claims to have learned of that event—8:40 A.M. If we credit NORAD's dubious claim that it learned of the Flight 11 hijacking only at 8:40 A.M., even then NORAD squandered a fighting chance to intercept Flight 11. NORAD's "scalded ape" story is palpably false. F-15 fighters departing Otis as late as 8:52 A.M. could, without undue effort, have reached New York in time to intercept Flight 175. The discrepancies in

NORAD'S (and Gen. Myers') accounts are numerous, consequential, and highly suspect. If Presidential authority was needed to shoot down airliners aimed at large buildings, such authority could, and ought to have, been obtained during the conference call that began shortly after 8:46 A.M. It is shocking that, as Flight 175 approached the South Tower, announcements continued to be made that that building was safe. Given the number and seniority of participants in the conference call, it is at best difficult in the extreme to ascribe to confusion or stress the failure to notify New York City authorities that a second airliner (off course and out of touch with air traffic control) was bearing down on the city. Hundreds of lives might have been saved, had such notice been given. However, had not both World Trade Center towers been reduced to clouds of fine, airborne dust, if either tower had been left standing with only a few hundreds dead, perhaps the public would not have been shocked into uncritical approval of military adventures and attacks on Constitutional freedoms that the Bush II Administration had had in the works long before 9/11.

545.   As has been shown, the defense system's response on 9/11 to the diversion of Flight 11 and Flight 175 was so sluggish, so inept, that it is impossible to believe that the top command did not want the attacks to succeed. Were the U.S. a parliamentary democracy, which of course it is not, on the facts as presented, one would think that the head of state would have been put to a vote of no confidence, and obliged to call for new elections. Were the U.S. a country in which the government is accountable to its citizens—which it is in theory but appears, dishearteningly, not to be in practice—if the president were not obliged by an indignant public, Congress and an aggressively-inquiring press to resign, in light of his bumbling, at least a great many heads within the military, NORAD, the FAA etc. would have "rolled." So far as has been made known publicly, none did. Not one.

546.   Even independently of other factors (e.g., the abundant warnings, the wish by PNAC, composed largely of Bush II Administration insiders *and even the president's brother Jeb,* for a "new Pearl Harbor," etc.) the response, or non-response to Flights 11 and 175 was so shockingly inept as to raise deep suspicions that the government wanted the attacks to play out, and so did nothing to stop them. Even more damning is consideration of what happened in respect of Flight 77.

**BEFORE STRIKING THE PENTAGON, FLIGHT 77 IS
ALLOWED TO FLY UNCONTESTED FOR ABOUT 50
MINUTES AFTER THE FIRST WTC STRIKE. THE
GOVERNMENT'S ACCOUNT IS, AGAIN, NONSENSICAL
AND INCONSISTENT.**

547.   Flight 77 took off from Dulles Airport near Washington at
8:20 A.M. Its last routine radio communication was made at 8:50:51,
and then it failed to respond to a routine instruction. Within "a few
minutes" after 8:48 A.M., and in all events by 8:56, at which time flight
controllers repeatedly called Flight 77 over the radio and received no
reply, "it was evident that Flight 77 was lost."

548.   NORAD's failure to intercept Flight 77, of course, becomes
all the more egregious, more indicative of "Stand Down" orders
intended to let the attacks proceed, in proportion to the time available
to it to mount an effective response. As we have seen, NORAD claims
it learned of the hijacking of Flight 11 only at 8:40 A.M., whereas if
established procedures had been followed, it ought to have learned of
this by 8:25 A.M. at the latest. In the case of Flight 77, amazingly,
whereas sometime between 8:48 A.M. and 8:56 A.M. air traffic controllers determined that Flight 77 had been hijacked, NORAD claims it
received word from the FAA only at 9:24 or 9:25 A.M., and even then
only that it "may" have been hijacked.

549.   This half-hour gap was disputed by the FAA in proceedings
before the Commission. Jane Garvey, FAA Administrator on 9/11, in a
statement released following her testimony, claimed that while formal
notification was logged in by NORAD only at 9:24 A.M., "information
about [Flight 77] was conveyed continuously during the phone bridges
[among the FAA, NORAD, the Secret Service and other agencies]
before the formal notification."

550.   A few days after 9/11, the *New York Times* reported,
"During the hour or so that American Airlines Flight 77 was under the
control of hijackers, up to the moment it struck the west side of the
Pentagon, military officials in a command center on the east side of
the building were urgently talking to law enforcement and air traffic
control officials about what to do." This seems more consistent with
the FAA's more recent claim that NORAD and other agencies knew
about the hijacking of Flight 77 long before 9:24 A.M.

551.   If Ms. Garvey is correct, then NORAD in the more than
two years since 9/11 has still not managed to adopt a plausible story,

and stick to it. If NORAD learned that Flight 77 had been hijacked, say, at 8:51 A.M., as the Pentagon impact occurred at 9:38 A.M., it would have had about 47 minutes to get a fighter plane over Washington, D.C. Let us leave aside for the moment the implausibility of the capital not being defended by fighters at Andrews Air Force Base, only ten miles away, and accept for the moment the story that the nearest high-alert status fighters available were at Langley, 129 miles from Washington. The maximum speed of the F-16s at Langley was "only" 1,500 MPH versus the 1,875 MPH of the F-15s at Otis. Then again, Langley is closer to Washington, D.C.—129 miles—than Otis is to New York (188 miles). At an average speed of 1200 MPH, which is 20 miles per minute, an F-16 fighter could have covered the 129 miles from Langley to Washington in about 6-1/2 minutes. NORAD has a "lot of explaining to do" concerning its failure to get a fighter over Washington in the approximately 47 minutes it had available for that task.

552.   NORAD's account, here again, simply should not be convincing to any fifth grader with a calculator. Supposedly, at 9:09 A.M. it ordered F-16s at Langley to battle stations alert.   However one pilot, code-named "Honey," relates that he was in one of the first planes to take off from Langley, but that battle stations alert was not sounded until 9:24 A.M.   NORAD claims that three F-16s were scrambled (ordered aloft) at 9:27 A.M. to intercept Flight 77, and took off three minutes later, at 9:30 A.M.   Here again, the NORAD timeline is inconsistent with "Honey's" recollection. Without giving exact times, he describes a series of events lasting much longer than six minutes, including waiting from "five to ten minutes" between two o f these events.

553.   Even crediting NORAD's account, however implausible, that it learned of the hijacking only at 9:24 A.M. but had planes taking off from Langley at 9:30 A.M., at 1200 MPH the F-16s *still* could have arrived on time, albeit with only 1-2 minutes to spare. Presumably, the pilots were motivated to travel quickly—on of them, Maj. Dean Eckmann, said he was told before scrambling that the World Trade Center had been hit by a plane.   Is it not, then, astounding, that in their May 2003 testimony, NORAD officials said that the F-16s did not use their afterburners, and flew at about 660 MPH to Washington? Even more astounding is the arrogance, the contempt that NORAD brass and the Enterprise have for the victims of 9/11 and the American public. Again using a calculator, it can be determined that, if

NORAD's timeline is to be believed, the F-16s were still 105 miles distant from Washington when Flight 77 crashed. If so, that means the planes covered a distance of only about 24 miles in the eight minutes from takeoff (9:30 A.M.) to the time Flight 77 crashed (9:38 A.M.). Actually, a fifth-grader should be able to do this calculation *without* a calculator. Twenty-four miles in eight minutes means the F-16s flew at 3 miles per minute. Three miles a minute times sixty minutes indicates an average speed of only 180 MPH, far from the 660 MPH the NORAD witnesses claimed.

554.   Indeed, NORAD and the pilots supposedly scrambled from Langley cannot even agree on where they were headed. "Honey" claimed that the F-16s were in fact flying toward New York City, not Washington. They were 30-40 miles to the east of Washington, not south of it, when they saw a black column of smoke coming from the city. They then changed course, and headed to Washington instead.

555.   Inconsistent with "Honey's" account of where the Langley F-16s were headed is that of two of the other pilots, who claimed their destination was always Washington, D.C. Advised, perhaps, that it is better not to be tied up in an untruth you may later have trouble extricating yourself from, NORAD's Maj. James Fox claims he dispatched the fighters without any target.

556.   At the May 2003 hearing, NORAD claimed the fighters from Langley were sent to fly *over the Atlantic Ocean* instead of heading directly toward Washington. This would be consistent with "Honey's" account of the fighters being too far east. NORAD officials admitted that, had the fighters traveled faster and headed directly toward Washington, they were capable of arriving there before Flight 77. NORAD's excuse was that hijacked airliners taking off within the United States were a "law enforcement issue," and that NORAD'S MISSION "was to protect [against] things coming towards the United States" from without.

557.   Again, NORAD's apparent contempt for our intellect is remarkable. Supposedly, we are to believe that F-16s were scrambled from Langley, to pursue and intercept hijacked Flight 77 that had made a U-turn roughly where West Virginia borders Kentucky, and was headed toward Washington, D.C. As it was known that two planes had been flown into the World Trade Center in New York City during the preceding 45 minutes, a government that admits to spending $40 billion annually on intelligence ought to have been able to figure out

(1) that Flight 77 was not headed in the opposite direction from its scheduled route to Los Angeles due to pilot error; (2) that whoever was in control of Flight 77 probably intended to fly it into a landmark building; and (3) Washington, D.C., by definition but especially because Flight 77 was headed in that direction, was a distinctly likely site of the intended attack.

558.   To cover what plaintiff alleges was a "Stand Down" order and that NORAD was ordered to and did allow Flight 77 to continue until the impact with the Pentagon, NORAD offers up the feeblest of fictions: that it had no jurisdiction over land, and it was the responsibility of law enforcement, not NORAD, to deal with aircraft headed toward Washington from the interior, NORAD'S task being limited to stopping planes coming in from outside the U.S., presumably from over the Atlantic. This story makes no sense. First, the Otis planes reportedly flew over land to reach New York City. Second, few "law enforcement" agencies have fighter aircraft, or any effective means (unaided by the military) to contest attacks by airplanes originating from within the U.S. and about to be flown into buildings. Third, if NORAD can protect Washington only from air attacks originating outside the U.S., it would make no sense to have the closest and, but for far-off Otis, the only available fighter aircraft at Langley, which is to say well inland, rather than at Andrews (or some other base closer to the coastline). Finally, if the Langley F-16s were tasked with intercepting Flight 77, was it hoped that the "terrorist hijackers," relatively inept pilots in control of an unwieldy, unarmed passenger airliner would—out of respect for NORAD'S jurisdictional scruple— join the F-16s out over the Atlantic?

559.   The failure to stop the strike on the Pentagon becomes all the more damning if one considers that, as calls poured in from fighter units volunteering assistance, it was not necessary to limit possible responses to Langley or Otis. Within minutes of the second crash at the World Trade Center, it was obvious to everyone that the nation was under attack. Calls started "pouring into NORAD and sector operations centers, asking 'What can we do to help?'" The Air National Guard commander in Syracuse, New York, told Col. Robert Marr, in charge of NORAD's Northeastern US sector, "Give me 10 minutes and I can give you hot guns. Give me 30 minutes and I'll have heat-seekers [missiles]. Give me an hour and I can give you slammers [Amraams]." Marr replied, "I want it all."

560.   Reportedly, Col. Marr said "Get to the phones. Call every Air National Guard unit in the land. Prepare to put jets in the air. The nation is under attack. Another NORAD commander, Maj. Gen. Eric Findley, claims he had his staff immediately order as many fighters in the air as possible. Yet, however sincere Col. Marr and Gen. Findley might be, the performance did not live up to the rhetoric. Col. Marr's response to Syracuse ANG may have delayed planes from taking off, whereas ostensibly it could have had planes with some weapons heading toward Washington by 9:20 A.M., which could have reached Washington before Flight 77 did.

561.   Another account says, "By 10:01 A.M., the command center began calling several bases across the country for help." A base in Toledo, Ohio, was one of those called at that time, and Toledo appears to have been the first base other than Otis, Langley, or Andrews to send up any fighters, which Toledo did at 10:16 A.M. Syracuse may have been next, finally putting fighters in the air at 10:44 A.M., *one hour and fifty-eight minutes after the impact at the North Tower.*

AN UNPRECEDENTED NATIONWIDE "GROUND STOP" ORDER MUST HAVE HAD WHITE HOUSE APPROVAL AND WAS THE FUNCTIONAL EQUIVALENT OF AN ORDER FOR THE MILITARY TO "STAND DOWN" AND ALLOW THE ATTACKS TO PROCEED.

562.   FAA Administrator Jane Garvey, "almost certainly after getting an okay from the White House, initiated a national ground stop" at 9:26 A.M. That measure forbade takeoffs, and required planes in the air to get down as soon as reasonable. The order—never implemented since the Wright Brothers first flew—"applied to virtually every single kind of machine that can take off—civilian, military, or law enforcement." *Note the inclusion of military planes.* Military and law enforcement flights were allowed to resume takeoffs at 10:31 A.M. A limited number of military flights were allowed to fly during the nationwide ground stop from 9:26 A.M. until 10:31, but the FAA has refused to reveal details. Later, *USA Today* claimed that Ben Sliney, FAA National Operations Manager, made the ground-stop decision. If true, this was indeed an audacious judgment call to have been made by Mr. Sliney *on his very first day on the job* as the "chess master of the air traffic system."

563.   Until the day following 9/11, Andrews Air Force Base boasted of "combat ready" fighters "in the highest state of readiness."

One would expect no less, as Andrews is the airport typically used by Air Force One and foreign dignitaries when flying to or from Washington, D.C. At the time of the first World Trade Center crash, three F-16 fighters assigned to Andrews were flying a training mission in North Carolina, 207 miles from Washington, D.C. Yet, it took about an hour after the North Tower impact before these fighters were recalled. They landed at Andrews only after Flight 77 had crashed into the Pentagon at 9:38 A.M. One of the fighters, piloted by Maj. Billy Hutchison, still had enough fuel to take off again without refueling, but the other two needed to refuel. By one report, Hutchinson took off with no weapons. "Hutchison was probably airborne shortly after the alert F-16s from Langley arrive over Washington, although 121st FS pilots admit their timeline-recall is fuzzy." If NORAD's timeline for the Langley F-16s is correct, Hutchinson did not depart Andrews until after 9:49 A.M. It has not been explained (1) why these planes from Andrews were not recalled earlier to protect Washington; and (2) why Hutchinson—who did not need to land for refueling—was not ordered directly to the skies over Washington, which were still unprotected.

564.   It appears NORAD was unwilling to use fighters from any but the two bases in the Northeast sector that they directly controlled, even if there were other bases or fighters already in the air that were closer. There was no legitimate reason for this. In 1999, it was widely reported that when golfer Payne Stewart's Learjet went off course, NORAD used fighters from a number of bases outside of NORAD's "official" seven bases to follow the aircraft as it crossed over several states before crashing. But on 9/11, NORAD appears to have been adamantly unwilling to use fighters from bases such as Andrews, even though Andrews is just ten miles from Washington. Andrews personnel learned about the national emergency through news coverage, and then a pilot called a friend in the Secret Service for more information. Shortly after the second crash at 9:03 A.M., it was the Secret Service—not NORAD—that called Andrews, asking that they get fighters ready. Again, a few minutes after the Pentagon crash at 9:38, it was the Secret Service that called Andrews, and said the fighters needed to "Get in the air now!"

565.   Yet, despite Andrews' claim to have "combat ready" fighters "in the highest possible state of readiness" when the command came to "get in the air," the fighters were not fully ready to take off. They had ammunition for "hot" guns, but AIM-9 missiles were located in a bunker on the other side of the base, and even though base command-

ers began the process of loading them shortly after 9:00 A.M., they still had not finished until about 40 minutes later. The next two fighters to take off from Andrews after Major Billy Hutchison were armed only with "hot" guns and non-explosive training rounds. Even though the Secret Service and NORAD had been sharing a conference call since shortly after the first North Tower impact at 8:46 A.M., NORAD claims it was unaware that the Secret Service ordered any planes into the air from Andrews.

566.   Lack of communication among Administration and military personnel on 9/11 would be comical, were the consequences not tragic. In May 2003 testimony, Transportation Secretary Mineta claimed that at about 9:25 or 9:26 A.M., a few minutes after his arrival at the bunker beneath the White House, he overheard an aide tell Vice President Cheney that a hijacked plane headed toward Washington was 50 miles away, then 30 miles away. When the plane was announced as being ten miles away, the aide asked the vice president, "Do the orders still stand?" Cheney replied, "Of course the orders still stand. Have you heard anything to the contrary?" Mineta inferred that the order was an order to shoot down the plane.

567.   Strange to say, if the president or the vice-president ordered incoming Flight 77 to be shot down before it reached Washington, *none of the pilots from Langley or Andrews appear to have been aware of any such orders!* One article pointed out, "If the airliner had approached much nearer to the White House it might have been shot down by the Secret Service, who are believed to have a battery of ground-to-air Stinger missiles ready to present the president's home." Given that the Pentagon is only two miles from the White House, the failure to use Stinger missiles to shoot down Flight 77 suggests that the Enterprise knew that the White House was not the intended target.

568.   Reports are also that Washington, D.C. air traffic controllers were kept in the dark concerning Flight 77, and did not learn of its approach until the last minute. One flight controller claimed she was the first to notice Flight 77 when it was about 12 to 14 miles away, and Vice President Cheney learned of it only after that. The head Washington flight controller claimed the Secret Service first alerted his tower of a hijacked plane coming his way, when it was only five miles away. According to another account, flight controllers detected Flight 77 just before 9:30 A.M., and told the Secret Service. Another account stated radar detected Flight 77 when it was 30 miles

away at 9:30 A.M., and still another account claimed detection at 9:33 A.M. An unanswered question is that, if Washington, D.C. flight control's radar did not detect Flight 77's approach from 9:24 A.M. and before, then whose radar did?

569.   NORAD admits official notice that Flight 77 was headed toward Washington at 9:24 A.M., and FAA Administrator Jane Garvey claimed a conference call discussed Flight 77 well before that time. It was not, however, until well after the Pentagon was hit, at 9:38 A.M., that orders were given to evacuate additional likely Washington targets such as the White House, the Capitol Building, the State Department and, indeed, the Pentagon itself. Had Flight 77 struck the Capitol instead of the Pentagon, most of the legislators would still have been inside. It is claimed, plaintiff submits not at all credibly, that Defense Secretary Rumsfeld and his top aides in their Pentagon offices remained unaware of any danger until after the Pentagon was actually hit, even though the conference call was being run out of the National Military Command Center inside the Pentagon itself. Vice President Cheney (according to Transportation Secretary Mineta) knew, and Defense Secretary Rumsfeld certainly ought to have known, of the approach of Flight 77. Why were no evacuation orders given for other Washington landmarks until after 9:38 A.M.? This remains unexplained. Had orders been given to begin evacuating the Pentagon at the time of the exchange between Vice President Cheney and the aide reported by Secretary Mineta, perhaps many of the 125 people who died inside the Pentagon on 9/11 would be alive today.

THE CRASH OF FLIGHT 93 IN SOMERSET COUNTY, PENNSYLVANIA. MORE EVIDENCE OF COMPLICITY AND UNANSWERED QUESTIONS.

570.   There are a host of unanswered questions also concerning Flight 93, the last of the four planes to be hijacked on 9/11. Flight 93's takeoff was delayed about 40 minutes, until 8:42 A.M. The FAA told NORAD at 9:16 A.M. that Flight 93 had been hijacked. The basis of that report is uncertain, as the transponder turned off only about 9:30 or 9:40 A.M. , and Flight 93 did not go off course until much later.

571.   The "timeline" for Flight 93 is the subject of secrecy and dispute. NORAD maintains that this plane crashed at 10:03 A.M. notwithstanding a seismic study, commissioned by the Army, that determined the time of the crash to be 10:06:05.

572.   Even murkier is when, or if, fighters were flown toward Flight 93 charged with intercepting it. NORAD'S first timeline said only that a fighter was 100 miles, or 11 minutes, away when Flight 93 crashed near Shanksville, in Somerset County, Pennsylvania.   That means the fighter was traveling about 545 MPH—again, inexplicably slow. NORAD's initial timeline also implies that the fighter allegedly in pursuit of Flight 93 had only traveled about 80 miles from Washington when Flight 93 crashed. If we assume the 545 MPH as a correct
average, that means the fighter left Washington about nine minutes before the crash, or 9:57 A.M. Consider the implications: before Flight 93 was reported hijacked at 9:15 A.M., two planes had been steered into the World Trade Center, the nation's defenses were in an uproar, and base commanders all around the country were phoning in, asking what they could do to help. Yet—if NORAD is to be believed— about 41 minutes elapsed before anyone got a plane into the air, head- ing in the direction of hijacked Flight 93.

573.   Secretary Mineta's impression that Cheney had given a shootdown order for Flight 77 at about 9:26 A.M. has been mentioned. It has also been claimed that, sometime after Flight 77 crashed, some- one from the White House spoke directly with pilots over Washington, and declared the Washington area a "free-fire zone."   In another account, the Secret Service told the pilots, "I want you to protect the White House at all costs."   Yet, it has been reported also that it was not until President Bush took off from Sarasota, Florida at about 9:56 A.M. that he had a short discussion with Vice President Cheney, and it was then that the president authorized the military to shoot down any plane under the control of hijackers.   Strange to say, none of the pilots over Washington claim to have heard any such order. "Honey," the lead pilot, claimed to have heard a garbled message about Flight 93 that the other pilots did not hear. He said, "The message seemed to convey that the White House was an important asset to protect . . . something like, 'Be aware of where [Flight 93] is, and it could be a target.'"   Both "Honey" and another pilot code-named "Lou" stated they were never given orders to shoot down any plane that day.

574.   All six of the first pilots to arrive over Washington were quoted in the press, and none of them indicated that he flew in pursuit of Flight 93. One article does say that Billy Hutchison's fighter from Andrews AFB "was to do ID that unknown [aircraft] that everybody was so excited about."   But the article containing that quote goes on to

describe how Hutchison began patrolling over Washington in low-flying loops instead.

575.   Furthermore, Hutchison's was the only fighter of the six that claimed to have been unarmed, but NORAD's most recent claim is that two unarmed fighters from Washington were sent after Flight 93. NORAD previously claimed that at some point after Flight 77 crashed at 9:38 A.M., two unarmed fighters in Michigan were ordered after Flight 93. These last-mentioned fighters are claimed to have been in the air since the time of the first attack at 8:46 A.M., raising the obvious question of why they were not recalled to be armed an hour earlier. NORAD seems to have forgotten these two fighters in its most recent timeline. Major General Paul Weaver, director of the Air National Guard, claimed that *no fighters were sent after Flight 93 at all.*

576.   Contradicting Gen. Weaver's claim of no fighters having been sent in pursuit of Flight 93, the day following 9/11 a New Hampshire flight controller claimed "that an F-16 fighter closely pursued Flight 93 . . . the F-16 made 360-degree turns to remain close to the commercial jet, the employee said. 'He must've seen the whole things,' the employee said of the F-16 pilot's view of Flight 93's crash." Details have been reported, too, of how Vice President Cheney was given notice when a fighter was 80 miles from Flight 93, when it was within 60 miles, and at least one additional notice. The vice president reportedly confirmed his order to shoot down Flight 93 after every update.

577.   Plaintiff submits that, where a purported investigation is being carried out at taxpayer expense of events that caused the deaths of 2,993 persons, it is conclusive proof that the proceedings are a farce, a coverup and a public-relations sham that any significant proof is received without the witnesses being sworn to testify truly and under the penalties of perjury. Such laxity has been the practice of the Commission, generally and particularly in respect of the NORAD commanders who testified. NORAD representatives lied brazenly—so greatly were their accounts internally inconsistent, and patently unbelievable, that the only reasonable conclusion is that they recognized the Commission for what it is—a comedy produced for C-Span, a bone tossed in the direction of activist groups of victims' families, and a means to postpone any true investigation, if not forever then at least until after the 2004 election. Judging by their conduct, the NORAD commanders were well aware that the Commissioners—or

a majority of them at least—had no expectation of being told even a plausible, roughly consistent set of lies, much less the truth.

578.   Late in 2001, for example, Maj. Gen. Larry Arnold wrote how NORAD's response on 9/11 was "immediate" and "impressive." Moving into a zone of untruth that may best be described as hallucinatory, Gen. Arnold claimed, "we were able to identify, track and escort suspected hijacked aircraft after the initial attacks," "our reaction time outpaced the process in some instances," "our well-practiced rapid response capability may very well have prevented additional surprise attacks on the American homeland saving countless lives."   Apart from the absurdity of such claims in light of such facts as are known and, of course, the outcome of the attacks, Gen. Arnold was flatly contradicted by current NORAD Commander Maj. Gen. Craig McKinley who, testifying to the Commission in May 2003 with Gen. Arnold seated at his side, admitted "We had not positioned prior to September 11, 2001, for the scenario that took place that day."   "McKinley admitted," another report stated, "that NORAD was utterly unprepared for the attack." Gen. McKinley called NORAD's 9/11 stance "a Cold War vestige."

579.   Not only did Gen. McKinley squarely contradict Gen. Arnold's referenced article that had boasted of NORAD's response, but Gen. Arnold himself testified lamely before the Commission that he did not think Flight 77 would be shot down on its approach to Washington, because even at that point, it was only "through hindsight that we are certain that this was a coordinated attack on the United States."

580.   Gen. Arnold's last-quoted statement is astonishing.   At the time in question, roughly 9:26 A.M., about 40 minutes had elapsed since a hijacked plane had crashed into the WTC North Tower.   Nearly half an hour had passed since the second impact at the South Tower. Flight 77, having made a "U" turn from its projected flight path, had been out of radio contact with controllers for about 35 minutes, and was bearing down on the nation's capital.   Yet, Gen. Arnold is suggesting that he — and perhaps other military and civilian leaders as he employs the pronoun "we"—were unsure that a "coordinated attack on the United States" was in progress.   Two possible conclusions, and two only, are possible: the General is an extravagant liar, or his acuity is so feeble that it is a terrible scandal that he achieved his rank, and a worse scandal that he was not dismissed from service in the wake of the attacks.

581.   Inspired, no doubt, by the manner in which Lt. Col. Oliver North parlayed brazen perjury covering up massive illegal sales of weapons (and drugs) and the creation and use of an extra-Constitutional parallel government to thwart laws passed by Congress into wealth and a lucrative career as a pro-Enterprise pundit, NORAD witnesses appearing before the Commission did not feel the need even to avoid lies that could readily be refuted—stating, for example, that CNN first began showing images of the North Tower of the World Trade Center on fire at 8:57 A.M., when it is easily verifiable that CNN began doing so at 8:48 A.M. It bears repeating: a so-called "Independent Commission" that countenances such mendacity from witnesses, and gives them a free pass from possible prosecution for perjury by excusing them from testifying under oath, invites, and indeed deserves, only contempt.

582.   Regardless of whether NORAD'S story of convenience at a given moment entails fighters flying toward Flight 93 from Michigan, on the one hand, or Washington, on the other, its account cannot withstand scrutiny. Three fully-armed fighters reached Washington, before the one unarmed, or the two partially-armed ones did. So why was not one of the first three, fully-armed fighters sent after Flight 93? Can anyone but a fool believe that, an hour and a half after NORAD had been notified of the first hijacking, NORAD—had Flight 93 not crashed, but remained aloft at about 10:16, at which time supposedly it might have been overtaken by an unarmed fighter from Washington— could not have done better than an unarmed fighter, that might not have been able to bring the hijacked plane down except by ramming it or other such maneuvers posing a grave risk to the fighter pilot's life?

583.   As will be shown, there is significant evidence that Flight 93 was shot down, and that it was tailed by a private jet owned by an enormously wealthy businessman who—the coincidences just keep coming—chanced to be hosting a charity event at the secure Air Force facility in Nebraska to which President Bush was flown on 9/11. Especially in light of the inspiring, albeit uncertain, story that passengers on Flight 93 fought the hijackers and may have recaptured control of the aircraft, Enterprise spinmeisters have sought to keep armed aircraft far from Flight 93 in their accounts of the moments preceding its crash.

584.   If the facts are viewed critically, however, the Enterprise, NORAD, and the Bush II Administration cannot have it both ways.

Either the brave passengers who exclaimed "Let's roll!" were blown out
of the sky by military (or CIA or other Enterprise) fire, or Flight 93
flew for fifty minutes, uncontested, after two planes had struck the
WTC and the government knew it had been hijacked. Small wonder,
then, that NORAD continues to hide behind lies and vague stories of
unarmed fighters, with the timeline kept as fuzzy as possible. NORAD
Commander Craig McKinley newly claimed at the May 2003 hearings
that NORAD was unaware of any shootdown order until five minutes
after Flight 93 had crashed.

585.   Additional questions are raised by the failure to escort Air
Force One when, at last, President Bush tore himself away from the
schoolchildren's "goat story" and left the Sarasota airport about 9:56
A.M. Interestingly, one of the president's security detail at the elementary school saw the second WTC crash at 9:03 A.M. and immediately
exclaimed, "We're out of here. Can you get everyone ready?" Two air
bases in Florida (Homestead and Tyndall) were among the seven in
NORAD'S system. One would think that, during the approximately
32-minute delay between the second WTC impact, and the time that
the commander-in-chief (the children's "briefing" regarding the pet
goat having been completed) left with his motorcade about 9:35 A.M.,
the president's security would have arranged for an armed fighter
escort to accompany Air Force One. It appears, however, that no fighters reached Air Force One until sometime between 11:00 A.M. and
11:30 A.M. (NORAD has not released full details). Reportedly, the
first fighters to reach Air Force One came from Ellington, near
Houston, long after Air Force One left Florida. If, somehow, the 9/11
attacks were not an "inside job," carried out with the secret blessing of
high officials in the Bush II Administration and the military and
"national security" agencies, the President's initial conduct following
word of the attacks was bizarre, and those responsible for his safety
were remarkably casual.

586.   One columnist wrote in May 2003, "The great majority of
people, sickened and overwhelmed by the horror of the attacks,
unquestioningly accepts the White House version [of what happened
on 9/11]. Many thousands, however, are patiently stitching together
the documented evidence and nothing the holes in the fabric of that
official story. A Florida columnist called the "restrained—even
failed—standard US military air defense protocols while the attacks
were occurring" a "real mystery" deserving of a serious investigation.

Regrettably, shockingly, few major media organizations have displayed any interest whatsoever in challenging the Official Story, or even acknowledging the discrepancies.

FURTHER PARTICULARS CONCERNING THE 9/11 FLIGHTS THAT REVEAL THAT THE OFFICIAL STORY IS FALSE, OR AT THE VERY LEAST IS UNPROVED AND REQUIRES A FULL INVESTIGATION AND NOT A COVER-UP

587.   Details concerning each of the four doomed flights of 9/11 render the Official Story unbelievable. Many facts have emerged into the public domain, mostly from official or from mainstream media sources, which make the Official Story offensive to the laws of physics, or to common sense. Plaintiff, obviously, has not the resources, the expertise, or the obligation in order to sustain her complaint under Rule 12(b)(6) to offer, especially at this juncture, definitive proof of alternatives to the various details of the Official Story so as to render them untrue as a matter of law.

588.   However, by describing just some of the many discrepancies, internal inconsistencies, absurdities and other fallacies, and by demonstrating that these many, glaring incongruities have been studiously avoided by two (2) "official" investigations into 9/11, plaintiff can and will show that overall the Official Story is utterly unworthy of belief and, that by avoiding these issues, both Congress and the Commission have, at best, proved nothing concerning the facts of who actually carried out the attacks and in what fashion, and more probably are acquiescing or participating in a cover-up—more precisely, a "modified limited hang-out," reducing the gravest of crimes, including treason and mass murder, to bureaucratic failures. Overall, the purported official "investigations" are merely a grand exercise in hiding from the public the truth concerning 2,993 counts of murder, and attacks first, carried out and then manipulated to produce two wars, the deaths of thousands of persons, and grave damage to the security, world standing, and Constitutional order of the United States.

589.   Again, plaintiff is undertaking the task not of proving any specific alternative scenario to comprehensively explain the 9/11 attacks, but to discredit the Official Story.

590.   As a preliminary matter, much of the evidence that could reveal what really happened to the four diverted planes remains secret

in government hands, or has disappeared. The flight data recorders from all of the planes except Flight 93 were allegedly unrecovered, or were too damaged to yield data. The same is true of the cockpit voice recorders.

591.   Except for a few minutes of a longer purported call from Flight 11 flight attendant Betty Ong, no audio recordings from any phone conversations with passengers or flight attendants have been released. None of the electronic records of the monitoring of the hijacked flights by air traffic control systems have been released. No interviews with air traffic controllers involved in the incident have been released. Reportedly, air traffic control personnel have been told to keep silent concerning what they know.

592.   shocking is that it recently came to light that at least six air traffic controllers, who dealt with two of the hijacked airliners on 9/11, made a tape recording that same day describing the events, *but the tape was destroyed by a supervisor without anyone making a transcript or even listening to it.* About 16 people met in a conference room before noon on 9/11 at the New York Air Route Traffic Control Center in Ronkonkoma, Long Island, and, passing around a microphone, each recorded his or her version of the events a few hours earlier. Later, however, an F.A.A. official "crushed the cassette in his hand, shredded the tape and dropped the pieces into different trash cans around the building." Curiously, as nearly all of the principal airports in the U.S. had video cameras in boarding areas (and other places) in 2001, no video shows any of the alleged hijackers at the four planes' airports of origin on 9/11. Upon information and belief, although the government claims to have identified remains of persons onboard Flight 77 via DNA testing, this claim is doubtful given that supposedly the entire aircraft was consumed by fire, and DNA becomes unusable in a fire more readily than an entire aircraft can be consumed. Few if any of the Flight 11 and Flight 175 passengers' remains were identified, and upon information and belief none of the passengers' remains on any of the four flights were returned to family members for burial.

FLIGHT 11—BOSTON'S LOGAN AIRPORT TO THE WORLD TRADE CENTER, NORTH TOWER

593.   The Official Story has it that Flight 11 took off from Boston's Logan Airport at 7:59 A.M., bound for Los Angeles. Its last normal communication with Boston air traffic control was at 8:14

A.M., when controllers cleared the flight for an altitude climb, which went unacknowledged.

594. At 8:24 A.M., flight controllers heard a heavily-accented male voice say to the passengers: "We have some planes. Just stay quiet and you will be OK. We are returning to the airport. Nobody move." A few seconds later, the same voice said: "Everything will be OK. If you try to make any moves, you'll endanger yourself and the airplane. Just stay quiet."

595. At 8:26 A.M., Flight 11's location was between Albany and Lake George, New York, and it was headed in a west-by-northwesterly direction. It made an abrupt turn of about 100 degrees, and headed southward, generally following the course of the Hudson River toward New York City.

596. Supposedly, Flight 11 flight attendant Madeline (Amy) Sweeney placed a cell phone call to her ground manager during the hijacking, at 8:22 A.M. There is an FBI transcript of this call, which was published on September 20, 2001. According to this transcript, Ms. Sweeney claims that hijackers had stabbed two fight attendants, and slit the throat of a business class passenger, killing him. According to an FAA memo that emerged on 9/11 but was later retracted, one passenger—remarkably, an American-Israeli dual national who was a member of an elite Israeli security service—was shot.

597. Especially revealing is that, according to the purported Sweeney transcript, the stabbings and the (possible) shooting *all occurred before the hijackers breached the cockpit.*

598. With approximately 80 passengers on board, it defies reason that multiple stabbings and even gunfire, and the commotion and screaming among terrified passengers that assuredly would have resulted, all could have occurred without the cockpit crew knowing that something was awry. Why, then, did not the pilots alert ground control, as they must have heard the disturbances, and were still free o communicate? The hijackers not yet having gained access to the cockpit—according to Sweeney's purported account—radio contact would still have been possible. At the very least, the pilot or co-pilot should have been able to send the emergency alert code, which can be activated form no less than four places in the cockpit of a Boeing 767, including the steering yoke.

599. Reviewing the transcript of Sweeney's supposed cell phone call from Flight 11 reveals additional incongruities which render the

Official Story incredible. According to the transcript, shortly after the
hijackers gained access to the cockpit, the plane quickly changed direction and began a sharp descent towards the World Trade Center—elic-
iting from Sweeney the chilling if inexplicable statements, "I see water
and buildings. Oh my God! Oh my God!" These are the last words on
the transcript. Sweeney is alleged to have retained her composure
throughout her call to an unbelievable degree. She also was reported
as having worked as a flight attendant, mostly in the northeastern U.S.,
for some twelve years. As a preliminary matter, the Manhattan skyline
is sufficiently distinctive and familiar that most Americans, to say
nothing of a veteran flight attendant, would have exclaimed "Oh my
God! We're going to hit Manhattan!" instead of referring vaguely to
"buildings" and "water."

600.   More critically, Sweeney's account is irreconcilable with the
known timeline. The transcript of the call indicates the breaching of
the cockpit, a sharp descent within sight of the New York skyline in
quick succession, followed by the abrupt termination of the call—
which, if genuine, must therefore have occurred within a few minutes
before impact. However, it is known that the sharp deviation of Flight
11 from its original course, roughly a 90 degree turn southward toward
New York City, occurred not far from Albany, New York. Albany is
about 150 miles—or about 18 minutes' flying time at 500 MPH—
north of Manhattan. If, consistent with the Sweeney transcript, the
hijackers breached the cockpit only when Flight 11 was within view of
Manhattan, why did the pilots, without voice communication with air
traffic control and without punching in the readily-accessible emergency alert code, make a sharp left-hand turn over Albany, New York,
roughly twenty minutes earlier?

601.   Inasmuch as the Sweeney transcript is an integral part
of Flight 11's Official Story, it requires of us the concurrent belief that
terrorists stabbed and, possibly, shot multiple passengers during a
25-minute interim, while pilots did not trouble to sound any alarm to
speak to air traffic control, but decided (apparently on their own, the
cockpit not yet having been breached) to turn from a westward course,
toward Los Angeles, and head for New York City.

602.   Also, while plaintiff does not have the entire Sweeney
transcript, news stories suggest that Sweeney announced the stabbings
and the killing of the business class passenger at the outset of her call.
If, at 8:22 A.M., several persons had already been stabbed and/or shot,

it is difficult to imagine that exhortations over the PA system could quell panic and screaming amongst the passengers.

603.   Sweeney counted <u>four</u> hijackers on Flight 11, and identified their seat numbers as being in rows 9 and 10. The FBI identified <u>five</u> hijackers, placing them all in row 8. (Both reports are anomalous if the hijackers are identifiable as Arabs, neither the reported names of the hijackers, nor indeed any Arab names, are on the manifest released to the public). The pilot, John Ogonowski, although never sounding the emergency alarm or speaking with controllers subsequent to 8:14 A.M., is claimed at intervals to have surreptitiously activated a cockpit microphone, over which was heard, we are told, a male voice with a thick Middle Eastern accent (for the first time at 8:24:38). If one speculates that Sweeney did, in fact, see four hijackers in the cabin while the fifth hijacker (unbeknownst to her) was in the cockpit directing the pilot, and thereby seeks to explain away the discrepancy between Sweeney's and the FBI's respective "head count" of terrorists, troubling questions persist. How did that one hijacker gain access to the cockpit? When did that occur? Why would only one hijacker be assigned to overcome at least two pilots in the cockpit? If but a single hijacker first intruded into the cockpit, while four others remained in the cabin, stabbing and shooting passengers, what explains that neither the pilot or co-pilot even managed to transmit the emergency alarm? If one hijacker successfully overpowered two pilots in the cockpit, was he armed with a firearm? If so, how did the weapon get on board the plane? If a man with a thick Middle Eastern accent was telling passengers over the public address system to remain quiet, should that not have indicated to Sweeney that the cockpit indeed had been breached, and indeed that this occurred by 8:24 A.M.? If one terrorist, perhaps armed sufficiently to succeed in preventing two pilots from transmitting electronic or voice alarms from 8:14 A.M. onward until impact at 8:46 A.M., why then (according to Sweeney) did other hijackers enter the cockpit only as the plane came within view of the New York City skyline?

604.   Also—again assuming the scenario of one hijacker in the cockpit and four in the cabin—as Flight 11 stopped responding to air traffic control at 8:14 A.M. and its transponder was turned off at 8:20 A.M., and hijackers intended to fly it into the World Trade Center in New York City, why was there a lapse of up to 12 minutes between the hijacking, which presumably occurred very close in time to 8:14 A.M., and the southward turn over Albany, New York that took place only at

8:26 A.M.? Sweeney's call was placed at 8:22 A.M., and she reported four hijackers. If, however, Sweeney did not see a fifth hijacker because that was the one who had penetrated the cockpit and effected the takeover of the plane, why would he not have admitted other terrorists to assist him in the cockpit, if his control there was not sufficiently firm, over a 12-minute period, to redirect the pilots to a course headed for New York?

605.   No less incredible is that, of the five passengers the FBI originally identified as the Flight 11 hijackers, three were later reported alive and residing in the Middle East. Indeed, a total of seven Arabs, of the nineteen originally implicated, have been shown to be alive. The FBI has sought to explain this away, by averring that these terrorists used false identification. On September 28, 2001, the FBI simply released a new list, substituting seven new terrorist perpetrators of the total of nineteen. To be sure, false identification papers can be obtained, and one can conceive of an airplane being hijacked by persons using false IDs. If that occurred on 9/11, however, given that all of the seven hijackers apparently acknowledged by the FBI as having been, at first, incorrectly identified perished in the attacks, what then was the evidence upon which the "new and improved" identifications issued on September 28th? Moreover, what exactly is the evidence that the other twelve hijackers—*i.e.*, those whose identities were not amended in
the Official Story—were not impostors? Why do zero Arab names appear on passenger lists first posted by the airlines? Given that the "evidence"—inconclusive, suspect, and troublingly scanty—of Arabs hijacking any of the aircraft emerged in part only on September 12th (e.g., the CNN report of Flight 77 passenger Barbara Olson's alleged telephone calls to her husband, U.S. Solicitor General Ted Olson, a known liar) would United and American have been so racist as to scrub all and any Arab names from passenger manifests before releasing them to the public? How did the FBI identify any hijackers, and so quickly?

606.   The Official Story has it that, of the nineteen Arab hijackers of 9/11, nine were required to undergo special security screenings—based on suspicious ID documents—before they boarded the planes. Given that all of the hijackers presumably are dead, and the airlines have been virtually immunized from liability by a grateful Congress, what is the justification for the continuing refusal to identify which of

the purported hijackers were subjected to closer scrutiny? One specu-
lative explanation as to how a hijacker may have gained access to Flight
11's cockpit is that it sometimes happens that off-duty pilots are
allowed access to the cockpit, as a sort of professional courtesy. If, con-
ceivably, that might explain a hijacker being in the cockpit of Flight 11,
is it not appropriate for it to be asked, and answered, whether there are
indications of that actually happening, and which of the Arabs (if any)
of the five supposedly on Flight 11 were examined due to doubtful ID
documents? Does it make sense (and how one might possibly explain)
that someone with a thick Middle Eastern accent, posing as a pilot, was
permitted access to the cockpit, on a flight where one or more Middle
Eastern men with questionable IDs were pulled aside and searched?

607. After the strike on the North Tower, New York City police
claimed to have found the passport of Mohammed Atta, ostensibly the
"crew chief" of the Flight 11 hijackers, 8 blocks from the World Trade
Center. A piece of "Atta's" luggage, which miraculously got left behind
at Logan Airport, emerged containing supposedly incriminating evidence Is this "evidence" even remotely credible? Consider: New York
City's two tallest buildings dissolved (tidily, so as not to adversely affect
real estate values nearby) into an unbelievably huge cloud of inconceiv-
ably fine powder. In the meantime, one hijacker's passport—which he
had thoughtfully brought along to display on entering Paradise, Flight
11 being a domestic flight, and a suicide mission—floated to earth
eight blocks away, a bit smudged but otherwise intact.

608. In addition, why has not the identity, the background, and
the seat location (9B) of the man supposedly killed (possibly, shot) in
business class by the hijackers not excited any but passing mention?
This was Daniel C. Lewin, a U.S. citizen with dual Israeli citizenship,
who was a former elite Israeli commando officer in a secret unit of the
Israeli Defense Force called Sayeret Matkal. While a member of the
Israeli Defence Force, Lewin reportedly received extensive anti-terrorist
training. It is reported also that Sayeret Matkal's mission was to infil-
trate Arab communities to gather intelligence and, in some instances,
conduct death-squad killings of Arabs—tasks, obviously, that require
Jews to become skilled at impersonating Arabs. The fact of Lewin's
mere presence on this flight is, at the very least, a remarkable fact that
begs for some explanation. We must add to this coincidence, however,
to additional facts that plaintiff deems to be very startling. First, in
February 2000, intelligence officials in Calcutta, India detained 11

members of what they thought was an al-Qaeda hijacking conspiracy. It was then discovered that the 11 supposed *tabliqis* or Muslim preachers all were Israeli nationals from the West Bank. Bangladeshi officials denied them permission to fly to Dhaka, but "seemingly under Israeli pressure," India allowed them to fly to Tel Aviv. Thus, although there is no indication that Daniel Lewin was involved in this prior incident, we may have a recorded instance in which Israelis, posing as Muslims, were boarding aircraft in numbers sufficient to pull off a hijacking. If we add, also, that Daniel Lewin was the business class passenger on Flight 11 who (according to Sweeney) was shot or had his throat cut, plus the million-to-one coincidence that Lewin (an Israeli commando from a unit that impersonated Arabs) chanced to have a seat assignment literally next to one of the "Arab terrorists," the lack of official and media curiosity becomes simply too much to bear.

609.   Thickening yet more the web of intrigue is that allegedly the Flight 11 (and other) hijack pilots learned to fly at the Venice, Florida based Huffman Aviation flight school, which has ties to the CIA as well as to fundamentalist Christian "charities" including Pat Robertson's "Operation Blessing" and Jerry Falwell's "World Help."

610.   Astonishingly, while the FBI and other federal agencies claimed and still claim to have been caught off guard by the attacks of 9/11, which came as a "bolt from the blue" in the middle of the night of September 11-12, 2001, less than 24 hours after the attacks, the Huffman Flight School was raided in the middle of the night, and the records from the flight school were loaded onto a C-130 cargo plane *with the President's brother, Florida Gov. Jeb Bush onboard,* and flown from Sarasota, Florida to Washington, D.C.

611.   Reportedly, the true owner of the Huffman Aviation flight school is a Republican, Wally Hilliard, who is the owner of a Learjet that was seized by federal agents in July 2000 at the Orlando Executive Airport, with more than 30 pounds of heroin onboard.

612.   During the same period in which Hilliard's charter jet service—at various times called Florida Air, Sunrise Airlines and Discover Air—allegedly was flying between Florida and Venezuela bringing illegal drugs into Florida, the service was being utilized at virtually no cost (despite the fact that Lear jets rent for up to $1,800 per hour) by Governor Jeb Bush. Indeed, both Jeb Bush and Florida Secretary of State (now U.s. Representative) Katherine Harris were publicly touting Hilliard's operation even after one of its planes (Lear jet #N351WB)

had been busted by DEA agents, armed with machine guns.

613.   Asked by 9/11 victims' family members how the FBI knew to go to Huffman Aviation within hours of the attacks, the FBI's response was "we got lucky."

HOW DID THE ALLEGED HIJACKERS GET VISAS TO ENTER THE UNITED STATES?

613.   Plaintiff admits to uncertainty concerning precisely how the attacks of 9/11 occurred. Possibly, Arab hijackers were involved, the Enterprise having learned of their plans, and electing to let them be carried out. Another possibility is that Arab hijackers were impersonated, perhaps with a foreign intelligence service playing a part. Possibly, there were no Arabs or hijackers onboard the commandeered flights at all.

614.   However, if it shall be shown that all or some of the nineteen men identified as the 9/11 hijackers were on the hijacked planes, or in any way participated in the attacks, the government has much to explain concerning how these individuals were permitted to enter the United States in the first place.

615.   Michael Springmann, former head of the Visa Bureau at the U.S. Consulate in Jeddah, Saudi Arabia, said that he was repeatedly ordered by high-level State Department officials to issue visas to unqualified applicants. His complaints to higher authorities at several agencies went unanswered. In an interview, he indicated that the CIA was indeed complicit in the attacks.

616.   According to Mindy Kleinberg's testimony before the Commission, fifteen of the nineteen hijackers' visas should have been denied because their applications were incomplete and incorrect. Most of the alleged hijackers were young, unmarried, and unemployed males—in short, "the classic over-stay candidates." A seasoned former Consular officer stated in National Review that "[s]ingle, idle young adults with no specific destination in the United States rarely get visas absent compelling circumstances."

617.   An article by Joel Mowbray that appeared in National Review Online stated that six separate experts had analyzed the visa application forms of 15 of the 19 alleged terrorists (the other four applications were unavailable) and agreed that all of the applications ought to have been denied on their face. Mr. Mowbray quotes Nikolai Wenzel, a former consular officer who analyzed the forms, as declaring

that the Department of State's issuance of the visas "amounts to criminal negligence." "Defying the conventional wisdom that al Qaeda had
provided its operatives with extensive training to game the system with
the right answers to guarantee a visa," Mr. Mowbray writes, "the applications were littered with red flags, almost all of which were ignored."

618.   A review of the further particulars in Mr. Mowbray's article
is very convincing that the details of the alleged terrorists' entries into
the United States is consistent with U.S. officials ignoring the rules over
and over again, to willfully admit to this country persons so manifestly
unqualified for visas, that they were probably either (1) persons suspected of planning attacks, that the Enterprise intended to let happen,
or (2) outright "patsies," or candidates to be blamed for such attacks.
Certainly, the 15 visa applications discussed in the article in the right-
wing National Review display no trace of the applicants being sophisticated, well-instructed members of an elite terrorist organization, skill-
fully slipping through cracks in the system to enter this country If
these men, or any of them, actually were persons involved in the 9/11
attacks, U.S. consular authorities "stood down" in allowing them entry
to the United States as badly as NORAD "stood down" on the morning
of 9/11 in failing to intercept any of the diverted planes. Plaintiff is not
aware that there has been any investigation, or that anyone has been
fired, in connection with the granting of these visas.

FOOTNOTES

[*Editor's note*: Below is a partial list of the
sources cited in the 151 footnotes that
accompanied the original text of this excerpt.]

New York Times, Asia Times Online, BBC, *Los Angeles Times,* Newhouse
News, *Ottawa Citizen, Code One Magazine, Aviation Week and Space
Technology,* ABC News, MSNBC, AP, Fox News, *Boston Globe,
Christian Science Monitor,* CNN, *Newsday, Guardian, Village Voice,*
NORAD, *FAA Regulations, Cape Cod Times, Air Force News, Dallas
Morning News, Wall Street Journal, Washington Post, Meet the Press,
Toledo Blade, USA Today,* Norman Mineta Testimony, *The Telegraph,*
CBS News, *New Jersey Star-Ledger,* UPI, *Sarasota Herald-Tribune,
Toronto Star,* Al-Jazeera.com, *National Review Online,* and *Newsweek.*

Sources

Introduction
PAGE

xv   Caution urged following 9/11—Jim Marrs, "Who's Truly Behind the Attack on America?" JimMarrs.com (Sept 12, 2001).

Section 1—The Events of September 11, 2001

[No notes for this section.]

Section 2—A Chronology of Events
2   9/11 chronology—Compiled from various mainstream news sources.

Section 3—Unresolved Questions Abound
6   US officials and stand-down orders—David Ray Griffin, *The New Pearl Harbor*, (Northhampton, MA: Olive Branch Press, 2004).

7   Chilling message—Ron Fournier, "'Air Force One Is Next,' Caller Said," Associated Press (Sept. 13, 2001).

7   Steganography—Editors, "Digital Moles in the White House?" WorldNetDaily.com (2001), http://www.worldnetdaily.com/news/article.asp? ARTICLE_ID=24594

Section 4—What Did President Bush Know?
8   Bush's remarks at school—Griffin, op. cit.; Associated Press (Aug. 19, 2002).

9   Andrew Card and 700 seconds—Ibid.

Section 5—Did War Games Aid the Terrorists?
10   NRO 9/11 exercise—Editors, "Agency Was to Simulate Plane Crash on September 11," Associated Press (Aug. 22, 2002).

11   Vigilant Warrior NORAD exercise—Richard A. Clarke, *Against All Enemies* (New York: Free Press, 2004).

11   Government set 9/11 date—Barbara Honegger, "Feature: The US Government, Not the Hijackers, 'Chose' the Date of the 9/11 Attacks," http://www.911pi.com/honegger.htm.

12   "Exceptions" explained—Author's interview with Barbara Honegger (May 6, 2004).

12   Hijacked planes as weapons—Steven Komarow and Tom
      Squitieri, "NORAD Had Drills of Jets as Weapons," *USA
      Today* (April 19, 2004).

13   Scenario "unrealistic"—Eric Schmitt, "War Games: Pentagon
      Rejected Pre-9/11 Hijacking Exercise," *New York Times*
      (April 14, 2004).

13   Mass Casualty Exercise—http://www.mdw.army.mil/news/
      Contingency_Planning.html

Section 6—Bush Creates the Premise for a War on Terrorism

14   Hunkered-down attitude—http://www.cbsnews.com/stories/
      2001/05/08/national/main290081.shtml

14   Unnamed intelligence source—Jon Rappoport, "Briefing on
      Al Quaeda," StratiaWire (Sept. 5, 2002).

Section 7—Who Authorized the bin Laden Evacuation?

15   Flying bin Ladens—Jane Mayer, "The House of Bin Laden,"
      The New Yorker (Nov. 12, 2001).

16   Bin Ladens flown from US—Craig Unger, "Saving the
      Saudis," *Vanity Fair* (October, 2003).

Section 8—What About the Hijackers Themselves?

17   No stone unturned—Editors, "They Saw It Happen,"
      America at War, (New York: Personality Profiles Presents,
      2001).

17   Some identified hijackers still alive—Editors, "Hijack
      'Suspects' Alive and Well," BBC News (Sept. 23, 2001).

18   Saudi Prince al-Faisal—
      http://911review.org/Wiki/HijackersAliveAndWell.shtml.

18   Arab names similar—Hanna Rosin, "Some Cry Foul
      as Authorities Cast a Wide Net," *Washington Post*
      (Sept. 28, 2001).

18   Kristin Breitweiser—Jim Miklaszewski, "US Had 12
      Warnings of Jet Attacks," NBC, MSNBC, Associated
      Press, and Reuters (Sept. 18, 2002).

19   Venice Airport, Florida—Daniel Hopsicker, *Welcome to
      Terrorland*, (Eugene, OR: The Madcow Press, 2004).

19   No Arabs on Flight 77—Thomas R. Olsted, MD, "Autopsy:
      No Arabs on Flight 77," SierraTimes.com (July 6, 2003),
      http://www.sierratimes.com/03/07/02/article_tro.htm.

20   Hani Hanjour's flight capabilities—
      http://www.newsday.com/ny-usflight232380680sep23.story

20   Passport found—"Terrorist Hunt," ABC News (Sept. 12, 2001);
      http://www.cnn.com/2001/US/09/16/gen.america.under.attack.

21   Trail left deliberately—Griffin, op. cit.

21   Terrorists looked for hookers—Editors, "Reports: Hijack
      Suspects Looked for Hookers in Boston," Reuters
      (Oct. 10, 2001).

22   Abu Zubaydah—Gerald Posner, *Why America Slept*, (New
      York: Random House, 2003).

22   Ari Fleisher—
      http://www.foxnews.com/story/0.2933.49226.00.html.

22   Abu Zubaydah's Saudi connections—Johanna McGeary,
      "Confessions of a Terrorist," *Time* (Sept. 8, 2003).

22   Posner—Ibid.

24   Sgt. Ali A. Mohamed—John Sullivan and Joseph Neff,
      "An Al Qaeda Operative at Fort Bragg," *Raleigh News &
      Observer* (Nov. 13, 2001).

25   Osama bin Laden background—Anonymous source,
      translated document provided to Frontline, Public
      Broadcasting System; http://www.angelfire.com/home/pearly/
      hjtmis1/ osama-bio.html.

26   Republicans suppress Saudi information—
      http://pub12.ezboard.com/fnuclearweaponsnuclear
      weaponsforum.showMessage?topicID=282.topic.

Section 9—What Really Happened at the Pentagon?

26   Pentagon survivor's story—Author's interview with April
      Gallop (April 18, 2004).

27   Steve Riskus—Thierry Meyssan, editor, *Pentagate*, (London:
      Carnot Publishing Ltd., 2002).

27   Where's the airplane?—http://www.asile.org/citoyens/
      numero13/pentagone/erreurs_en.htm.

28   Francois Grangier—Meyssan, op. cit.

29   Witnesses—Ibid.

29   Rumsfeld's missile quote—http://www.defenselink.mil/news/
      Nov2001/t11182001_t1012pm.html.

30   Chaney's comments—Secretary Norman Mineta's testimony
      to the National Commission on the September 11 Terrorist
      Attacks; http://www.cooperativeresearch.org/timeline/2003/
      commissiontestimony052303.html.

30   NORAD procedural change—DDOD 3025.15 (Feb. 18, 1997);
      CJCSI 3610.01A (June 1, 2001).

31   Jerry Russell—http://www.rumormillnews.com/cgi-bin/
      forum.cgi?read=46729.

Section 10—Explosions at the World Trade Center?

32   Controlled implosions—Olivier Uyttebrouck, "Explosives
      Planted in Towers, N.M. Tech Expert Says," *Albuquerque
      Journal* (Sept. 11, 2001).

33   Romero reverses—John Fleck, "Fire, Not Extra Explosives,
      Doomed Buildings, Expert Says," *Albuquerque Journal*
      (Sept. 21, 2001).

33   Louie Cacchioli—Editors, "New York City," People.com
      (Sept. 12, 2001), http://people.aol.com/people/special/
      0.11859.174592-3.00.html

33   Lt. Paul Isaac Jr.—Randy Lavello, "Bombs in the Building:
      World Trade Center 'Conspiracy Theory' Is a Conspiracy
      Fact," http://www.prisonplanet.com/analysis_lavello_050503_
      bombs.html.

34   Teresa Veliz and bombs—Dean E. Murphy, "Teresa Veliz:
      A Prayer to Die Quickly and Painlessly," *September 11:
      An Oral History* (New York: Doubleday, 2002).

34   Ross Milanytch—*America at War*, op. cit.

34   Steve Evans of BBC—Christopher Bollyn, "New York
      Firefighters' Final Words Fuel Burning Questions about 9-
      11," *American Free Press* (Aug. 19, 2002).

35   Explosion at base of building—Col. Donn de Grand Pre,
      "Many Questions Still Remain about Trade Center Attack,"
      American Free Press (Feb. 11, 2002).

35   Tom Elliott—Peter Grier, "A Changed World, Part 1: The
      Attack," *The Christian Science Monitor* (Sept. 17, 2001).

36   CNN videotapes smoke from WTC 6—Christopher Bollyn,
      "Unexplained 9/11 Explosion at WTC Complex," *American
      Free Press* (July 22, 2002).

37   Ben Fountain and drills—http://www.unityinamerica.com/
      stories/survivorStoriee.asp; www.prisonplanet.com/
      011904wct7.html.

37   Mayor Giuliani warned—http://www.prisonplanet.com/
      eye_witness_account_from_new_york.html;
      http://physics911.org/net/modules/wfsection/article.php?
      articleid=15.

Section 11—Firefighters Thought the Fires Were Controllable

38   Firefighters Palmer and Bucca—Bollyn (Aug. 19, 2002),
      op. cit.

38   Transcripts—http://www.prisonplanet.com/eye_witness_
      account_from_new_york.html.

39   Loizeaux's speculation—Ibid.

40   Seismic evidence of two shocks—Christopher Bollyn,
      "Seismic Data Refutes Official Explanation," *American Free
      Press* (Sept. 9, 2002).

40   Arthur Lerner-Lan and Eric Hufschmid—Ibid; Eric
      Hufschmidt, *Painful Questions* (Goleta, CA, Endpoint
      Software, 2002).

41   Sooty smoke—Ibid.

41   Thomas Eager and "clips"—http://www.worldnewsstand.net/
      2001/towers/trusseseager. html

42   How could debris crush 100 steel and concrete floors—
      Hufschmid, op. cit.

Section 12—What Caused the Collapse of Building 7?

43   Building 7 fires—Ibid.

43   Larry Silverstein—Editors, "America Rebuilds," PBS-TV
      (Sept. 2002).

Section 13—FEMA's Report: Cause of WTC Collapses Unknown

44   WTC steel sold for scrap—Bill Manning, "Selling Out the
      Investigation," *Fire Engineering* (Jan. 2002).

45   Evidence treated like garbage—Francis Brannigan, "WTC
      'Investigation'? A Call to Action," *Fire Engineering*
      (Jan. 2002).

45   W. Gene Corley and team complaints—Avery Comarow,
      "After the Fall," *US News & World Report* (May 13, 2002).

46   National Construction Safety Team report—
http://www.nist.gov/public_affairs/releases/ncst_first_
report.htm.

Section 14—Tracks of Foreknowledge Revealed

49    $30 billion—Editors, "The Road to Sept. 11," *Newsweek*
(Oct. 1, 2001).

49   Kenneth Katzman—http://www.washingtonpost.com/wo-dyn/
articles/A14120-2001Sep11.html.

49   State Dept. Warning—Phillip Matier and Andrew Ross,
"State Department Memo Warned of Terrorist Threat,"
San Francisco Chronicle (Sept. 14, 2001).

50   Snider resigns from joint committee—Tabassum Zakaria,
"Head of Congressional Probe into Sept. 11 Quits," Reuters
(April 29, 2002).

50   Small teams of investigators—Greg Miller, "Tactics Impede
Investigation," *Los Angeles Times* (May 4, 2002).

51   FBI investigates leaks—Christopher Newton, "FBI Asks
Lawmakers to Take Lie Detector Test in Sept. 11 Leak
Investigation," Associated Press (Aug. 2, 2002).

51   Attack will be spectacular—John Doughtery, "Panel: Attack
on US 'Inevitable'," *WorldNetDaily* (Sept. 21, 2001).

51   US officials warned—Jeff Johnson, "Congress Was Warned
Two Months Before 9/11 Attacks," NewsMax.Com
(Sept. 19, 2002).

51   Sen. Richard Shelby—Miklaszewski, op. cit.

51   Sen. Bob Graham—Ibid.

52   McCain co-sponsors inquiry—Lisa Stein, "Private Eye," Top
of the Week, *U.S. News & World Report* (Oct. 7, 2002).

52   Eleanor Hill noted consistent theme—Editors, "US 'Failed
to Heed' Terror Warnings," BBC News (Sept. 18, 2002).

52   Rep. Ray Lahood—Miklaszewski, op. cit.

53   Terrorist trained to crash airliners—Yossef Bodansky,
Target America: Terrorism in the US Today (New York:
Shapolsky Publishers, 1993).

53   Italian wiretaps—Sebastian Rotella and Josh Meyer,
"Wiretaps May Have Foretold Terror Attacks,"
Los Angeles Times (May 29, 2002).

54   Spanish wiretaps—Ibid.

54   Cayman Islands warning—Chris Hansen, "Warning Signs," MSNBC (Sept. 23, 2001).

54   Taliban warning—Kate Clark, "Revealed: The Taliban Minister, the US Envoy and the Warning of September 11 that Was Ignored," The Independent (September 7, 2002); http://news.independent.co.uk./world/politics/story.jsp?story=331115.

55   Manila warning—Editors, "Flashback: Airliner Terror Plan Was Code-Named 'Project Bojinka'," World Tribune.com (Sept. 25, 2001).

55   Air France Flight 8969—Matthew L. Wald, "Earlier Hijackings Offered Signals that Were Missed," New York Times (Oct. 3, 2001).

55   Philippine warnings—Dorian Zumel Sicat, "Abu's Long-Standing Ties to Global Terrorism Bared," The Manila Times (Feb. 15, 2002).

55   Terry Nichols and terrorists—Dorian Zumel-Sicat, "RP Cops Aware of Long-Term Rightwing, Muslim Connection," The Manila Times (April 26, 2002), http://www.manilatimes.net/national/2002/apr/26/top_stories/20020426top6.html.

56   Chinese manual—http://www.newsmaxstore.com/nms/showdetl.cfm?&DID=6&Product_ID=886&CATID=9&GroupID=12.

56   China enters WTO—http://www.cnn.com/2001/WORLD/asiapcf/central/11/10/china.WTO/.

57   Dr. Koryagina—http://www.newsmax.com/archives/articles/201/10/3/212706.shtml.

58   Egyptian warning—Patrick E. Tyler and Neil MacFarquhar, "Egypt Warned US of Al Qaeda Plot, Mubarak Asserts," The New York Times (June 4, 2002).

58   Atwan warning—Editors, "Expert: Bin Laden Warned of 'Unprecedented' US Attack," Reuters News Service (Sept. 11, 2001).

59   Arab MBC channel—Editors, "US Airlines May Be a Terror Risk Over Next Three Days," Airjet Airline World News (June 23, 2001).

59   Letter to New York Times—http://judiciary.senate.gov/oldsite/childers.htm.

Section 15—The FBI Couldn't, or Wouldn't, Connect the Dots

61   Carnivore and FBI memos—Editors, "FBI 'Carnivore' Glitch Hurt Al Qaeda Probe," Reuters (May 29, 2002); http://www.cnn.com/2002/US/05/28/attack.carnivore.reut

62   "most committed tracker"—Lawrence Wright, "The Counter Terrorist," *The New Yorker* (Jan. 14, 2002).

62   "dealt with dolts"—Ibid.

62   Jamal Ahmed al-Fadl—Ibid.

63   Groups' ability to strike—Wright, op. cit.

63   No government support—Wright, op. cit.

63   Valarie James—Wright, op. cit.

63   Something big to happen—Wright, op. cit.

64   FBI not protecting—Wes Vernon, "Agent: FBI Could Have Prevented 9/11," NewsMax.com (May 31, 2002).

64   Senior officials thwart efforts—Ibid.

64   Phoenix suspicions—Editors, "FBI Agent Warned of Suspicious Flight Students Last Summer," Fox News (May 3, 2002).

65   Agent Williams' memo—Richard Behar, "FBI's 'Phoenix' Memo Unmasked," Fortune.com (May 22, 2002).

65   FBI agents indicted—Alex Berenson, "Five, Including FBI Agents, Are Named in a Conspiracy," *New York Times* (May 23, 2002).

65   Assistant US Attorney Kenneth Breen—Whitley Strieber, "Is the FBI Penetrated?" UnknownCountry.com (May 25, 2002), http://www.unknowncountry.com/journal/print.phtml?id=95

65   Mission jeopardized—Vernon, op. cit.

66   Gary Aldrich—http://www.newsmaxstore.com

66   FBI and Clinton White House—James Risen, "CIA's Inquiry on Al-Qaeda Aide Seen as Flawed," *New York Times* (Sept. 22, 2002).

66   FBI Agent Ivan C. Smith—Paul Sperry, "Why FBI Missed Islamic Threat Agents: Clinton Shifted Counterterror Efforts to Fighting 'Right-Wing' Groups," *WorldNetDaily* (July 25, 2002).

66   40 boxes of evidence—Ibid.

66   Commerce Dept. report sanitized—Ibid.

67   FBI Director Robert Mueller—Eric Lichtblau and Josh Meyer, "Terrorist Signs Were Missed, FBI Chief Says," *The Los Angeles Times* (May 30, 2002).

67   Randy Glass—John Mintz, "US Reopens Arms Case in Probe of Taliban Role," *The Washington Post* (Aug. 2, 2002); Wanda J. DeMaarzo, "Feds Reopen Probe of Florida Arms Deal," *The Miami Herald* (Aug. 2, 2002).

68   David Schippers— http://www.infowars.com/transcript_schippers.html.

70   Sibel Edmonds—Andrew Buncombe, "I Saw Papers that Show US Knew Al-Qaeda Would Attack Cities with Aeroplanes," *The Independent* (April 2, 2004); http://news.independent.co.uk/world/americas/story.isp?story=507514.

71   Al-Shibh's wire to Moussaoui—Spotlight, "The Strange Case of Mr. M." *U.S. News & World Report* (Sept. 23, 2002).

71   Ramzi al-Shibh in custody—Lisa Stein, "Man of the Hour," *US News & World Report* (Sept. 23, 2002).

71   FBI docs in Moussaoui's cell—Lisa Stein, op. cit.

72   Colleen Rowley—http://www.counterpunch.org/sperry0613.html; http://www.apfn.org/apfn/WTC_whistleblower1.htm.

72   Rowley testimony defused—Steve Perry, "How All the President's Men Buried Coleen Rowley," *Counterpunch* (June 13, 2002).

73   Ashcroft rejects FBI request for $50 million—Julian Borger, "Bush Held Up Plan to Hit Bin Laden," *The Guardian* (Aug. 5, 2002).

Section 16—Missed Opportunities at the CIA

74   Echelon like vacuum cleaner—Ned Stafford: "Newspaper: Echelon Gave Authorities Warning of Attacks," Newsbytes.com (Sept. 13, 2001).

74   French probe Echelon—Warren P. Strobel, "A Fine Whine from France," *US News & World Report* (July 17, 2000).

74   Osama's big news—Ben Fenton and John Steele, "Bin Laden Told Mother to Expect 'Big News'," *Daily Telegraph* (Oct. 2, 2001).

75   Osama as Tim Osman—Mike Blair, "Public Enemy No.1 Was Guest of Central Intelligence Agency," *American Free Press* (Jan. 7 & 14, 2002).

75   "Olberg" in Durenberger's office—Ibid.

76   "it's unconscionable"—Interview, "Has Someone Been Sitting on the FBI?" *News Night*, BBC Television (June 11, 2002).

77   Kahlid al-Midhar and Nawaq Alhazni—Risen, op. cit.

77   Khalid Shekh Mohammed—Ibid.

77   Mohammed identified before 9/11—Ibid.

78   FBI tracked Mohammed Atta in Germany—Audrey Gillan, Giles Tremlett, John Hooper, Kate Connolly and Jon Henley, "Dozens Detained as Net Spreads from US to Europe," *The Guardian* (Sept. 27, 2001), http://www.guardian.co.uk/waronterror/story/0.1361. 558871.00.html.

78   Osama bin Laden in Dubai—Alexandra Richard, translation by Tiphaine Dickson, "The CIA Met Bin Laden while Undergoing Treatment at an American Hospital Last July in Dubai," *Le Figaro* (Oct. 11, 2001); http://www.globalresearch.ca/articles/RIC111B.html.

79   CIA team in Afghanistan—Editors, "Newspaper: Afghans Tracked Bin Laden," In brief, *USA Today* (Dec. 24, 2001).

79   CIA's James Pavitt—http://www.cia.gov/cia/public_affairs/ speeches/pavitt_04262002.html.

80   Delmart "Mike"Vreeland—http://www.fromthewilderness. com/free/ww3/index.html#vree.80.

82   LAPD cocaine bust—Ibid.

82   Attorney Galati—Nick Pron, "Did This Man Predict 9-11? Strange Story of a Jailed Spy Unfolds in Toronto Court," *Toronto Star* (Feb. 5, 2002).

83   Internet domain names—Jeff Johnson, "Internet Domain Names May Have Warned of Attacks," Cybercast News Service (Sept. 19, 2001); http://www.middleeastwire.com/ atlarge/stories/20010919_3_meno.shtml.

83   Editor Russ Kick—Russ Kick, "September 11, 2001: No Surprise," *Everything You Know Is Wrong* (New York: The Disinformation Company, 2002).

84　Willie Brown's warning—Phillip Matier and Andrew Ross, "Willie Brown Got Low-Key Early Warning about Air Travel," *San Francisco Chronicle* (Sept. 12, 2001).

84　Pentagon officials won't fly—Evan Thomas and Mark Hosenball, "Bush: 'We're At War'," *Newsweek* (Sept. 24, 2001).

85　Ashcroft uses charter jets—Jim Stewart, "Ashcroft Flying High," CBS News (July 26, 2001).

85　David Welna report—http://www.thememoryhole.org/tenet-9-11.htm.

85　Rumsfeld lays off blame—http://www.defenselink.mil/news/Nov2001/t11182001_t1012pm.html.

86　Senior officials warned—Risen, op. cit.

86　Bush warned at Crawford—Hirsh and Isikoff, op. cit.

86　Kearn on different circumstances—Editors, "September 11 Attacks Might Have Been Prevented, Inquiry Chairman Says," *AFP Worldwide* (March 22, 2004); http://www.afp.com/english/home/.

Section 17—Selling Stocks Short Indicates Foreknowledge

87　$15 billion worldwide—Christopher Bollyn, "Revealing 9/11 Stock Trades Could Expose the Terrorist Masterminds," *American Free Press* (May 13, 2002).

88　Richard Crossley—James Doran, "Millions of Shares Sold Before Disaster," *The Times* (Sept. 18, 2001), http://www.thetimes.co.uk/article/0.2001320007-20011323297.00.html.

88　U.S. Treasury notes—Ibid.

88　Dylan Ratigan—Ibid.

88　Michael Ruppert—Kellia Ramares and Bonnie Faulkner, "The CIA's Wall Street Connections," *Online Journal* (Oct. 12, 2001).

89　Alex Popovic—Marcy Gordon, "SEC Investigating Trading in Shares of 38 Companies: Asks Brokerages to Review Records," *Associated Press* (Oct. 2, 2001).

89　Harvey Pitt: Ibid.

90   Other suspicious trading—Michael C. Ruppert, "Suppressed Details of Criminal Insider Trading Lead Directly into the CIA's Highest Ranks," *From The Wilderness Publications* (Oct. 9, 2001).

90   Tracks lead to Deutsche Bank—Ibid.

90   "Buzzy" Krongard— http://www.cia.gov/cia/information/krongard.htm.

91   Promis software—Carl Cameron, Fox News (Oct. 16, 2001).

92   Don Radlauer—Bollyn, op. cit.

92   Walter Burien—http://www.serendipity.li/wot/burien01.htm.

93   Chicago affidavit—Alex Jones, op. cit.

93   Jerry Bremer—Elizabeth Neuffer, "Officials Aware in 1998 of Training," *Boston Globe* (Sept. 15, 2001).

94   Credibility gap—Hirsh and Isikoff, op. cit.

Section 18—What About Israeli Foreknowledge?

94   Germans say US and Israelis warned—Ned Stafford, "Newspaper: Echelon Gave Authorities Warning of Attacks," *The Washington Post*, Newsbytes (Sept. 13, 2001).

94   Odigo message warnings—Editors, "Instant Messages to Israel Warned of WTC Attack," *The Washington Post* (Sept. 28, 2001).

95   CEO Micha Macover—Yuval Dror, "Odigo Says Workers Were Warned of Attack," *Ha'aretz Daily* (Nov. 3, 2001).

95   ZIM American Shipping Co.—Christopher Bollyn, "Who Knew? Israeli Company Mum about WTC Pullout," *American Free Press* (Dec. 10, 2001).

95   4,000 Israelis reported missing—Editors, "Thousands of Israelis Missing Near WTC, Pentagon," *Jerusalem Post* (Sept. 12, 2001).

96   Israelis film WTC—Editors, "The White Van: Were Israelis Detained on Sept. 11 Spies?" ABC News (June 21, 2002), http://abcnews.go.com/sections/2020/DailyNews/2020_whitevan_020621.html.

96   Maps in car—Paulo Lima, "Five Men Detained as Suspected Conspirators," *The Bergen Record* [New Jersey] (Sept. 12, 2001).

96   Foreign Counterintelligence Investigation—Marc Perelman, "Spy Rumors Fly on Gusts of Truth," *Forward* (March 15, 2002).

97   Stoffer and Berlet—Ibid.

97   DEA report leaked—Ben Fenton, "US Arrests 200 Young Israelis in Spying Investigation," Telegraph (July 3, 2002); http://www.telegraph.co.uk/news/main.jhtml?xml=/news/2002/03/07/wspy07.xml&sSheet.

97   Guillaume Dasquie—Christopher Bollyn, "120 Spies Deported," *American Free Press* (March 25, 2002).

98   Carl Cameron quotes investigators—Michael Collins Piper, "Israel Knew: Israel Conducts Massive Spying Operation in US," *American Free Press* (Dec. 24, 2001).

98   *Le Monde* on cell phones from vice consul—John F. Sugg, "Israeli Spies Exposed," Weekly Planet [Tampa] (April 2, 2002).

98   National Counterintelligence Center warning—Ibid.

99   Military bases and petroleum facilities—Justin Raimondo, "The 'Urban Myth' Gambit," Antiwar.com (March 13, 2002).

99   Served in intel or signal intercepts—Ibid.

99   German paper Die Zeit—Rob Broomby, "Report Details US 'Intelligence Failures,'" BBC News (Oct. 2, 2002).

100   Reversed wiretaps—Charles R. Smith, "US Police and Intelligence Hit by Spy Network," NewsMax.com (Dec. 19, 2001); http://www.newsmax.com/archives/articles/2001/12/18/224826.shtml

100   Insulated from foreign influence—Charles R. Smith, "FBI Investigates Foreign Spy Ring—US Companies Deny Involvement," NewsMax.com (Jan. 16, 2002), http://www.newsmax.com/archives/articles/2002/1/16/110443.shtml.

101   Pipes and conspiracy theories—Daniel Pipes, "An Israeli Spy Network in the United States?" *Jewish World Review* (March 11, 2002).

101   Hands off Israel—Raimondo, op. cit.; Smith (Jan. 16, 2002).

101   Lisa Dean and Brad Jansen—Smith (Sept. 19, 2001).

101   Daniel Pipes advocates Isreali victory—Michael Sherer, "Daniel Pipes, Peacemaker?" MotherJones.com (May 26, 2003).

103   IASPS "Clean Break" paper—
http://www.israeleconomy.org/strat1.htm.

104   Israeli policy foisted on Bush—Lyndon LaRouche, "The
Pollard Affair Never Ended!" http://www.larouchein2003.com.

104   CFR and Israel—Jim Marrs, *Rule by Secrecy* (New York:
HarperCollins Publishers, 2000).

105   Gen. Hameed Gul—Michael Collins Piper, "Former Pakistani
Intelligence Chief Alleges Rogue Spook Agencies Behind
Error Attacks," *American Free Press* (Dec. 5, 2001).

106   Werthebach and von Bulow—Christopher Bollyn, "European
Spooks Say Mideast Terrorists Needed State Support,"
American Free Press (Dec. 24, 2001).

106   Mossad has capability—"US Troops Would Enforce Peace
Under Army Study," *The Washington Times* (Sept. 10, 2001).

107   Chossudovsky on Pakistani ISI intelligence link to 9/11—
http://www.globalresearch.ca/articles/CH0111A

Section 19—Remote Controlled Aircraft a Reality

108   Global Hawk in Afghanistan—Editors, "Operational Debut
for Global Hawk," *Jane's Aerospace* (Oct. 8, 2001),
http://www.janes.com/serospace/military/news/misc/
globalhawk_ppv.shtml.

108   First flight—News Release, "Global Hawk Completes First
Flight," United States Department of Defense (March 2,
1998), http://www.defenselink.mil/news/Mar1998/
b03021998_bt091-98.html.

109   Global Hawk made history—http://www.dsto.defence.gov.au/
globalhawk/releases/parlsec18801.html.

109   Andreas Von Buelow—Joe Vialls, "'Home Run' Electronically
Hijacking the World Trade Center Attack Aircraft,"
http://geocities.com/mknemesis/printer.html.

110   Joe Vialls—Ibid.

111   NFERS white paper—http://www.kinetx.com.

112   Hijackers flying skills—"Hijacker Suspects Tried Many
Flight Schools," *The Washington Post* (Sept. 19, 2001).

113   Alhazmi and Al-Mahar—"San Diegans See Area as Likely
Target," *The Washington Post* (Sept. 24, 2001).

113   Transponder explanation—Vialls, op. cit.

114   Objective is loss of national sovereignty—Col. Donn de Grand Pre, "The Enemy Is Inside the Gates," *American Free Press* (Feb. 11, 2002).

115   Glen Cramer—John Carlin, "Unanswered Questions—The Mystery of Flight 93," *The Independent* (Aug. 13, 2002).

116   Seismic boom recorded—Robb Magley, "Seismic Event: The Final Moments of Flight 93," http://members.fortunecity. com/seismicevent/; author's email correspondence (Feb. 15, 2003).

116   Cheney acknowledges shoot-down order—Editors, "Cheney Says Military Was Ordered to Shoot Down Planes," Online NewsHour, Public Broadcasting Service (Sept. 16, 2001).

117   Paul Wolfowitz—Ibid.

117   Bill Wright—Carlin, op. cit.

117   Wally Miller—Ibid.

118   Elaine Scarry—Emily Eakin, "Professor Scarry Has a Theory," *New York Times* (Nov. 19, 2000); http://news.independent. co.uk/world/americas/story.jsp?story=323958.

119   Gary North— http://www.mycountryrightorwrong.net/mcrow3.htm.

Section 20—The Official 9/11 Inquiry: Another Warren Commission?

124   Bush and complaining commission—Editors, "Chairman Says Commission Needs More Time," NBC, MSNBC and news services, (Feb. 13, 2004); http://www.msnbc.msn.com/id/4232892/.

124   Chairman Thomas H. Kean—Ibid.

125   Vice Chairman Lee Hamilton—Griffin, op. cit.

125   Max Cleland—Greg Pierce, Inside Politics, "9/11 Former Sen. Max Cleland Now Export-Import Bank," *Washington Times* (Nov. 25, 2003), http://washingtontimes.com/ national/20031124-124430-3305r.htm.

126   Ashcroft's testimony was deceptive—*Center for American Progress Daily Report* (April 12, 2003), http://www.americanprogress.org.

126   Ashcroft erroneously claims funds for counter terrorism— http://slate.msn.com/id/2098783.

127   Ben-Veniste easy on Ashcroft—http://www.911commission.
        gov/hearings/hearing10/staff_statement_9.pdf.

127   Clarke's claims electrified country—*Center for American
        Progress Daily Report* (April 22, 2003),
        http://www.americanprogress.org

130   Rice's lies according to Sibel Edmonds—Andrew Buncombe,"I
        Saw Papers that Show US Knew Al-Qa'ida Would Attack Cities
        with Airplanes," *The Independent* (April 2, 2004).

131   Sibel Edmonds harassed by FBI—Tom Flocco, "DOJ Asked
        FBI Translator to Change Pre-9/11 Intercepts," (March 24,
        2004), http://www.tomflocco.com.

131   Edmonds terminated—A statement released by Edmonds'
        attorneys (June 19, 2002); http://www.thememoryhole.org/
        spy/edmonds.htm.

131   Ellen Mariani's lawsuit—Copy of suit filed Nov. 26, 2003
        in US District Court, Eastern District of Pennsylvania, Case
        No. 03-5273.

132   Report on Saudis—Linda Robinson, "What's in the Report?"
        US News & World Report (August 11, 2003).

133   Sen. Bob Graham—Ibid.

134   Carmen bin Laden—Unger, op. cit.

Section 21—What Do We Know Now?

[*No notes for this section.*]

Give the gift of
One Planet:
A Progressive Vision for Enforceable Global Law
to your friends

☐ YES, I want _____ copies of
One Planet
at $16.00 each—Please include:
$4.95 shipping for the first book and
$1.00 for each additional book.
CA residents add 7.25% sales tax.

Name _____

Address _____

City _____ State _____ Zip _____

Phone _____

Email _____

Total _____

☐ Check or money order   ☐ Visa   ☐ Mastercard

Card # _____ Exp. _____

Signature _____

Call our Toll Free order line: 1.888.267.4446
Fax your order to: 415.453.4723
Order online: www.OriginPress.com

Please make your check payable and mail to:

Origin Press
P.O. Box 151117
San Rafael, CA 94915